Play Therapy With Children

Play Therapy With Children

Modalities for Change

Edited by
Heidi Gerard Kaduson
and Charles E. Schaefer

 AMERICAN PSYCHOLOGICAL ASSOCIATION

Published by
American Psychological Association
750 First Street, NE
Washington, DC 20002
https://www.apa.org

Order Department
https://www.apa.org/pubs/books
order@apa.org

In the U.K., Europe, Africa, and the Middle East, copies may be ordered from Eurospan
https://www.eurospanbookstore.com/apa
info@eurospangroup.com

Typeset in Charter and Interstate by Circle Graphics, Inc., Reisterstown, MD

Printer: Sheridan Books, Chelsea, MI
Cover Designer: Gwen J. Grafft, Minneapolis, MN

Library of Congress Cataloging-in-Publication Data

Names: Kaduson, Heidi, editor. | Schaefer, Charles E., editor.
Title: Play therapy with children : modalities for change / edited by
  Heidi Gerard Kaduson and Charles E. Schaefer.
Description: Washington, DC : American Psychological Association, [2021] |
  Includes bibliographical references and index.
Identifiers: LCCN 2020025340 (print) | LCCN 2020025341 (ebook) |
  ISBN 9781433833595 (paperback) | ISBN 9781433834592 (ebook)
Subjects: LCSH: Play therapy. | Children—Counseling of. | Psychotherapist
  and patient.
Classification: LCC RJ505.P6 P573 2021 (print) | LCC RJ505.P6 (ebook) |
  DDC 618.92/891653—dc23
LC record available at https://lccn.loc.gov/2020025340
LC ebook record available at https://lccn.loc.gov/2020025341

https://doi.org/10.1037/0000217-000

Printed in the United States of America

10 9 8 7 6 5 4 3 2 1

Contents

Contributors

Cindy Bridgman, MSW, University of Michigan, Ann Arbor, MI, United States

Teresa Dias, LMHC, RPT, MA, Expressive Therapist, Ellenhorn's PACT team (Program for Assertive Community Treatment), Arlington, MA, United States

Elisabeth Etopio, PhD, University at Buffalo, The State University of New York, Buffalo, NY, United States

Eliana Gil, LMFT, RPT-S, ATR, PhD, Founder, Partner, and Senior Clinical Consultant, Gil Institute for Trauma Recovery and Education, Fairfax, VA, United States

Deanne (DeeDee) Ginns-Gruenberg, MA, Oakland University, Rochester, MI, United States

Elizabeth Kjellstrand Hartwig, LPC-S, LMFT, RPT-S, PhD, Texas State University, San Marcos, TX, United States

Kevin B. Hull, PhD, Hull and Associates, P.A., Lakeland, FL, United States

Nikole R. Jiggetts, LCSW, RPT-S, CTS, Replay Counseling Center, LLC, Richmond, VA, United States

Heidi Gerard Kaduson, RPT-S, PhD, Director, The Play Therapy Training Institute, Monroe Township, NJ, United States

Richard Lamb, PhD, East Carolina University, Greenville, NC, United States

Julie Meighan, MEd, The Open University, Milton Keynes, England, United Kingdom

Clair Mellenthin, LCSW, RPT-S, Wasatch Family Therapy, Salt Lake City, UT, United States

Sonia Murray, NNEB, DipSW, BAPT-RPT, Jogo Behaviour Support, Northampton, Northamptonshire, England, United Kingdom

Julie Blundon Nash, RPT-S, PhD, Riverside Psychological Associates, LLC, Centerbrook, CT, United States

Mary Anne Peabody, LCSW, RPT-S, EdD, University of Southern Maine, Lewiston, ME, United States

Siobhán Prendiville, MA, MEd, Children's Therapy Centre, Westmeath, Ireland

Charles E. Schaefer, RPT-S, PhD, Professor Emeritus of Clinical Psychology, Fairleigh Dickinson University, Teaneck, NJ, United States

Jacqueline M. Swank, LMHC, LCSW, RPT-S, PhD, University of Florida, Gainesville, FL, United States

Daniel S. Sweeney, LMFT, LPC, RPT-S, PhD, George Fox University, Portland, OR, United States

Susan A. Taylor, LCSW-C, CMA, RPT-S, Center for Resilience and Connection, Baltimore, MD, United States

Jo L. Weaver, NCC, MS, University of Florida, Gainesville, FL, United States

Play
Therapy
With
Children

INTRODUCTION

The Therapeutic Powers of Play

HEIDI GERARD KADUSON AND CHARLES E. SCHAEFER

Play is the singular central activity of childhood and an essential wellspring of children's cognitive, emotional, and social development (Fisher, 1992; Ginsburg et al., 2007). Because play is the language of the child, it provides a way for children to express their troublesome experiences through a natural healing process. Play is an activity that is best defined by its eight distinctive characteristics (Barnett, 1990; Gray, 2011; Schaefer & Drewes, 2014):

- It is freely chosen.
- It is intrinsically motivated.
- It values means over ends.
- It involves multiple positive affects.
- It is personally directed.
- It includes active involvement.
- It includes nonliterality/pretense.
- It includes flexibility.

Play not only fosters human development and well-being but also is a powerful healing force for overcoming psychopathology. It is noteworthy that the dramatic decline in children's free play, particularly outdoor play, over the

https://doi.org/10.1037/0000217-001
Play Therapy With Children: Modalities for Change, H. G. Kaduson and C. E. Schaefer (Editors)

past century has been accompanied by an increase in childhood depression and anxiety (Gray, 2011).

THERAPEUTIC POWERS OF PLAY

Specific change agents in play initiate, facilitate, or strengthen the impact of play therapy. These are referred to as the *therapeutic powers of play* (Schaefer & Drewes, 2014). On the basis of a review of the literature and clinical experience, Schaefer and Drewes (2014) identified 20 core therapeutic powers of play, which are grouped into four categories:

- *Facilitates Communication*: Self-Expression, Access to the Unconscious, Direct Teaching, Indirect Teaching

- *Fosters Emotional Wellness*: Catharsis, Abreaction, Positive Emotions, Counterconditioning Fears, Stress Inoculation, Stress Management

- *Increases Personal Strengths*: Creative Problem Solving, Resiliency, Moral Development, Accelerated Development, Self-Regulation, Self-Esteem

- *Enhances Social Relationships*: Therapeutic Relationship, Attachment, Social Competence, Empathy

PLAY THERAPY

The Association for Play Therapy (https://www.a4pt.org) defined *play therapy* as "the systematic use of a theoretical model to establish an interpersonal process wherein trained play therapists use the therapeutic powers of play to help clients prevent or resolve psychosocial difficulties and achieve optimal growth and development." Noteworthy in this definition is the central role ascribed to the aforementioned therapeutic powers of play. Play therapy represents a unique and rapidly expanding form of mental health treatment. Although primarily applied to children, it is also proving effective with adolescents (Gallo-Lopez & Schaefer, 2005) and adults (Schaefer, 2003).

Play therapy has been the treatment of choice for children for many decades. An accurate understanding of how play therapy works to cause change involves looking into the therapeutic factors that operate to produce a treatment effect and affect change (Holmes & Kivlighan, 2000; Yalom, 1995). They represent the middle abstraction between theories and concrete techniques. Humanistic and psychodynamic theories, as well as cognitive behavioral theories, comprise the highest level of abstraction. They offer a framework for understanding the origin and treatment of problematic behaviors. Therapeutic factors, the middle level of abstraction, refer to specific clinical strategies—for example, catharsis, counterconditioning, and contingency management for obtaining the desired change in a client's dysfunctional behavior. Techniques or modalities are the lowest level of abstraction; they are observable clinical procedures designed to implement the therapeutic factors—for example, sand play, doll play, puppets, and storytelling.

Ever since play therapy was developed in the first half of the 20th century, different theoretical domains have allowed varied approaches and numerous theoretical foundations (i.e., client centered, Jungian, psychodynamic, Adlerian, cognitive behavioral, or attachment based) to be used during play therapy (Brown, 2015). Because no one single play therapy theory has proven equally effective with all the different psychological disorders of youth, prescriptive play therapists select from both directive and nondirective play therapy theories an intervention that has strong empirical support for the client's specific presenting problem. Therapists then modify it as needed for each client, based on the client's strengths, limitations, developmental status, and preferences (Kaduson et al., 2020). The fundamental goal of prescriptive psychotherapy is to tailor the intervention to the presenting problem and personal characteristics of the client. In formulating a treatment plan, prescriptive psychotherapists seek to answer Gordon Paul's (1967) question "*What* treatment, by *whom*, is most effective for *this* individual, with *that* specific problem, with *which* set of circumstances, and *how* does it come about?" (p. 111; italics in original). Therefore, the treatment is truly client centered rather than focused on the personal preferences of the therapist.

Numerous research studies have begun to establish play therapy as an intervention with empirical support for a broad range of childhood disorders, including internalizing, externalizing, and developmental problems (Opiola & Bratton, 2018; Reddy et al., 2005, 2016). Other studies (e.g., Shen, 2016) have investigated the ways in which culture impacts the effectiveness of play therapy and have concluded that it can be successful with children of diverse cultures. However, these studies are not specific to the modalities in this volume, although many of the therapists use at least one or more of these interventions. Therefore, it is recommended that future research do more specific analysis of these modalities.

Much like the broader field of psychotherapy, the field of play therapy has been gradually shifting away from model-specific treatments to more integrated and prescriptive models (Drewes, 2011a, 2011b; Schaefer & Drewes, 2010, 2011, 2014). These models focus more on multimodal methods of assessing children's needs, matching these needs with interventions based on an understanding of the therapeutic mechanisms common in most models of child therapy and the factors that establish and maintain the therapeutic relationship. Through the prescriptive approach to play therapy (Kaduson et al., 2020), the therapists can have one or more theoretical orientations from which they tailor interventions to the presenting problem and personal preferences of the client.

TRAINING FOR PLAY THERAPISTS

As long as they have a strong theoretical foundation, play therapists can become competent in a variety of interventions and modalities through their training. This multimodal approach will allow them to integrate different modalities if necessary to tailor their treatment to clients with specific co-occurring disorders. By providing a state-of-the-art overview of the effective ways to practice each modality, front line child therapists, including psychologists, counselors, social workers, and other health professionals, can arm themselves with interventions that would facilitate treatment of children through play therapy. Therefore, this book will be an asset to any beginning child and play therapists as well as to experienced child clinicians who wish to expand their therapeutic tool kit.

Skill development in the clinical application of the play therapy modalities requires approved training, repetition, and a dedication to supervised practice so that an acceptable level of competency is achieved. Training in play therapy follows the guidelines of the Association for Play Therapy, which developed a credentialing process for play therapists to help identify the core knowledge and skills mental health professionals of any discipline who practiced play therapy should have. In 2001, the association launched its first web-based continuing education program to make high-quality training available to anyone with internet access. The association established standards for Approved Providers of Play Therapy Continuing Education (Association for Play Therapy, 2010). Each year, thousands of hours of continuing education are offered across the country by such approved providers. Through this approval process there are now approved training sites, online webinars, and an e-learning center so that one can acquire the skills necessary, as well as the supervision needed.

OVERVIEW OF THE VOLUME

The purpose of this book is to provide a detailed understanding of 15 play therapy modalities. These modalities are at the core of how one would practice play therapy. Starting with the "classic" modalities, such as sandtray, doll play, block play, and drawings, the authors illustrate how the clinician can use these modalities in play therapy sessions. With the use of popular modalities, such as bibliotherapy, storytelling, puppetry, and guided imagery, play therapists can use verbal communication to achieve therapeutic goals. Additionally, recent focus upon modalities, such as sensory play, drama play, and music/movement play, has been integrated into play therapy to include the whole body in the intervention. Board game play, electronic game play, and virtual reality play complete the book with exciting additions to the play therapist's modality options.

Each chapter of this book focuses on one of these play modalities written by notable child clinicians with particular expertise in one or more of these play techniques. Critical information such as therapeutic benefits, core techniques, clinical application, and empirical support is included for each modality. Through their extensive experience, these clinicians have learned to implement the modalities in an effective and child friendly manner, which is reflected in their case illustrations.

REFERENCES

Association for Play Therapy. (2010). *History speaks: Frey interview.* http://youtu.be/6cxO0UQZFuo

Barnett, L. A. (1990). Developmental benefits of play for children. *Journal of Leisure Research, 22*(2), 138–153. https://doi.org/10.1080/00222216.1990.11969821

Brown, S. D. (2015). Foreword. In D. A. Crenshaw & A. L. Stewart (Eds.), *Play therapy: A comprehensive guide to theory and practice* (p. xi). Guilford Press.

Drewes, A. A. (2011a). Integrating play therapy theories into practice. In A. A. Drewes, S. C. Bratton, & C. E. Schaefer (Eds.), *Integrative play therapy* (pp. 21–35). John Wiley & Sons. https://doi.org/10.1002/9781118094792.ch2

Drewes, A. A. (2011b). Integrative play therapy. In C. E. Schaefer (Ed.), *Foundations of play therapy* (2nd ed., pp. 349–364). John Wiley & Sons.

Fisher, E. (1992). The impact of play on development: A meta-analysis. *Play & Culture, 5,* 159–181.

Gallo-Lopez, L., & Schaefer, C. E. (2005). *Play therapy with adolescents.* Jason Aronson.

Ginsburg, K. R., the American Academy of Pediatrics Committee on Communications, & the American Academy of Pediatrics Committee on Psychosocial Aspects of Child and Family Health. (2007). The importance of play in promoting healthy child development and maintaining strong parent–child bonds. *Pediatrics, 119*(1), 182–191. https://doi.org/10.1542/peds.2006-2697

Gray, P. (2011). The decline of play and the rise of psychopathology in children and adolescents. *American Journal of Play, 3*(4), 443–463.

Holmes, S. V., & Kivlighan, C. (2000). Comparison of therapeutic factors in group and individual treatment processes. *Journal of Counseling Psychology, 47*(4), 478–484. https://doi.org/10.1037/0022-0167.47.4.478

Kaduson, H. G., Cangelosi, D., & Schaefer, C. E. (2020). *Prescriptive play therapy: Tailoring interventions to specific childhood problems.* Guilford Press.

Opiola, K., & Bratton, S. (2018). The efficacy of child parent relationship therapy for adoptive families: A replication study. *Journal of Counseling and Development, 96*(2), 155–166. https://doi.org/10.1002/jcad.12189

Paul, G. L. (1967). Strategy of outcome research in psychotherapy. *Journal of Consulting Psychology, 31*(2), 109–118. https://doi.org/10.1037/h0024436

Reddy, L. A., Files-Hall, T. M., & Schaefer, C. E. (Eds.). (2005). *Empirically based play interventions for children*. American Psychological Association. https://doi.org/10.1037/11086-000

Reddy, L. A., Files-Hall, T. M., & Schaefer, C. E. (Eds.). (2016). *Empirically based play interventions for children* (2nd ed.). American Psychological Association. https://doi.org/10.1037/14730-000

Schaefer, C. E. (2003). *Play therapy with adults*. John Wiley & Sons.

Schaefer, C. E., & Drewes, A. A. (2010). The therapeutic powers of play and play therapy. In A. A. Drewes & C. E. Schaefer (Eds.), *School-based play therapy* (2nd ed., pp. 3–16). John Wiley & Sons. https://doi.org/10.1002/9781118269701.ch1

Schaefer, C. E., & Drewes, A. A. (2011). The therapeutic powers of play and play therapy. In C. E. Schaefer (Ed.), *Foundations of play therapy* (2nd ed., pp. 15–26). John Wiley & Sons.

Schaefer, C. E., & Drewes, A. A. (2014). *The therapeutic powers of play: 20 core agents of change*. John Wiley & Sons.

Shen, Y. (2016). A descriptive study of school counselors' play therapy experiences with the culturally diverse. *International Journal of Play Therapy, 25*(2), 54–63. https://doi.org/10.1037/pla0000017

Yalom, I. D. (1995). *The theory and practice of group psychotherapy* (4th ed.). Basic Books.

1

SANDTRAY THERAPY

DANIEL S. SWEENEY

Sandtray therapy is a wonderful application of Jung's (1957/1985) powerful assertion that "often the hands will solve a mystery that the intellect has struggled with in vain" (para. 181). This expressive and projective therapy has remarkable and adaptable qualities as a therapeutic intervention. For clients, it is (a) beautiful, in its creative nature; (b) raw, in its ability to touch deep and sensitive areas of the psyche; and (c) safe, in its ability to explore these areas in a projective and expressive manner. Who knew that the powerful tools of sandtray, facilitated by a trained and experienced sandtray therapist, could be so powerful? The basic tools of a tray, sand, and miniature figures can indeed make a deep and lasting impact. This chapter provides the reader with a summary of the philosophy behind it, therapeutic benefits and core techniques of this valuable intervention, the empirical support for it, and a case illustration of its use with a child.

A significant advantage of sandtray therapy is that it can incorporate a broad array of technical and theoretical psychotherapeutic approaches. It can be nondirective or directive, can be largely nonverbal or quite verbal, and can frequently incorporate techniques from a variety of therapeutic approaches. These qualities make sandtray therapy a truly cross-theoretical intervention.

https://doi.org/10.1037/0000217-002
Play Therapy With Children: Modalities for Change, H. G. Kaduson and C. E. Schaefer (Editors)

Homeyer and Sweeney (2017a) emphasized that sandtray therapy is indeed cross-theoretical, not atheoretical.

I wish to point out that sandtray therapy interventions and techniques should always be theoretically based. Sweeney (2011a) asserted that theory is always important, but theory without technique is basically philosophy. At the same time, techniques may be quite valuable, but techniques without theory are reckless and could be damaging. Sweeney (2011a) further asserted that

> all therapists are encouraged to ponder some questions regarding employing techniques: (a) Is the technique developmentally appropriate? [which presupposes that developmental capabilities are a key therapeutic consideration]; (b) What theory underlies the technique? [which presupposes that techniques should be theory-based]; and (c) What is the therapeutic intent in employing a given technique? [which presupposes that having specific therapeutic intent is clinically and ethically important]. (p. 236)

The definition of sandtray therapy reflects this contention that it is a cross-theoretical approach. As such, it does not include theory-specific language. Homeyer and Sweeney (2017a) offered the following definition:

> Sandtray therapy is an expressive and projective mode of psychotherapy involving the unfolding and processing of intra- and inter-personal issues through the use of specific sandtray materials as a nonverbal medium of communication, led by the client or therapist and facilitated by a trained therapist. (p. 6)

Sandtray therapy includes a variety of approaches, which cannot be fully discussed in this chapter. The most widely used approach is sandplay therapy (Kalff, 2003). It is important to note the specific and intentional term *sandtray therapy* in this chapter, as opposed to *sandplay therapy*. Sandtray therapy includes any theoretical and technical use of sandtray materials in the psychotherapeutic process. Sandplay therapy is the well-defined Jungian approach to sandtray therapy. Although I fully endorse sandplay therapy, the distinction is an important one.

The history of sandtray therapy begins in the 1920s, when British pediatrician Margaret Lowenfeld (1979) was looking for a developmentally appropriate way to allow children to express their emotional and psychological inner worlds. She was seeking a

> medium which would in itself be instantly attractive to children and which would give them and the observer a language, as it were, through which communication could be established . . . if given the right tools, they would find their way to communication of their interior experience. (p. 281)

Lowenfeld developed an approach to working with children using miniature toys and a sandtray. As clients created their "worlds" in the sandtray, Lowenfeld's approach was named the *world technique*.

Sandtray work with children was expanded and promoted by Dora Kalff, a Swiss Jungian analyst. Kalff (2003) learned of Lowenfeld's work and studied with her in London. She adapted the procedure, calling her approach Sandplay—to differentiate it from Lowenfeld's World Technique. As just mentioned, the term *sandplay* is the Jungian approach, although it has been widely (and, some would argue, inappropriately) used outside of Jungian circles. Kalff (1971) acknowledged Lowenfeld's important contribution: "She understood completely the child's world and created with ingenious intuition a way which enables the child to build a world—his world—in a sandbox" (p. 32).

As this chapter moves on to further discuss sandtray therapy, a point should be made about its unique quality of creating a safe place for clients to tell their story. As we consider safety, it is helpful to remember van der Kolk's (2002) contention that trauma always involves *speechless terror*—that traumatized clients are fundamentally not able to put feelings into words and are thus left with overwhelming emotions that cannot be fully verbalized. He further stated that as long as clients "are unable to talk about their traumatic experiences, they simply have no story, and instead, the trauma is likely to be expressed as an embodiment of what happened" (van der Kolk, 2003, p. 311). Sandtray provides a safe place to tell their stories.

THERAPEUTIC BENEFITS

Multiple benefits and rationales for the sandtray therapy process have been posited (Homeyer & Sweeney, 2017a, 2017b; Sweeney, 2016) using the therapeutic powers of play:

- Sandtray therapy inherently gives expression to nonverbalized emotional issues. Like other expressive and projective therapies, sandtray provides a *language* for clients unable or unwilling to verbalize. In this case, the sandtray therapy process is the *language*, and the sandtray miniatures are the *words*. Along with this, clients do not need creative or artistic ability to participate, which may be the case for other art-related interventions. As such, sandtray facilitates self-expression (Bennett & Eberts, 2014) as one of the therapeutic powers in *The Therapeutic Powers of Play* (Schaefer & Drewes, 2014).

- Sandtray therapy naturally has a unique kinesthetic quality. The innate and novel sensory and kinesthetic experience in sandtray therapy serves as an extension of foundational attachment needs. Attachment, as a therapeutic power of play, is further discussed by Whelan and Stewart (2014).

- Sandtray therapy serves to create an indispensable therapeutic distance for all-aged clients. When clients are experiencing challenges expressing themselves through verbalization, they can often do so through a projective medium such as sandtray therapy, which allows for their unconscious expression. Oftentimes, it is simply easier for traumatized clients to "speak" through sandtray miniatures than to directly verbalize pain.

- The therapeutic distance that sandtray therapy furnishes creates a safe place for abreaction to occur. Clients who have experienced trauma fiercely need a therapeutic setting in which to abreact. This therapeutic distance provides a place where unexpressed issues can emerge in the context of safety—and thus be safely relived—as well as providing the opportunity to experience the associated negative emotions. This abreactive element is another crucial therapeutic power of play (Prendiville, 2014; Schaefer & Drewes, 2014).

- Related to this, sandtray therapy is an effective intervention for traumatized clients. When considering the neurobiological effects of trauma (Badenoch & Kestly, 2015; De Bellis & Zisk, 2014; Gaskill & Perry, 2014; van der Kolk, 2014), provision of an expressive intervention is crucial. For example, with prefrontal cortical dysfunction, overactivation of the limbic system, and deactivation of the Broca's area—the part of the brain responsible for speech (van der Kolk, 2014)—this approach clearly points to the benefit of nonverbally based interventions. This clear neurobiological interference with cognitive processing and verbalization clearly invites the use of an expressive intervention such as sandtray therapy.

- Sandtray therapy is effective in overcoming client resistance. The inherently engaging and nonthreatening nature of sandtray therapy often captivates the involuntary (e.g., the vast majority of children) or reticent client. For children who are resistant or perhaps even fear verbal engagement, sandtray therapy can provide a safer means of therapeutic connection. This fostering of the therapeutic relationship is further discussed as a therapeutic power of play in Stewart and Echterling (2014).

- Sandtray therapy provides an effective (and possibly necessary) communication medium for the client with poor verbal skills. Combining the always essential element of providing developmentally appropriate therapeutic interventions for child clients, therapists also encounter clients who have poor verbal skills (e.g., stuttering). Sandtray therapy helps clients who experience language deficits or delays, physiological challenges, and/or social difficulties.

- Conversely, sandtray therapy cuts through verbalization used as a defense. For clients, even children, who are verbally astute or may use verbalization as a means to resist or manipulate, sandtray therapy provides a means of legitimate or undefended communication. Sandtray therapy can assist some clients who use verbal rationalization and intellectualization as a defense because it can cut through these defenses.

- The potential challenge of transference can be effectively addressed and processed through sandtray therapy. The cross-theoretical sandtray therapy process provides an agent for transference issues to be safely identified and thus addressed. In sandtray therapy, the miniatures and tray become the objects of transference (rather than the therapist), thus an effective means through which transference issues are identified and appropriately focused on within the therapeutic relationship.

- Finally, it is clear that in the deeper intrapersonal and interpersonal issues are accessed more thoroughly and more rapidly through sandtray therapy. The cumulative benefits and rationales for sandtray therapy just noted establish a therapeutic milieu where complex and profound presenting issues can be safely approached. Many clients are, not surprisingly, psychologically and neurobiologically guarded when addressing challenges to their injured self, and the safety of sandtray therapy serves to create safety, decrease defenses, and increase therapeutic interaction. This access to the unconscious is discussed as another therapeutic power of play by Crenshaw and Tillman (2014).

- These benefits and rationales are ultimately based on Margaret Lowenfeld's simple observation: "Children think with their hands" ("A Short Biography of Margaret Lowenfeld and the Margaret Lowenfeld Trust," 2019, para. 3). Although this applies to clients of all ages, this supposition is particularly important for sandtray therapy with children.

CORE TOOLS AND TECHNIQUES

As noted earlier in this chapter, sandtray therapy has the ability to be both cross-theoretical and cross-technical. Before discussing a variety of possible techniques, the sandtray therapist must initially assemble a variety of basic tools.

Sandtray Tools

The tools of the sandtray therapy process should be intentionally selected, not merely collected. The essential components consist of the sandtray, the sand, and the sandtray miniatures. It is not possible to discuss these tools at length, but some comments are necessary.

The size of the tray and its shape are crucial and may vary according to theoretical tray. Sandplay therapists prefer a standard rectangular size, which is approximately 30 in. × 20 in. × 3 in. (Kalff, 2003; Turner, 2005). This size is frequently used by sandtray therapists from across theoretical orientations. Trays can be another shape, such as round, square, or octagonal, but the size should not be substantially bigger or smaller. Generally, a group or family sandtray experience will need a larger tray. A helpful guideline is that the sandtray for a single client should be able to be viewed in a single glance. Also, trays are often painted blue on the inside, to represent water and sky (Homeyer & Sweeney, 2017a; Turner, 2005).

It is important to recognize that the tray is more than merely a container for the sand. It is also a container of the psyche. Jung's (1977) discussion about the notion of *temenos* is highly valuable. The Greek word *temenos* refers to the sacred space surrounding a temple or an altar. Jung used the concept to describe a deep inner space within people where *soul-making* occurs. Within this, temenos speaks of a boundary between what is sacred and what is profane. For Jung, and within the context of this chapter, the therapy experience as a whole is one involving temenos. This is true of the sandtray therapy process but is also true of the sandtray itself. Thus, the tray is a container of the psyche and incorporates temenos, where the sacred is kept separate from the profane.

Inside this container is the sand. Sand texture can range between coarse and fine, and the color can vary. These determinations can be made on the basis of the theoretical approach and the therapist's personal preference (Homeyer & Sweeney, 2017a). Sand is tactile and kinesthetic, and it is an essential part of the sandtray therapy process.

The selection of miniatures is important and should be approached by sandtray therapists with purposeful and intentional consideration. Therapists should have a variety of miniatures within a variety of categories— keeping in mind that a broad collection is important but a large total of miniatures may be inappropriate. Some sandtray therapists are very enthusiastic in the collection process. The general recommendation is to have about 400 to 500 miniatures. Although some sandtray therapists have collections in the thousands, this has the potential to overwhelm already overwhelmed clients. Homeyer and Sweeney (2017a, pp. 27–31) provided recommendations regarding general miniature categories for a balanced collection:

- People: family groups, occupations, different stages of life, historical figures, soldiers, various racial and ethnic peoples
- Animals: prehistoric, wild/zoo, farm/domestic, birds, sea life, insects
- Buildings: houses, schools, castles, forts, lighthouses, churches/temples/mosques
- Transportation: cars, trucks, helicopters, planes, motorcycles, covered wagons
- Vegetation: trees (with and without leaves), bushes, cacti, flowers
- Fences/gates/signs: barricades, railroad tracks, traffic lights, traffic cones
- Natural items: seashells, rocks, fossils, twigs, brambles
- Fantasy: wizards, wishing wells, dragons, unicorns, cartoon characters, children's movie characters, treasure chests
- Spiritual/mystical: religious figures, crystal balls, gold, chalices, pyramids
- Landscaping and accessories: sun, moon, stars, caves, tunnels, monuments, bridges, mailboxes
- Household items: furniture, tools, dishes, utensils
- Miscellaneous items: medical items, alcohol bottles, weapons
- Tools to smooth and move the sand: spatula, brush

This is not an exhaustive list, by any means. Miniatures should be reflective of the clients' culture, keeping in mind such issues as race, ethnicity, gender identity, sexual orientation, socioeconomic status, and religion.

Sandtray Protocol

Similar to the sandtray materials, the sandtray therapy protocol will vary according to therapeutic theory and style. However, Homeyer and Sweeney (2017a) detailed basic elements that are considered important in the overall process: (a) room preparation, (b) introduction to the client, (c) creation of the sandtray, (d) postcreation process, (e) sandtray cleanup, and (f) documentation of the session. These are briefly discussed next.

Room Preparation

It is the responsibility of the therapist to ensure that the sandtray materials are organized, including checking that there no buried items in the tray and ensuring that the sand is somewhat flat. The miniatures should be arranged in an orderly and consistent manner. I prefer that they are displayed on shelves and organized by category. This consistency creates an atmosphere of predictability and safety. The therapist should sit in a nonintrusive place but also remain fully involved. This means not interrupting the developing dynamic between the client and the media. The furniture in the room should facilitate client movement between the tray(s) and the collection of miniatures.

Introduction to the Client

The therapist may use a nondirective or directive approach. A nondirective approach involves giving minimal directions to the client, allowing the creation to be largely the result of the client's interaction with the miniatures, tray, and sand. This may simply involve a prompt from the sandtray therapist to the client, such as, "Create a scene [or Build a world] in the sand, using as many or as few of the miniatures as you'd like." A directive approach might be used when the therapist would like to address a specific issue, or perhaps seems necessary when clients are overwhelmed with a free and unstructured experience. Giving definitive instructions may feel more protective for these clients. This may simply involve a prompt from the sandtray therapist to the client, such as, "I'd like you to create a tray about what it is what like to be bullied" or "If you woke up tomorrow and this problem that brought you into therapy was totally gone, make a tray of what that would look like."

Creation of the Sandtray

During the client's creation of the sandtray scene, the therapist should honor both the process and the product (scene). Kalff (2003) discussed the need to create a "free and protected" space. This involves the previously discussed Jungian concept of temenos. Clients must believe they are fully safe— emotionally, psychologically, spiritually, and physically. The interaction between the therapist and client will again depend on the therapist's approach and style. Some therapists are very verbally interactive, and others remain largely silent during the client's creative process. In sandtray therapy with children, it may be helpful for the therapist to verbally track the process, as is often done in traditional play therapy.

Postcreation Process

It is helpful for the client and therapist to sit on the same side while viewing the sandtray creation. Some sandtray therapists prefer to allow the creative process and product to stand alone, with little to no discussion, arguing that this in itself activates the client's internal healing process. Others use the creative process and creations as a springboard for discussion and continued verbal and nonverbal work with the client. This is generally my process, and experience demonstrates that clients discover insights regardless of whether it is a directed or nondirected experience. Kestly (2014) and Badenoch (2008) have suggested spending process time helping clients bridge the creative, symbolic, emotional, right-brain hemisphere with the therapeutic work in the logical, sequential, verbal, left-brain hemisphere. This recommendation is valuable but should be done with great care so that the *therapeutic distance* that was previously discussed does not get lost in pressuring clients to verbalize.

Sandtray Cleanup

The cleanup element may vary depending on the therapeutic approach of the sandtray therapist. Some like to dismantle the tray with the client, with the goal to further promote the egalitarian process. This relates to the parallel work done as a play therapist. In play therapy, the view is that play as the language and the toys as the words—thus, in sandtray therapy, the miniatures are the words. The miniatures and the creation are fundamentally the expression of the client's emotional life and inner self. As such, it is not considered appropriate in any way to communicate that the client's emotional expression needs to be "cleaned up" and is therefore unacceptable. This belief is consistent with Weinrib's (1983) assertion: "To destroy a picture in the patient's presence would be to devalue a completed creation, to break the connection between the patient and his inner self, and the unspoken connection to the therapist" (p. 14). Having said this, other perspectives, such as Adlerian and cognitive behavioral play therapy (e.g., Drewes, 2009; Kottman & Meany-Walen, 2015), support engaging in a therapist–client cleanup partnership as a means to promote the therapeutic relationship.

Documentation of the Session

Typically, photographs of the completed sandtray creations are taken and placed in the client's file. This should be done with the client's permission—for children, this would involve the legal guardian. These photos are quite helpful for reviewing the progress of clients over a period of time. It is important to note that although these photos are a crucial part of documenting the sandtray therapy process, there is the standard importance of accompanying case notes, which may vary according to therapeutic setting, documentation standards, and therapist preference.

A wide variety of sandtray therapy techniques fit into the aforementioned general structure, ranging from theory-specific interventions to prescriptive practice. For a broad array of interventions, see Homeyer and Sweeney (2017a). Additionally, sandtray therapy can be used with groups of children and in the family therapy process. Sandtray therapy can also be used in a psychoeducational context, as well as psychotherapeutically.

CLINICAL APPLICATIONS

Very few presenting problems, diagnostic considerations, or symptom constellations would be considered inappropriate for sandtray therapy. The typical childhood referrals are for general externalizing (e.g., oppositional defiant disorder, conduct disorder, attention-deficit/hyperactivity disorder) and internalizing problems (e.g., anxiety and depressive disorders) and trauma or stress problems (e.g., posttraumatic stress disorder, attachment disorders, adjustment disorders). These all respond well to sandtray therapy interventions. Children on the autistic spectrum will also benefit from sandtray therapy.

Having posited this sweeping endorsement, certainly some children will find the sensory experience of sand and related materials to be overwhelming. Children with sensory processing challenges may be repulsed by it. Children and adults who are experiencing psychosis can be overloaded by the sandtray process. Any aged client with a fragile psyche can benefit from the non-threatening nature of sandtray therapy. At the same time, this client can be devastated by the tactile quality that makes sandtray so beneficial for others. Therapists should thus be well trained in and sensitive to how clients respond. Some children find the sand "dirty"—and a negative reminder of their own "dirty" experiences. This can be true for clients of any age.

As with other interventions in this book, all projective, expressive, and experiential techniques can be activating for children. Sandtray therapists should do relevant client screening and continued monitoring for the appropriateness of the expressive medium. Related to this, therapists should assess the client's readiness and willingness to move into expressive modalities. This essentially involves the clinical and ethical assessment on the part of the therapist.

CASE ILLUSTRATION

This case is a brief adaptation of a case discussed in Homeyer and Sweeney (2017a), which involves two girls (6 and 8 years of age), and to protect patient confidentiality, identifying details have been changed. It is worth noting that sandtray therapy was not an initial part of the treatment plan. Also, the following description represents only one session but illustrates the benefits of using sandtray therapy. The presenting issue involved a case in which the girls were having a challenging time emotionally and behaviorally adjusting to the current divorce process of their parents. Diagnostically, although the children were described as oppositional, a diagnosis of adjustment disorder

(*Diagnostic and Statistical Manual of Mental Disorders*, fifth ed.; American Psychiatric Association, 2013) was considered a more appropriate fit. Because their emotional and behavioral challenges were in response to their parents' challenges, a variety of diagnostic considerations could be made.

The treatment plan initially involved seeing the girls in sibling group play therapy (Sweeney et al., 2014) and concurrently seeing the parents in filial therapy (Landreth & Bratton, 2019). A significant part of the parent intervention was to create a predictable parent–child experience in each home. Although the use of sandtray therapy was not originally planned, this case illustrates one beneficial use of sandtray—that is, sandtray therapy can be an effective intervention shift at any point in the therapeutic process. This is also an example of *prescriptive play therapy* (e.g., Kaduson et al., 2020).

This particular sandtray therapy experience came about as a result of a scheduling misunderstanding. On a week when the parents were expected for continued filial therapy training, the father brought in the two girls. Standard play therapy equipment was not available that week; however, sandtray therapy materials were. With the work that I do with young children, the use of sandtray miniatures is unusual unless there is a particular intervention in mind.

When the sandtray materials were introduced to the girls, specific directive instructions were given. The girls were told, "On one side, build what your world was like before the divorce. On the other side, build what your world is like now." There was some hesitancy about the girls' ability to comprehend what was meant by the term *world*, but they did not at all seem inhibited.

The 8-year-old girl chose to divide the tray in half using tombstones. This was certainly a vivid depiction of the "death" of their parents' marriage. The metaphorical (and arguably right-brained) display of her recognition of the apparently unchanging termination of her parents' relationship was remarkable.

On the left side of the tray, there was a couple, with the female figure clearly leaning toward the male figure. In their own (developmentally appropriate) words, both girls described this as a representation of how their parents were frequently arguing and underscored that the leaning woman depicted how their mother was particularly loud and aggressive with her words.

In the lower portion of the tray's left half were two girl miniature figures far from the adult figures; the girl figures' faces were against the side of the tray. I believe that this demonstrated the girls' emotional and physical need to hide from their parents when they were fighting.

On the right side of the tray, the scene was divided in half with fences. Unlike the thorough separation of the sides of the tray sides using tombstones, the divisions of this side of the tray with fences seemed somewhat open and porous. The state of child custody at the time (permanent custody arrangements were not yet established) was joint physical custody, and the girls often experienced their parents interacting.

The top half of the right side showed the girls' description of living with their mother. They chose a miniature in academic regalia (female in white graduation gown and cap), as they clearly recognized the relationship between this figure and school, stating that their mother had recently gone back to school. They also perceived that, between school and their mother's social life ("She's dating"), she didn't have time for the girls. Notably, in this section of the tray the two girl figures they'd selected for themselves were facing away from their mother. Also, these figures were larger than all other figures in the tray. Perhaps this spoke of their desire, albeit ignored, to be noticed at home.

On the bottom half of this side, the girls' miniatures were facing the figurine chosen for their father. Perhaps this reflected the fact that the father was noted to be more relational in the filial therapy process. Of interest, the girls selected a judge figure for their father and did not discuss this selection. It is possible that this represented some part of the girls' perception of their father—or possibly, with the custody issue not yet resolved, it could have symbolized their awareness of the judge's power and authority in this process.

Although this was not an ongoing sandtray therapy case, the vivid depiction of the girls' perception of the divorce and relationship dynamics is an example of the therapeutic power of sandtray therapy and the therapeutic powers of play (Schaefer & Drewes, 2014). Significantly, the majority of the benefits and rationale of sandtray therapy noted earlier can be seen in this extraordinary intervention.

EMPIRICAL SUPPORT

The majority of the sandtray therapy literature has been theoretical, practice, and case study related. Thus, there is limited outcome research. However, there is emerging evidence for sandtray therapy being an effective expressive intervention.

It should first be noted that many sandtray interventions are adaptations of empirically based interventions. These include cognitive behavioral interventions (Homeyer & Sweeney, 2017a; Sweeney & Homeyer, 2009) and solution-focused sandtray therapy interventions (Nims, 2007; Sweeney, 2011b; Taylor, 2009).

There are two solid outcome studies regarding group sandtray therapy (Flahive & Ray, 2007; Shen & Armstrong, 2008). Flahive and Ray (2007) used a pretest/posttest control group design with 56 nine- to 12-year-olds who were referred by teachers for disruptive classroom behaviors; peer interaction challenges; and/or symptoms of anxiety, depression, or being withdrawn. Students in the treatment group had slight improvement, and the control group displayed worsening behavior. Teachers also reported significant changes in internalizing behaviors between the groups and externalizing behavior improved, as reported by both caregivers and teachers (Flahive & Ray, 2007).

Shen and Armstrong (2008) studied 37 seventh-grade girls, also using a pretest/posttest control group design, noting changes in self-esteem. The treatment groups consisted of four girls meeting twice a week, for a total of nine sessions, and completing directed sandtrays focusing on self-esteem issues. Results demonstrated that participants in the self-esteem–focused treatment groups showed improvement on measures of scholastic competence, physical appearance, global self-worth, and behavioral conduct (Shen & Armstrong, 2008).

Although using a small sample size ($N = 26$) in a study comparing sandtray therapy and behavioral modification with fourth-grade students (Zarzaur, 2005), teachers' perception of students' ability to adapt and reduction of specific unwanted behaviors was equally beneficial in both interventions. In a larger study, involving sandplay therapy with 56 children and adolescents (M age $= 10$ years), von Gontard et al. (2010) found a reduction of total and internalizing behavioral issues.

There is clearly a need for further research to establish the efficacy of sandtray therapy as an empirically based psychotherapeutic intervention. This is consistent with Kestly's (2014) and Bratton's (2015) call for greater research in play and sandtray therapy, as well as the dissemination of this research to establish greater credence to these important fields.

SUMMARY AND CONCLUSION

Spare (1981) wrote the following about sandplay, which I believe applies to all sandtray interventions:

> As with every aspect of clinical practice, meaningful use of sandplay is a function of our own human hearts, and of the ever ongoing interplay between our own centers and the centers, hearts, and needs of those we are privileged to see in psychotherapy. (p. 208)

This speaks to the application of theories and techniques to the child's soul and reflects Jung's (1928) encouragement: "Learn your theories as well as you can, but put them aside, when you touch the miracle of the living soul" (p. 361).

Having shared a few philosophical thoughts, some last comments. Sandtray therapy is a powerful intervention, in part because it is so flexible and adaptive. These elements lend themselves to its ability to deeply impact clients in deep intrapsychic and interpersonal ways. In this short chapter, sandtray therapy is seen as genuinely cross-theoretical—almost any therapeutic approach or technique can be adapted, it can be prescriptive, and it can be as directive or nondirective as the therapist or therapeutic situation calls for. This can occur through sandtray therapy—facilitated by a trained, intentional, and empathic sandtray therapist.

REFERENCES

American Psychiatric Association. (2013). *Diagnostic and statistical manual of mental disorders* (5th ed.).

A short biography of Margaret Lowenfeld and the Margaret Lowenfeld Trust. (2019). Sussex Academic Press. http://www.sussex-academic.com/sa/titles/psychology/LowenfeldBiography.htm

Badenoch, B. (2008). *Being a brain-wise therapist*. W. W. Norton.

Badenoch, B., & Kestly, T. (2015). Exploring the neuroscience of healing play at every age. In D. A. Crenshaw & A. L. Stewart (Eds.), *Play therapy: A comprehensive guide to theory and practice* (pp. 524–538). Guilford Press.

Bennett, M. M., & Eberts, S. (2014). Self-expression. In C. E. Schaefer & A. A. Drewes (Eds.), *The therapeutic powers of play: 20 core agents of change* (pp. 11–24). John Wiley & Sons.

Bratton, S. C. (2015). The empirical support for play therapy: Strengths and limitations. In K. J. O'Connor, C. E. Schaefer, & L. D. Braverman (Eds.), *Handbook of play therapy* (2nd ed., pp. 651–668). John Wiley & Sons. https://doi.org/10.1002/9781119140467.ch35

Crenshaw, D., & Tillman, K. (2014). Access to the unconscious. In C. E. Schaefer & A. A. Drewes (Eds.), *The therapeutic powers of play: 20 core agents of change* (pp. 25–38). John Wiley & Sons.

De Bellis, M. D., & Zisk, A. (2014). The biological effects of childhood trauma. *Child and Adolescent Psychiatric Clinics of North America, 23*(2), 185–222, vii. https://doi.org/10.1016/j.chc.2014.01.002

Drewes, A. A. (Ed.). (2009). *Blending play therapy with cognitive behavioral therapy: Evidence-based and other effective treatments and techniques*. John Wiley & Sons.

Flahive, M. W., & Ray, D. (2007). Effect of group sandtray work with adolescents. *Journal for Specialists in Group Work, 32*(4), 362–382. https://doi.org/10.1080/01933920701476706

Gaskill, R. L., & Perry, B. D. (2014). The neurobiological power of play: Using the neurosequential model of therapeutics to guide play in the healing process. In C. A. Malchiodi & D. A. Crenshaw (Eds.), *Creative arts and play therapy for attachment problems* (pp. 178–196). Guilford Press.

Homeyer, L. E., & Sweeney, D. S. (2017a). *Sandtray therapy: A practical manual* (3rd ed.). Routledge.

Homeyer, L. E., & Sweeney, D. S. (2017b). Sandtray therapy: A variety of approaches. In B. A. Turner (Ed.), *The Routledge international handbook of sandplay therapy* (pp. 328–338). Routledge.

Jung, C. G. (1928). *Contributions to analytical psychology*. Harcourt Brace.

Jung, C. G. (1977). *Symbols of transformation*. Princeton University Press.

Jung, C. G. (1985). *The collected works of C. G. Jung* (Vol. 16, para. 181). Princeton University Press. (Original work published 1957)

Kaduson, H. G., Schaefer, C. E., & Cangelosi, D. (Eds.). (2020). *Basic principles and core practices of prescriptive play therapy*. In H. G. Kaduson, D. Cangelosi, & C. E. Schaefer (Eds.), *Prescriptive play therapy: Tailoring interventions for specific childhood problems* (pp. 3–13). Guilford Press.

Kalff, D. M. (1971). *Sandplay: Mirror of a child's psyche*. C.G. Jung Institute.

Kalff, D. M. (2003). *Sandplay: A psychotherapeutic approach to the psyche*. Temenos Press.

Kestly, T. A. (2014). *The interpersonal neurobiology of play: Brain-building interventions for emotional well-building*. W. W. Norton.

Kottman, T., & Meany-Walen, K. (Eds.). (2015). *Partners in play: An Adlerian approach to play therapy* (3rd ed.). American Counseling Association. https://doi.org/10.1002/9781119272205

Landreth, G. L., & Bratton, S. C. (2019). *Child–parent relationship therapy (CPRT): An evidence-based 10-session filial therapy model* (2nd ed.). Routledge. https://doi.org/10.4324/9781315537948

Lowenfeld, M. (1979). *The world technique*. George Allen & Unwin.

Nims, D. R. (2007). Integrating play therapy techniques into solution-focused brief therapy. *International Journal of Play Therapy, 16*(1), 54–68. https://doi.org/10.1037/1555-6824.16.1.54

Prendiville, E. (2014). Abreaction. In C. E. Schaefer & A. A. Drewes (Eds.), *The therapeutic powers of play: 20 core agents of change* (pp. 83–103). John Wiley & Sons.

Schaefer, C. E., & Drewes, A. A. (Eds.). (2014). *The therapeutic powers of play: 20 core agents of change*. John Wiley & Sons.

Shen, Y.-P., & Armstrong, S. A. (2008). Impact of group sandtray therapy on the self-esteem of young adolescent girls. *Journal for Specialists in Group Work, 33*(2), 118–137. https://doi.org/10.1080/01933920801977397

Spare, G. (1981). Are there any rules? (Musings of a peripatetic sandplayer). In K. Bradway, K. A. Signell, G. Spare, C. T. Stewart, L. H. Stewart, & C. Thompson (Eds.), *Sandplay studies: Origins, theory and practice* (pp. 195–208). C.G. Jung Institute.

Stewart, A. L., & Echterling, L. G. (2014). Therapeutic relationship. In C. E. Schaefer & A. A. Drewes (Eds.), *The therapeutic powers of play: 20 core agents of change* (pp. 157–169). John Wiley & Sons.

Sweeney, D. S. (2011a). Group play therapy. In C. E. Schaefer (Ed.), *Foundations of play therapy* (2nd ed., pp. 227–252). John Wiley & Sons.

Sweeney, D. S. (2011b). Integration of sandtray therapy and solution-focused techniques for treating noncompliant youth. In A. A. Drewes, S. C. Bratton, & C. E. Schaefer (Eds.), *Integrative play therapy* (pp. 61–73). John Wiley & Sons. https://doi.org/10.1002/9781118094792.ch4

Sweeney, D. S. (2016). Sandtray therapy: A neurobiological approach. In E. Prendiville & J. Howard (Eds.), *Creative psychotherapy: Applying the principles of neurobiology to play and expressive arts-based practice* (pp. 157–170). Routledge.

Sweeney, D. S., Baggerly, J., & Ray, D. C. (2014). *Group play therapy: A dynamic approach*. Routledge. https://doi.org/10.4324/9780203103944

Sweeney, D. S., & Homeyer, L. E. (2009). Sandtray therapy. In A. A. Drewes (Ed.), *Blending of play therapy and cognitive behavioral therapy: Evidence-based and other effective treatments and techniques* (pp. 297–318). John Wiley & Sons.

Taylor, E. R. (2009). Sandtray and solution-focused therapy. *International Journal of Play Therapy, 18*(1), 56–68. https://doi.org/10.1037/a0014441

Turner, B. A. (2005). *The handbook of sandplay therapy.* Temenos Press.

van der Kolk, B. (2014). *The body keeps the score: Brain, mind, and body in the healing of trauma.* Penguin Books.

van der Kolk, B. A. (2002). In terror's grip: Healing the ravages of trauma. *Cerebrum, 4,* 34–50.

van der Kolk, B. A. (2003). The neurobiology of childhood trauma and abuse. *Child and Adolescent Psychiatric Clinics of North America, 12*(2), 293–317, ix. https://doi.org/10.1016/S1056-4993(03)00003-8

von Gontard, A., Löwen-Seifert, S., Wachter, U., Kumru, Z., Becker-Wördenweber, E., Hochadel, M., Schneider, S., & Senges, C. (2010). Sandplay therapy study: A prospective outcome study of sandplay therapy with children and adolescents. *Journal of Sandplay Therapy, 19*(2), 131–139.

Weinrib, E. L. (1983). *Images of self: The sandplay therapy process.* Sigo Press.

Whelan, W. F., & Stewart, A. L. (2014). Attachment. In C. E. Schaefer & A. A. Drewes (Eds.), *The therapeutic powers of play: 20 core agents of change* (pp. 171–183). John Wiley & Sons.

Zarzaur, M. C. (2005). The effectiveness of sandtray therapy versus classroom behavior management on the improvement of school behavior of kindergarten through fourth-grade students [Master's thesis]. *Dissertation Abstracts International, 65*(11-A), 4121.

2 DOLL PLAY

JULIE BLUNDON NASH

Doll play has long been a part of children's lives and cultures. From early Victorian era wives collecting and creating family lives in miniature as a way to showcase wealth to rural children in the 1800s covering corncobs in scraps of fabric (e.g., Laura Ingalls Wilder's first doll in 1871; Wilder, 2016) to children in the 2000s connecting mechanical dolls to computers to update their capabilities, dolls are known in many formats and serve multiple functions.

Dolls come in many types, including baby dolls, plush dolls (both human and animal), worry dolls, and anatomically correct and specific dolls. They have been used in home, school, and therapeutic settings to encourage children's sense of self, teach nurturance, gain insight into children's thoughts and emotions, assess aggression, support sexual abuse disclosures, reduce anxiety related to medical procedures, and learn about familial relationships. Considerable research supports the use of dolls to reduce anxiety and cognitive disturbances for people dealing with dementia, but for the purposes of this chapter, only doll play with children is discussed.

https://doi.org/10.1037/0000217-003
Play Therapy With Children: Modalities for Change, H. G. Kaduson and C. E. Schaefer (Editors)

In 1897, a book by Granville Stanley Hall and Alexander Caswell Ellis titled *A Study of Dolls* was published, which the authors identified as the first "serious attempt" to study "one of the chief toys of children . . . so nearly universal" (p. 1) amongst multiple socioeconomic and ethnic groups. The authors noted that dolls were mentioned in historical literature from the 15th century on, in multiple areas of the world, used for play as well as cultural and religious activities and showcasing wealth and status. This is perhaps the earliest suggestion of the role of dolls in therapeutic play, as Hall and Caswell suggested that all of children's unconscious ideas are represented in their doll play and that "almost anything within these large topics can be explored by the observing, tactful adult, without danger of injuring that naivete of childhood which is both its best trait and its chief charm" (p. 68).

Research has continued to examine the access to the unconscious that doll play provides as well as multiple assessment opportunities and therapeutic benefits. Whereas early research focused on doll play primarily as a means to gain insight about children's lives, thoughts, relationships, and emotions (e.g., Baruch, 1941), developments have been made to research the use of doll play to assess aggression (e.g., Levin & Turgeon, 1957; Sears, 1951) and fantasy worlds (Marshall & Doshi, 1965). More recent research has included examination of a child's view of the world and racial identities (Jesuvadian & Wright, 2011), as well as use in assessment of attachment and clinical issues (e.g., Cole & Piercy, 2007; Dubois-Comtois & Moss, 2008). Multiple techniques that harness the therapeutic benefits and power of doll play have been developed from this research and from clinical experience; these techniques are discussed later in this chapter, along with the therapeutic benefits of doll play, clinical applications, a case illustration, and further exploration of relevant research and findings.

THERAPEUTIC BENEFITS

Doll play supports and is supported by multiple therapeutic powers of play. From the earliest observations and writings about doll play, it was clear that this play encourages self-expression and access to the unconscious (Hall & Ellis, 1897). In 1943, Sargent recognized that play with dolls allowed children to identify and project their current conflicts (both internal and external) and literally play these out while in spontaneous play, thus encouraging the powers of creative problem solving and abreaction. Techniques have been created to specify the doll play such that behavioral modifications and new solutions can be developed and used (Mann, 1957). Such play also allows for the power of indirect teaching to be used, as children can learn new skills such as feeding and dressing (motor skills development), help to overcome hurdles in skills such as toilet training, and develop and accept nurturing behaviors (Kiley et al., 2012). The latter is also a key component when using the therapeutic power of empathy.

The ability to hold and manipulate a doll allows a child a sense of miniaturization, as the child is able to be larger and more powerful than the character represented by the doll. This characteristic of doll play allows for the therapeutic powers of stress inoculation and counterconditioning of fears to be more fully utilized. For example, when children are able to practice through doll play, they are able to experience major life events, such as the arrival of a new sibling or entering a new school, on a small and manageable scale. Hurdles in development that may be difficult or cause fear, such as toilet training, bathing, riding a school bus, or separating from a loved one, can be played out through doll play, allowing the child to experience the fear and challenge on a smaller scale and overcome that anxiety, thus creating a positive foundation for experiencing the actual event. Doll play has been used successfully in medical settings to reduce children's anxiety of medical procedures through exposure, teaching, and practice (e.g., Gaynard et al., 1991).

These abilities to manipulate and practice on smaller representations, as well as to develop and practice new skills, allow for the therapeutic powers of social competence, moral development, and self-regulation to be addressed. To become socially competent, one must develop both social skills and the ability to successfully use those skills (Nash & Schaefer, 2011). Being able to play with these skills through doll play allows children to develop them and fill in learning gaps as needed, resulting in the opportunity to apply social skills to real-life situations in a more seamless way. The same is true of moral development and self-regulation. By being able to manipulate the experience of these skills in nonthreatening and controlled situations, children open themselves to the healing powers of play in these realms.

CORE TECHNIQUES

Specific techniques have been developed to highlight the use of dolls, including doll play narratives, assessments, adaptive doll play, doll play interviews, and use in medical and forensic settings. The use of dolls during unstructured play therapy should not be discounted. Doll play has long been seen as useful in delineating relationships, acquiring and practicing skills, working through trauma, and developing nurturance skills.

One of the earliest applications of doll play that has continued to be used therapeutically through the years is narrative based, in which a child is given dolls and a setting and asked to create a story with the combination (Levin & Wardwell, 1962). In narrative doll play, specific sentence or question stems are given to children for them to complete through play and words. Stems can be specifically chosen to correspond to presenting problems or needs of the child, as well as attachment and family dynamics (Murray, 2007). Multiple assessment batteries have been published to this effect, including the MacArthur Story Stem Battery (Bretherton & Oppenheim, 2003), Attachment Doll Play Assessment (George & Solomon, 2016), and Attachment Story Completion Task (Bretherton et al., 1990). In these assessments, children and/ or adult interviewers choose dolls to represent families, and the interviewer presents the child with a specific story stem. As the child plays out the story, the interviewer may prompt the play with specific predetermined statements, and themes are identified and classified (George & Solomon, 2016).

Although these assessments are primarily completed for research studies, the clinical value cannot be ignored. Less methodologically stringent methods can be used in the therapy setting to provide some exploratory play and to gather more specific information. These methods would take more of an interview format and allow the child to be flexible in his or her play (C. H. Ammons & Ammons, 1952). Another method would be having dolls available for children to use spontaneously as needed, with further discussion as appropriate. For instance, Stein et al. (2004) presented a case study in which a 9-year-old child spontaneously played out a domestic violence scene between dolls and was then able to answer verbal questions about her experiences.

A child might be encouraged to create a story using dolls, with the therapist responding in doll play based on the child's presenting needs (Sniscak, 2001). The two can create the setting and conversation in back-and-forth communication, with the therapist expressing the feelings and behaviors appropriate to the situation, thus exposing the child to these in a safe setting. Various solutions might be presented for a problem and allowed to be played out and experienced. Doll play can also be used in this way to prepare a child for a stressful situation such as a court trial, new school situations, or parental separation (Sniscak, 2001). More specific stories can be created that include a beginning, middle, and end to specifically move a child through a challenging situation such as parental separation and learning new routines, and parents can be encouraged to use this technique at home (Brennan, 2001).

Specific dolls have been patented for use in medical settings to allow a child to practice and prepare for medical procedures. These dolls include things such as wounds, tracheostomy sites, injection sites, veins, stomas, catheter openings, and feeding tubes. The purpose of these dolls is to allow people to learn about various medical procedures and practice in a hands-on environment (Aponte, 1994). Such tools are clinically applicable for some children and have been adapted into medical settings via these specific dolls as well as more nondescript dolls that are offered with medical tools (e.g., Gaynard et al., 1991).

Anatomical dolls that include genitalia can be used as toys with children who have experienced sexual abuse (Marvasti, 2001). In these cases, doll play would be used for education and trauma play. A child who chooses to use these dolls may reenact an episode of sexual abuse because of over-stimulation to reduce internal tension and increase mastery over the event, which is typical of posttraumatic play (Marvasti, 2001). A child might also use these dolls for abreactive play in which he or she acts out the traumatic episode and the therapist encourages mastery and introduction of helper figures to create a mastery ending.

Anatomically correct dolls can also be used during forensic interviews to serve a number of functions. An evaluator might use the dolls to prompt or explain questions, or to break the ice or comfort during the interview process (Everson & Boat, 1994). Evaluators might use the dolls to stimulate a child's memory of alleged events or demonstrate specific questions (Everson & Boat, 1994).

A therapist might introduce worry dolls to a child to provide a medium to explore anxiety and worry. Traditional Guatemalan worry dolls are tiny at 1 to 2 inches tall and are given in sets of multiple dolls. They have bright colors of threads and yarns and are easy to tuck into a hand (Nieves-Grafals, 2001). Children are encouraged to tell one worry to each doll and place them underneath their pillows at night so that the dolls can remove the worries as the children sleep (McInnis, 2012).

The use of dollhouses in play therapy has been seen as a projective tool, with the use of the house representing the relationship with the therapist or family, or more specifically, family dynamics (Murray et al., 1999; Nilsson, 2000; Sweeney & Rocha, 2000). Allowing free play in the dollhouse can show positive and negative family relationships, as well as interactions in school settings (Murray et al., 1999). In terms of a relationship with the therapist, observing how a child plays with the outer and inner worlds of the house (with interactions and restrictions) can potentially indicate how the child is allowing a therapist access to his or her inner world (Nilsson, 2000). Anecdotally, the application of dollhouses with children experiencing parental divorce has been useful in clinical settings, especially if two houses are provided. This has allowed children to work through separation and attachment issues, along with new developments in their custody and living situations.

Many of the techniques described using doll play in therapy involve some structured work on the part of the therapist but allow for flexibility and creativity on the part of the child. These techniques and uses of doll play are often similar across presenting issue (e.g., anxiety, depression, acting out), as the ability to miniaturize and manipulate the small doll figures helps facilitate healing.

CLINICAL APPLICATIONS

Doll play has been shown to be useful with specific childhood problems, in addition to the benefits of spontaneous, unprompted doll play in typical childhood behaviors. In particular, doll play has benefits in forensic work, medical care settings, trauma care, and dealing with anxiety and attachment needs.

Anatomically correct dolls have historically been used during investigations with children who disclosed sexual abuse. The forensic interviewing side of this use of dolls is outside the scope of this chapter, but there are other uses for these dolls in a therapeutic setting. For example, anatomically correct dolls could be used to process a sexual trauma by allowing for a stimulus to approach the work (Johnston, 1997) or to begin and then proceed through the healing stages (Gil, 1991).

Doll play is also appropriate for other types of childhood trauma that result in symptoms of posttraumatic stress disorder (Cole & Piercy, 2007), interpersonal trauma including witnessing domestic violence (Stein et al., 2004), and hospitalizations (Gaynard et al., 1991). The ability to take control over terrifying situations in miniature and create mastery endings (often through the abreactive healing process) encourages this healing and creation of new coping skills. Thus, doll play can also help prevent trauma reactions when a significant event is anticipated, such as a surgery or serious medical issues. Child Life departments in hospital settings encourage professionals to use dolls and doll-sized equipment to familiarize children with items they will encounter in their medical journeys and to interact with these pieces prior to use (Thompson, 2018). Allowing children to play out the upcoming situations permits control and mastery to be obtained and anxiety to decrease.

Play with dolls is also being used in pediatric medical settings to help prevent and alleviate anxiety, fear, and medical trauma through more behaviorally based interventions as well. Interviews of multiple pediatric health care providers in a variety of settings show that play with dolls is used to educate children and their families about procedures, such as modeling how to work an insulin pump to treat diabetes or what to expect with an upcoming procedure. Dolls are also used to deliver information in a child-friendly and understandable way, and this has helped siblings understand what is happening to and with their loved ones (Stenman et al., 2019).

Attachment is another area in which doll play can be significantly impactful. Multiple studies have elucidated the use of doll play to determine relationships within the family system and changes therein (e.g., R. B. Ammons & Ammons, 1949; McHale et al., 1999; Murray et al., 1999; Oppenheim, 1997). Thus, clinicians can use this knowledge to guide doll play and accompanying narratives to support specific clinical needs, including help with separation anxiety (Danger, 2003; Murray, 2007) or upcoming familial changes.

CASE ILLUSTRATION

The following is a composite sketch of a client, drawn from experiences of children of similar ages, which protects patient confidentiality by changing identifying details. Jack is a 6-year-old boy who was referred for treatment prior to a surgical procedure that would result in a 2-week recovery in which he could be at home but with significant restrictions on his activity level. As Jack is prone to anxiety and often has larger-than-expected reactions to scary and challenging events, his parents sought treatment to help prepare him for the procedure and the resulting recovery restrictions. Jack is a smart and typically healthy child from an intact family whose history was remarkable for an episode of mononucleosis when he was 3. During that episode, he needed to be restrained for a blood draw and spontaneously played out his trauma around that event and reached abreactive healing. Thus, the use of doll play to prepare him this time was recommended.

Jack was introduced to the play space and given time to examine and interact with most of the toys. He knew that he was coming to the office to practice for his procedure and was aware that he would both get to play with the available toys and be introduced to some that would help him understand his surgery. He was agreeable to this and chose a doll dressed as a lion for his practice. Jack was asked what he knew about the hospital ("It's where sick people go to get better") and his surgery ("The doctor needs to fix a part of me"). He was able to point out on the doll which part of him needed to be fixed. With the therapist's help, he took his doll to the toy hospital and into the waiting room, where he sat him down with two dolls to represent his parents.

At this point, Jack was introduced to some of the medical tools that would be placed on his body, with straws and pipe cleaners cut to represent tubing, dust masks for surgical masks, and so on. He was able to play with these items and prep his doll for surgery with the therapist's guidance. He focused on making sure that the tubes were in the correct place and retaped them a few times before feeling settled enough to move on to the next portions. When Jack was ready, and his body indicated that anxiety had reduced, he placed the doll on the bed and listened to the description of the operating room. He wheeled the toy bed down to the operating room and positioned his doll near the doctors and lights. Jack practiced deep breathing and counting at this point to become familiar with the "sleepy medicine" that his doll was receiving. He then wheeled his doll to the recovery room, where he was reunited with the parent dolls and given juice and an ice pop. Jack took the straws and pipe cleaners home to practice taping them and become more familiar with them with his own toys.

The hospital where Jack was having his surgery offered Child Life classes and visits, and his parents took him to see the real space next. He brought his doll to the hospital, and the Child Life professionals walked him through the same process in the prep and operating rooms. He also visited the recovery room. His parents reported that Jack seemed a bit overwhelmed by these spaces and spent time prepping and talking to his doll for the next 2 nights about the procedure. On the day of the surgery, he was slightly anxious but able to manage quite well.

In the days following Jack's surgery, he appeared more down and crankier than usual. His parents scheduled another appointment, and Jack gravitated toward the dolls. He took the one he had used previously and engaged some others in outdoor play (running, jumping, riding on bicycles). The doll dressed as a lion was kept on the sidelines for this play and told he needed to sit still and just watch. This was not surprising, as Jack himself was being made to sit out from these more high-impact activities. Through this doll play, he was able to express his frustration at this and helped the doll count how many more days he would have to sit out, and he came up with alternate activities. After he played, his parents and therapist talked with him about some things he could do for the rest of the recovery time that he did not usually get to do during the week (e.g., watch movies, play on electronics, participate in family board game nights) to help him feel less frustrated about missing his usual play activities. His parents reported that he was able to complete his recovery days successfully.

EMPIRICAL SUPPORT

Multiple studies support the use of doll play in both assessment and clinical settings. Validated assessment procedures have been used to identify attachment patterns and classification across ages and in multiple countries (George &

Solomon, 2016; Kayoko, 2006). Research has also indicated associations between attachment and parental caregiving through mother–child interactions as seen in children's doll play, as doll interactions that were coherent and reciprocal were indicative of secure attachments and positive, consistent maternal interactions (Dubois-Comtois et al., 2011; Dubois-Comtois & Moss, 2008). Doll play research also indicates that children's representations of disorganized and dysregulated caregiving often mirrors the same real-life attachments and caregiving (George & Solomon, 2016). Children are able to distinguish between family relationships and interactions in play situations, thus shedding light on awareness of family climate and dynamics (McHale et al., 1999). Research indicates that doll play can be successfully used with preschoolers to observe moral development and predict behavioral problems in addition to these attachment pieces (Woolgar, 1999).

When reviewing doll play narratives of children who had been adopted recently, Steele and colleagues (2003) found influences of maternal state of mind and attachment in this play as well. In particular, the researchers noted that when mothers showed insecure attachment patterns, the children showed higher levels of aggression in their doll play narrative completions.

Doll play has been used frequently in research to determine temperament and aggressive and anxious traits. For instance, research indicates that although there are no statistical differences between genders across displays of aggressive behaviors, boys showed more instances of physical aggression than did girls (Sears, 1951; Tallandini, 2004). Some research on aggressive behavior indicates that children are more spontaneous during doll play compared with interview methods (Raya, 1986). Anxiety risk can be determined through doll play, specifically when examining children of mothers who have social phobia when children are approaching socially challenging events like beginning school (Pass et al., 2012).

It is interesting to note that the types of dolls presented to children can have an impact on food intake. Anschutz and Engels (2010) found that when girls were presented with thin dolls, average-sized dolls, or blocks as a control, food intake during a taste test was impacted. Specifically, those who played with average-sized dolls ate more than the girls in the other conditions. The girls' body image was also examined and was not found to be impacted by condition.

In terms of use of dolls with children referred for sexual abuse, research has indicated that anatomical dolls do not lead to sexualization of children and overstimulation in general, and it should not be used as a sole means for identifying history of abuse but could be appropriate for assessing sexual knowledge (e.g., Cohn, 1991; Everson & Boat, 1990; Realmuto et al., 1990; Simkins & Renier, 1996). In particular, anatomically correct dolls have been shown to serve seven primary functions during sexual abuse evaluations: "comforter, icebreaker, anatomical model, demonstration aid, memory stimulus, diagnostic screen, and diagnostic test" (Everson & Boat, 1994, p. 113).

When using anatomically correct dolls in a therapeutic setting rather than forensic, research has shown that some children use the dolls to show thematic play behaviors indicative of being stuck in a trauma until the child is able to successfully work through the trauma reactions (Klorer, 1995). This is consistent with Terr's work on posttraumatic play, which shows that children often engage in compulsive repetition of specific themes or behaviors in play, using an unconscious link to the trauma. This reactive play does not relieve the original anxiety or fear from the trauma until the child is able to overcome those reactions (e.g., Terr, 1981). Thus, use of anatomically correct dolls in a therapeutic setting can help children both show how and where they are stuck in their trauma reactions and help them process the events and work toward resolution.

SUMMARY AND CONCLUSION

In conclusion, doll play has a rich history of use in both clinical and research settings, in addition to natural play experiences of children. From the normative and spontaneous play of children across the ages, dolls hold an important place in the history of play as well as play therapy. Dolls can be used to examine and promote many things such as attachment, nurturance, new learning of skills, reduction of fears, processing of trauma, development of interpersonal dynamics, practice of social skills, and creative problem solving. The use of dolls should be encouraged across gender, socioeconomic status, and nationality to support the development of children as well as to help them overcome presenting clinical concerns.

REFERENCES

Ammons, C. H., & Ammons, R. B. (1952). Research and clinical applications of the doll-play interview. *Journal of Personality, 21*(1), 85–90. https://doi.org/10.1111/j.1467-6494.1952.tb01861.x

Ammons, R. B., & Ammons, H. S. (1949). Parent preferences in young children's doll-play interviews. *Journal of Abnormal Psychology, 44*(4), 490–505. https://doi.org/10.1037/h0060384

Anschutz, D. J., & Engels, R. C. M. E. (2010). The effects of playing with thin dolls on body image and food intake in young girls. *Sex Roles, 63*(9–10), 621–630. https://doi.org/10.1007/s11199-010-9871-6

Aponte, M. (1994). *Educational medical mannequin* (U.S. Patent No. US5314339A). U.S. Patent and Trademark Office. https://patents.google.com/patent/US5314339A/en

Baruch, D. W. (1941). Aggression during doll play in a preschool. *American Journal of Orthopsychiatry, 11*(2), 252–259. https://doi.org/10.1111/j.1939-0025.1941.tb05802.x

Brennan, C. A. (2001). The parent adaptive doll play technique. In H. G. Kaduson & C. E. Schaefer (Eds.), *101 more favorite play therapy techniques* (pp. 294–298). Jason Aronson.

Bretherton, I., & Oppenheim, D. (2003). The MacArthur Story Stem Battery: Development, administration, reliability, validity, and reflections about meaning. In R. N. Emde, D. P. Wolf, & D. Oppenheim (Eds.), *Revealing the inner worlds of young children: The MacArthur Story Stem Battery and parent-child narratives* (pp. 55–80). Oxford University Press.

Bretherton, I., Ridgeway, D., & Cassidy, J. (1990). Assessing internal working models of the attachment relationship: An attachment story completion task for 3-year-olds. In M. T. Greenberg, D. Cicchetti, & E. M. Cummings (Eds.), *Attachment in the preschool years: Theory, research, and intervention* (pp. 273–308). University of Chicago Press.

Cohn, D. S. (1991). Anatomical doll play of preschoolers referred for sexual abuse and those not referred. *Child Abuse & Neglect, 15*(4), 455–466. https://doi.org/10.1016/0145-2134(91)90029-D

Cole, E., & Piercy, F. (2007). The use of dolls to assist young children with PTSD symptoms. *Journal of Family Psychotherapy, 18*(2), 83–89. https://doi.org/10.1300/J085v18n02_07

Danger, S. (2003). Adaptive doll play: Helping children cope with change. *International Journal of Play Therapy, 12*(1), 105–116. https://doi.org/10.1037/h0088874

Dubois-Comtois, K., Cyr, C., & Moss, E. (2011). Attachment behavior and mother–child conversations as predictors of attachment representations in middle childhood: A longitudinal study. *Attachment & Human Development, 13*(4), 335–357. https://doi.org/10.1080/14616734.2011.584455

Dubois-Comtois, K., & Moss, E. (2008). Beyond the dyad: Do family interactions influence children's attachment representations in middle childhood? *Attachment & Human Development, 10*(4), 415–431. https://doi.org/10.1080/14616730802461441

Everson, M. D., & Boat, B. W. (1990). Sexualized doll play among young children: Implications for the use of anatomical dolls in sexual abuse evaluations. *Journal of the American Academy of Child & Adolescent Psychiatry, 29*(5), 736–742. https://doi.org/10.1097/00004583-199009000-00010

Everson, M. D., & Boat, B. W. (1994). Putting the anatomical doll controversy in perspective: An examination of the major uses and criticisms of the dolls in child sexual abuse evaluations. *Child Abuse & Neglect, 18*(2), 113–129. https://doi.org/10.1016/0145-2134(94)90114-7

Gaynard, L., Goldberger, J., & Laidley, L. N. (1991). The use of stuffed, body-outline dolls with hospitalized children and adolescents. *Children's Health Care, 20*(4), 216–224. https://doi.org/10.1207/s15326888chc2004_4

George, C., & Solomon, J. (2016). The Attachment Doll Play Assessment: Predictive validity with concurrent mother–child interaction and maternal caregiving representations. *Frontiers in Psychology, 7*, Article 1594. https://doi.org/10.3389/fpsyg.2016.01594

Gil, E. (1991). *The healing power of play: Working with abused children.* Guilford Press.

Hall, G. S., & Ellis, A. C. (1897). *A study of dolls.* E. L. Kellogg.

Jesuvadian, M. K., & Wright, S. (2011). Doll tales: Foregrounding children's voices in research. *Early Child Development and Care, 181*(3), 277–285. https://doi.org/10.1080/03004430903293172

Johnston, S. S. M. (1997). The use of art and play therapy with victims of sexual abuse: A review of the literature. *Family Therapy, 24*(2), 101–113.

Kayoko, Y. (2006). Assessing attachment representations in early childhood: Validation of the attachment doll play. *Japanese Journal of Educational Psychology, 54*(4), 476–486. https://doi.org/10.5926/jjep1953.54.4_476

Kiley, C., Yeh, K., & Hutchison, L. (2012, November 15). Why kids should play with baby dolls (yes, even boys!). *Mama OT.* http://mamaot.com/why-kids-should-play-with-baby-dolls-yes-even-boys/

Klorer, G. (1995). Use of anatomical dolls in play and art therapy with sexually abused children. *The Arts in Psychotherapy, 22*(5), 467–473.

Levin, H., & Turgeon, V. F. (1957). The influence of the mother's presence on children's doll play aggression. *Journal of Abnormal Psychology, 55*(3), 304–308. https://doi.org/10.1037/h0047448

Levin, H., & Wardwell, E. (1962). The research uses of doll play. *Psychological Bulletin, 59*(1), 27–56. https://doi.org/10.1037/h0043014

Mann, L. (1957). Persuasive doll play: A technique of directive psychotherapy for use with children. *Journal of Clinical Psychology, 13*(1), 14–19. https://doi.org/10.1002/1097-4679(195701)13:1<14::AID-JCLP2270130104>3.0.CO;2-D

Marshall, H. R., & Doshi, R. (1965). Aspects of experience revealed through doll play of preschool children. *The Journal of Psychology, 61*(1), 47–57. https://doi.org/10.1080/00223980.1965.10544794

Marvasti, J. A. (2001). Using anatomical dolls in psychotherapy with sexualized children. In H. G. Kaduson & C. E. Schaefer (Eds.), *101 more favorite play therapy techniques* (pp. 312–316). Jason Aronson.

McHale, J. P., Neugebauer, A., Asch, A. R., & Schwartz, A. (1999). Preschoolers' characterizations of multiple family relationships during family doll play. *Journal of Clinical Child Psychology, 28*(2), 256–268. https://doi.org/10.1207/s15374424jccp2802_12

McInnis, C. L. (2012). *Worry dolls.* Retrieved from http://www.lianalowenstein.com/FeaturedTechWorryDolls.pdf

Murray, L. (2007). Future directions for doll play narrative research: A commentary. *Attachment & Human Development, 9*(3), 287–293. https://doi.org/10.1080/14616730701455452

Murray, L., Woolgar, M., Briers, S., & Hipwell, A. (1999). Children's social representations in dolls' house play and theory of mind tasks, and their relation to family adversity and child disturbance. *Social Development, 8*(2), 179–200. https://doi.org/10.1111/1467-9507.00090

Nash, J. B., & Schaefer, C. E. (2011). Social skills play groups for children with disruptive behavior disorders. In A. A. Drewes, S. C. Bratton, & C. E. Schaefer (Eds.), *Integrative play therapy* (pp. 95–104). John Wiley & Sons. https://doi.org/10.1002/9781118094792.ch6

Nieves-Grafals, S. (2001). Brief therapy of civil war-related trauma: A case study. *Cultural Diversity & Ethnic Minority Psychology, 7*(4), 387–398. https://doi.org/10.1037/1099-9809.7.4.387

Nilsson, M. (2000). The dolls' house: Dream or reality? A borderline girl's psychotherapy. *Journal of Child Psychotherapy, 26*(1), 79–96. https://doi.org/10.1080/007541700362177

Oppenheim, D. (1997). The attachment doll-play interview for preschoolers. *International Journal of Behavioral Development, 20*(4), 681–697. https://doi.org/10.1080/016502597385126

Pass, L., Arteche, A., Cooper, P., Creswell, C., & Murray, L. (2012). Doll play narratives about starting school in children of socially anxious mothers, and their relation to subsequent child school-based anxiety. *Journal of Abnormal Child Psychology, 40*(8), 1375–1384. https://doi.org/10.1007/s10802-012-9645-4

Raya, P. A. (1986). Anger expressions of Filipino children as measured by the interview and doll play techniques. *Philippine Journal of Psychology, 19*, 55–60.

Realmuto, G. M., Jensen, J. B., & Wescoe, S. (1990). Specificity and sensitivity of sexually anatomically correct dolls in substantiating abuse: A pilot study. *Journal of the American Academy of Child & Adolescent Psychiatry, 29*(5), 743–746. https://doi.org/10.1097/00004583-199009000-00011

Sargent, H. (1943). Spontaneous doll play of a nine-year-old boy. *Journal of Consulting Psychology, 7*(5), 216–222. https://doi.org/10.1037/h0056884

Sears, P. S. (1951). Doll play aggression in normal young children: Influence of sex, age, sibling status, father's absence. *Psychological Monographs, 65*(6), i–42. https://doi.org/10.1037/h0093598

Simkins, L., & Renier, A. (1996). An analytical review of the empirical literature on children's play with anatomically detailed dolls. *Journal of Child Sexual Abuse, 5*(1), 21–45. https://doi.org/10.1300/J070v05n01_02

Sniscak, C. C. (2001). Play-Mates: The use of dolls in the therapeutic setting. In H. G. Kaduson & C. E. Schaefer (Eds.), *101 more favorite play therapy techniques* (pp. 285–290). Jason Aronson.

Steele, M., Hodges, J., Kaniuk, J., Hillman, S., & Henderson, K. (2003). Attachment representations and adoption: Associations between maternal states of mind and emotion narratives in previously maltreated children. *Journal of Child Psychotherapy, 29*(2), 187–205. https://doi.org/10.1080/0075417031000138442

Stein, M. T., Heyneman, E. K., & Stern, E. J. (2004). Recurrent nightmares, aggressive doll play, separation anxiety and witnessing domestic violence in a 9 year old girl. *Journal of Developmental and Behavioral Pediatrics, 25*(6), 419–422. https://doi.org/10.1097/00004703-200412000-00006

Stenman, K., Christofferson, J., Alderfer, M. A., Pierce, J., Kelly, C., Schifano, E., Klaff, S., Sciolla, J., Deatrick, J., & Kazak, A. E. (2019). Integrating play in trauma-informed care: Multidisciplinary pediatric healthcare provider perspectives. *Psychological Services, 16*(1), 7–15. https://doi.org/10.1037/ser0000294

Sweeney, D. S., & Rocha, S. L. (2000). Using play therapy to assess family dynamics. In R. E. Watts (Ed.), *Techniques in marriage and family counseling* (Vol. 1, pp. 33–47). American Counseling Association.

Tallandini, M. A. (2004). Aggressive behavior in children's dolls' house play. *Aggressive Behavior, 30*(6), 504–519. https://doi.org/10.1002/ab.20059

Terr, L. C. (1981). "Forbidden games": Post-traumatic child's play. *Journal of the American Academy of Child Psychiatry, 20*(4), 741–760. https://doi.org/10.1097/00004583-198102000-00006

Thompson, R. H. (Ed.). (2018). *The handbook of child life: A guide for pediatric psychosocial care* (2nd ed.). Charles C Thomas.

Wilder, L. I. (2016). *Little house in the big woods.* HarperCollins Publishers.

Woolgar, M. (1999). Projective doll play methodologies for preschool children. *Child Psychology and Psychiatry Review, 4*(3), 126–134. https://doi.org/10.1017/S1360641799002026

3

BLOCK PLAY

MARY ANNE PEABODY

Children are natural builders. Constructing and deconstructing with blocks, children often test their theories about the physical and social world. They create block structures to share their thoughts, beliefs, and interests based on culture and experience, tempered by their developmental level. A child's innate impulse to construct with blocks starts early in life and appears to be a universal human tendency (Schaefer, 2016). Accordingly, this innate desire makes blocks one of the most versatile play materials available to children.

Ample research supports the importance of block building in early childhood settings (Barton et al., 2018; Yelland, 2011), providing a normative context for children's play individually and collectively. Playing with blocks contributes to children's early mathematical development, including numerical knowledge, shape recognition, spatial reasoning, and problem-solving skills (Kamii et al., 2004; Ness & Farenga, 2007; Seo & Ginsburg, 2004; Wellhousen & Kieff, 2001). As children grow older, they often develop newer or more sophisticated ways to build, adding to their abilities in creative problem solving, mental imagery, visual spatial ability, mathematical skills,

https://doi.org/10.1037/0000217-004
Play Therapy With Children: Modalities for Change, H. G. Kaduson and C. E. Schaefer (Editors)

and geometric skills (Pirrone & Di Nuovo, 2014; Wolfgang et al., 2003). There is also support for associating block play with later math achievement (Stannard et al., 2001; Wolfgang et al., 2001).

In further studies, block play has been shown to contribute to children's language and literacy skills (Cohen & Uhry, 2007; Wellhousen & Kieff, 2001). Hanline et al. (2001) found a predictive relationship between block play complexity and later reading ability and self-regulation. Expanding on block play as a social activity, research has suggested that children engage in more complex language interactions with peers during classroom block play settings (Kersh et al., 2008; Sluss & Stremmel, 2004). Cartright (1974) used blocks in group play settings to help child clients gain skills in planning ahead, seeking each other's help, and learning to understand differences. Likewise, Rogers (1985) reported that block play enhanced children's friendship skill development and served as a catalyst for exchanging positive social interaction.

Therefore, when examining the literature on children's block play in educational settings, when children are given time to plan and construct with blocks, multiple opportunities for learning and development occur socially, emotionally, cognitively, linguistically, and physically (Hirsch, 1996; Pollman, 2010; Tunks, 2013; Wellhousen & Kieff, 2001). With the interconnected nature of block play across various learning domains and ages, it is clear that the benefits of block play are undisputable.

Despite the wealth of research supporting block play in educational settings, studies on the therapeutic impact of blocks in play therapy appear to be a relatively neglected topic (Schaefer, 2001). This is quite surprising given blocks or bricks are often mentioned in the play therapy material lists across various theoretical orientations. Landreth (2012) identified different shapes and sizes of building blocks in his recommended toys and materials list for child-centered play therapy, stating that blocks allow for creativity and emotional release through the building and knocking down of structures. Kottman and Meany-Walen (2018) placed building blocks in the pretend/fantasy toy category of Adlerian play therapy, whereas O'Connor (2000) discussed the pros/cons of construction toys (LEGO bricks, Lincoln Logs, Tinkertoys, and Erector sets) during his explanation of Level III play materials in Ecosystemic play therapy. Gaskill and Perry's (2017) identified stacking blocks, or playing with manipulatives such as LEGO bricks, as a relational/affective activity in their Neurosequential therapeutics approach of a play therapy model.

LEGO bricks, a form of blocks, are used in a specific intervention with children with autism called LEGO-based therapy (LeGoff et al., 2014; MacCormack et al., 2015). LEGO-based therapy is a directive group social skills intervention using children's interest in LEGO bricks as a motivator for socialization. Additionally, Thomsen (2018) recently explored the therapeutic use of LEGO bricks for boosting self-esteem and promoting the emotional well-being of children.

Specific to play therapy, Kestly (2014) adapted the LEGO Serious Play methodology to family play therapy, and Peabody (2015) used an adapted version in play therapy clinical supervision. Briefly, the LEGO Serious Play methodology involves several rounds of brick building, storytelling, and reflection to aid in communication and problem solving (Kristiansen & Rasmussen, 2014; The LEGO Group, 2010). When used in family play therapy or play therapy supervision, the therapist offers a specific directive prompt (Kestly, 2014; Peabody, 2015) whereby the client then builds a series of three-dimensional LEGO metaphoric models to represent feelings, reflections, struggles, or potential solutions.

In this chapter, the therapeutic use of block and brick play is explored by first conceptualizing four therapeutic powers of play as mediators of change in clients. Next, three core techniques are described, followed by clinical applications across individual, group, and family play therapy. Next, a case illustration highlights how blocks and bricks may be used throughout the play therapy process. Finally, empirical support for therapeutic block play is examined, and the chapter concludes with suggestions for future studies within the field of play therapy.

THERAPEUTIC BENEFITS

Foundational to play therapy is the belief that play behaviors are active forces that initiate, facilitate, or strengthen behavior change (Schaefer & Drewes, 2014). Dependent on the individual client treatment plan and the training or theoretical orientation of the therapist, block and brick play has tremendous potential to activate different therapeutic powers of play. To illustrate this, four therapeutic powers of play have been selected: self-expression, creative problem solving, self-regulation, and social competence. In choosing these four, the author recognizes that other therapeutic powers of play could be further examined and that the chosen four may overlap. Readers are urged to become well versed in all therapeutic powers of play that produce change in a client (Schaefer & Drewes, 2014).

Self-Expression

Landreth (2012) shared that children are naturally comfortable with using play activities, materials, and toys as ways to express themselves. The freedom inherent in blocks allows children to create anything they desire. Children can build walls or fortresses, they can invite their play therapist to join them inside their structure, or they can build a barrier that excludes the therapist. Children can add to their block creations by including miniatures, figures, puppets, or natural items like leaves or rocks as symbolic representations for experiences, thoughts, and feelings. As self-expression crosses all therapeutic orientation models, blocks and bricks can be useful along the continuum of nondirective, directive, and integrative approaches.

Block building provides emotional release for both comfortable and uncomfortable emotions. On one end of this continuum, mastery and accomplishment build self-esteem and ego strength. Conversely, block building may heighten frustration, such as in a young child struggling to balance a tower or a more experienced builder creating a complex structure. Learning to cope with frustration and gaining skills in perseverance are parts of the therapeutic self-expression process.

Creative Problem Solving

Bagiati and Evangelou (2016) found that young children demonstrated considerable problem-solving knowledge during block play. As children move through the various stages of building (stacking towers, creating elaborate designs, and reenacting their world), they have opportunities to experiment, make mistakes, problem solve, and find solutions. Block play allows children to practice both divergent and convergent thinking during problem solving. Divergent problem solving generates many options and choices, such as manipulating and arranging objects in varying constructions. Convergent problem solving involves assessing why the structure is not working as planned, what adjustments are necessary to make, and decision making on how to proceed.

This type of creative problem solving requires the ability to give organization to one's mental processes, often holding several pieces of information in mind while trying to navigate another task. The ability to problem solve requires the ability to think flexibly, which may be difficult for some children who are in therapy (Russ & Wallace, 2014). Children who struggle with self-regulation, a common referral issue for play therapy, often need support and directed teaching that could be met with opportunities for block and brick play.

Self-Regulation

Bodrova and Leong (2005) defined *self-regulation* as a deep internal mechanism that underlies mindful, intentional, and thoughtful behaviors of children (p. 32). Self-regulated children can suppress their impulses long enough to think about possible consequences of their behavior and to consider different actions that may be more appropriate. This ability to be intentional, thoughtful, and futuristic involves both thinking and behavioral skills (Blair, 2002).

Block building inherently requires planning ahead, frustration tolerance, and impulse control (Schaefer, 2016). For impulsive children who tend to act first, then remember what they should have or could have done later, the opportunity to playfully practice cognitive planning and impulse control is valuable. Anticipating block-building structural difficulties and slowing down before building as you think through possible adjustments are important ingredients of thinking ahead and inhibiting impulses. Additionally, while solving structural challenges, children may learn persistence and how to cope with feelings of frustration, anger, or disappointment.

Therefore, block play can provide a foundation for children to develop self-control and frustration tolerance while gaining self-confidence. Each of these skills is embedded in the ability to regulate internal emotions and external impulsive behavior. Because the primary context in which young children learn self-regulation is often through imaginative and extended play experiences (Bodrova & Leong, 2005), block building can be a way to strengthen these lifelong self-regulation skills.

Social Competence

When block or brick building is a social activity, it can be a training ground for acquiring and practicing socially necessary skills. Block and brick play provides experiences that foster social development as children work together and come to understand that others have different perspectives through playful exchanges. When children build with others, they are provided ample opportunities to make and implement plans, or in the case of disagreement, they can attempt to negotiate with others, compromise, or find mutually agreed-upon solutions. These are highly sophisticated skills, and children initially may need the support of adults to navigate these critical skills.

Imagine two children building with blocks, and one decides to knock down the other's tower. The child on the receiving end must try to cope with the feelings and use words to convey to the other child how she or he is feeling. Alternatively, building with others can provide opportunities whereby children experience a sense of communal accomplishment, pride, and satisfaction.

CORE TECHNIQUES

Given the popularity, versatility, and accessibility of blocks and bricks, three popular play therapy techniques are shared.

Jenga Variations

The Hasbro game Jenga and its many generic adaptations have been used therapeutically to build rapport, to identify and discuss feelings, and for social skill training. Therapists have written questions or feeling words directly on the blocks, or applied stickers with questions to the blocks, or paired different colored blocks with different feeling words. Totika is a commercially available therapeutic game (https://www.playtherapysupply.com) that uses question cards across different age levels (child–teen–adult) to start topical conversations on topics such as self-esteem, life skills, divorce, values, and beliefs. As the popular game requires little preparation or explanation, it is easily adaptable across multiple presenting issues.

Guided Teaching Techniques

More recently, the LEGO Education company created bricks with various emotional expressions with accompanying structured social and emotional learning activities (https://education.lego.com/en-us). The learning sets include cards, activities, and lesson plans created for helping young children recognize and understand feelings, express preferences, resolve conflicts, and learn about relationships. Although developed for the early childhood classroom setting, the materials and stories are easily transferable to the play therapy setting.

Another popular technique, created by Heidi Kaduson to promote a child's self-control, is Beat the Clock (Kaduson, 1997, pp. 139–141). The goal of the technique is for the child to stay focused for a select period while building with blocks and simultaneously resisting distractions created by the therapist. The child begins with a collection of 10 poker chips and is challenged to neither look up or around nor talk despite signs of distraction. If they do engage in distractible behaviors, the therapist takes a chip from their collection. The child is encouraged to stay focused because the child will also collect tokens after a specified amount of time. After accumulating a certain number of chips, the child can redeem the chips for a prize. When the children are successful with this technique, they feel a sense of accomplishment and competence, while extending time on task despite distractions (Kaduson, 1997). Although block building is often the activity of choice, children could also draw, stay still, or attempt to keep a straight face during the therapist-generated distractions.

Unstructured Play

If a therapist is using a nondirective approach to play therapy, blocks or bricks in the playroom could be considered a developmental mastery toy (Holliman et al., 2013). For many children, they have experience with building with LEGO bricks using detailed instructions for a specified purpose, so a play therapist can switch that by allowing free-form building. This unstructured play opportunity allows clients to stay within the comfort of a familiar material while offering a challenge without a template (Kronengold, 2017; O'Connor, 2000).

CLINICAL APPLICATIONS

Because block and brick building has such a universal appeal to enhance developmental skills across many domains, most children can benefit from the competence building that block or brick play provides. If the clinical setting allows for dyad, group, or family play therapy, the benefits for social skill applications are heightened.

Children With Trauma Backgrounds

Children with histories of trauma have experienced a loss of control, and at times their behaviors may appear maladaptive as they attempt to cope with elevated levels of competing needs, thoughts, physical symptoms, and emotions. These overwhelming experiences may cause some children to go back and forth between their response styles in unpredictable ways (Ohnogi & Drewes, 2016).

A sensitive therapist understands that trauma work is often erratic and intermittent and respects the child's need to move toward and away from trauma-related content (Goodyear-Brown, 2010). Valuing the rhythmic movement inherent in trauma play requires an understanding of the importance of pacing. A nuanced observation of children's block building reveals a natural pacing element embedded in the process. Typically, the building phase occurs as a quiet, slow, or methodical process. Conversely, the knocking-down phase is loud, quick, and exciting. When the therapist facilitates the intersection of construction or deconstruction pacing, along with the movement toward and away from difficult content, a reestablishment of the child's sense of power and control may occur.

Children who have been involved in natural or human-made disasters may reenact scenes with the building materials with themes of destruction and rescue, grief, and loss. Care must be taken to understand the advances in trauma treatment and when reenactment might be retraumatizing for children (Gil, 2006, Terr, 1990). Therapists can model appropriate ways to handle catharsis and clarify when, for whom, and how catharsis in play therapy can be helpful or hurtful (Schaefer & Mattei, 2005). It is imperative to stay current with the research and knowledge around trauma and reenactment play, catharsis, and skillful limit setting as part of the training, competencies, and ongoing clinical supervision of all play therapists.

Because of the open-ended and nondescriptive nature of block play, children experiencing trauma may be drawn to the element of destruction. Block play has a destructive appeal, not necessarily an aggressive appeal, and as such this destructive appeal can make some adults uncomfortable (Hewitt, 2001). It is important for play therapists to consider their own reactions and comfort level in the "destructive" side of block play and use supervision to explore this concept of the play therapy process.

Children With Social Communication Needs

Children with autism, dysregulation issues, and other neurodevelopmental disorders often are resistant to group therapy because of increased anxiety around the required demands or unfamiliarity with needed skills in social situations (LeGoff et al., 2014). LEGO-based therapy is a social skills intervention for school-age children that harnesses children's interest in LEGO construction to make social interactions interesting (LeGoff, 2004). It is one of the most researched interventions that uses LEGO bricks with children diagnosed with autistic spectrum disorder and others with communication and social developmental difficulties (LeGoff et al., 2010; Owens et al., 2008).

Using a naturalistic and directive approach to treatment, LEGO-based therapy is delivered in 30-minute sessions, once per week. A triage of children jointly build LEGO models, each with assigned roles of Engineer, Builder, and Supplier. The activity provides opportunities for children to use their problem-solving, creativity, attention, verbal and nonverbal communication, collaboration, and social interaction skills (LeGoff et al., 2010). It has been suggested that children on the autism spectrum have a strong urge to systemize—to predict patterns and changes in events (Baron-Cohen, 2008). Consequently, playing with LEGO bricks appeals to children with this diagnosis, as the toy itself is suited to being systemized because of its predictable and systematic nature (Owens et al., 2008).

Family Play Therapy

Kestly (2014) used a modification of LEGO Serious Play to restore a family's social engagement and family problem solving. By building models based on a directed prompt chosen by the therapist, family members move through the right–left–right brain hemispheric progression (McGilchrist, 2009). First, the right hemisphere of the brain is used as family members build with their hands, then the left hemisphere is used as individual family members tell a story about their model, and finally the right hemisphere through a metaphorical understanding at a creative higher level (Kestly, 2014). Additionally, by limiting the number and types of brick materials, the feeling of containment is maintained, thereby validating each family member's contribution, regardless of age or rank, while modeling active listening to one another (Kestly, 2014). Furthermore, this approach allows playful exchanges between parents and children that enhances connection.

CASE ILLUSTRATION

The following case illustration is a composite sketch of clients presenting with chronic medical concerns, and confidentiality is protected by changes to names and identifying details. Five-year-old Sam was referred to play therapy after his parents reported increased emotional meltdowns and bedtime fears that seemed to coincide with entering kindergarten. Sam was no stranger to managing stress, separation, or meeting a new therapist. Being born without lower extremities, Sam had undergone 10 surgeries in his short life, with another planned in 2 months. His parents described the impact of repeated hospitalizations on their family, but they also shared excitement that Sam had reached the developmental milestone of kindergarten entry.

Despite his numerous medical treatments and disruptions of routines, Sam possessed a range of coping strategies and resiliency that were immediately evident. He wheeled himself from the waiting room into the playroom, spun around in a full circle, and immediately ripped apart the Velcro seat belt holding him in his wheelchair. He independently climbed out of the chair onto the floor and subsequently used the strength of his upper body and arms to maneuver wherever he wanted.

In his first few play therapy sessions, Sam exhibited play themes related to exploratory play, control, and safety. Specifically, he engaged in sorting behaviors (sorting the wooden block sizes and the dishes into categories), fixing play (construction tools used to fix the dollhouse), and instability play (tools, cups, dishes, and small blocks falling from the sky). He would play rather intensely and then immediately stop, physically climb back into his wheelchair, and proceed to the whiteboard to draw. He seemed to have developed the emotional regulation skill of knowing when he needed to take a break.

In the middle of our fourth session, he grabbed the miniature bear family, a small police car, and a similar-sized fire truck. He unbuckled himself and moved toward the wooden block and LEGO bricks. Sam began to build as he engaged in private speech, self-narrating out loud his building plans. "This is my new house," he proclaimed, setting up the block rooms carefully, including a garage for the police car and fire truck. Sam continued to build for the remainder of the session. He was disappointed when our time was up, but like so many children, he returned right to this same building process in the following session. His story was not yet built, finished, or shared.

Suddenly, Sam's play changed. Danger entered the block house in the form of LEGO brick bombs dropped by Sam. "Danger, danger," he called out. In response to the reflection of how scared the bear family must be feeling. "No worries . . . they will get out. They can climb down the stairs, down the ladders." Upon closer examination, Sam had placed LEGO window-shaped bricks and ladders on the edges of the wooden blocks, providing safety escapes for each room. As this therapist reflected that the bear family was figuring out how to get to safety, Sam frantically exclaimed, "Where's the dog? Somebody get the dog! The dog can't climb the ladders. Don't forget the dog. Don't forget the dog! He can't climb! Find him!"

Sure enough, Sam had placed the small LEGO brick dog underneath the block and brick destruction. "Save him, save him. The firemen and police are stuck too!" As Sam had now placed this therapist in a role, the whisper voice technique was used (Kottman, 2011). In this technique, the therapist maneuvered between three distinct voices, including the voice of the rescuer; the whisperer voice, which involved asking Sam questions of what to do or say next so he remained in control of the story; and the regular voice of the therapist offering emotionally facilitative responses. Remaining in control of the play process, Sam led the bear family out through the windows, as he repeated, "Someone has to carry the dog out, he can't climb! Hurry up, don't forget him. The teacher doesn't know he's still in there!"

His fear of being unable to physically escape was being played out. The use of the word "teacher" when the original structure had been a home was significant. As often happens in play therapy, the home became school, the bear family became his kindergarten class, and the bear students began to climb through the windows and down the slides. His rescue play, certainly frantic at points, shifted and resulted in resolution play. The teacher bear finally found the LEGO dog and carried it on her back through the window and down the slide to safety. Sam abruptly announced, "Let's build a school with slides and ramps everywhere," again taking control of the play environment.

The blocks and bricks could be anything Sam wanted or needed. Blocks, as the ultimate expressive toy, easily allowed him to engage in several thera-peutic powers of play, such as self-expression, emotional release, fear manage-ment, and creative problem solving. Bears, bombs, dogs, teachers, rescue plans, ramps, and windows came to life. Sam could play and express his fears, his need to know that others would take care of him, and how he could take control over his own play scenes.

At the end of the session, this therapist asked for a parent consultation, in which the themes of the play were shared and a plan developed. Sam's parents would share with the new teacher the importance of explicitly explaining to Sam the overall safety plan for all children and specifically any accommodations for Sam. Because the school was scheduled to practice safety drills for both fire and lockdown scenarios, Sam could be helped in advance to process this new information, environment, and experience.

Sam continued in play therapy for several weeks, and as the kindergarten routine became normalized, his unsafe play subsided. For Sam, block and brick play was the ultimate open-ended material choice. He used blocks and bricks to build and create, communicate, destroy, rescue, cope, prepare for upcoming stressful events, and process unfamiliar experiences. As the unfamiliar became more familiar, he was emotionally stronger to face the next steps in his ever-changing life.

EMPIRICAL SUPPORT

A growing body of empirical support for block play has supported correlational evidence for gains in mathematics, spatial, and literacy skills (Ramani et al., 2014; Verdine et al., 2014), gross and fine motor skills (Pirrone & Di Nuovo, 2014), and executive functioning (Schmitt et al., 2018). The empirical studies conducted in educational settings highlight that block and brick building have tremendous potential across various child developmental domains (Hirsch, 1996; LeGoff, 2004; Pollman, 2010; Tunks, 2013; Wellhousen & Kieff, 2001).

Despite blocks and bricks often appearing on play therapy material lists, block play is a relatively neglected topic in the play therapy literature (Schaefer, 2016). The capacity of block play to activate various therapeutic powers of play beyond those described in this chapter, along with the versatility and interest that block play holds for children across disparate treatment difficulties, paves the way for future exploration.

Specifically, two areas for exploration include children's executive functioning and social learning. Charles Schaefer (2016) reminded us that block building requires planning, frustration tolerance, and impulse control, which are skills involved in executive functioning and skills that many play therapy clients struggle navigating. As previously stated, educationally based research has found that block play enhances children's executive functioning (Schmitt et al., 2018). Although we can potentially extrapolate the results into a clinical setting, it behooves play therapist researchers to replicate this study within a play therapy context.

Furthermore, for the therapist who conducts sibling or small-group therapy, including many school-based play therapists, LEGO-based therapy (LeGoff et al., 2014) has strong empirical support, specifically with children presenting with communication and social developmental difficulties (LeGoff et al., 2010; Owens et al., 2008). Therefore, a play therapist seeking to apply empirically supported interventions using bricks and blocks can look to this body of literature (LeGoff et al., 2010; Owens et al., 2008) during case formulation and when developing their treatment plans.

SUMMARY AND CONCLUSION

This chapter explored the nature of and empirical support for block and brick play in educational and therapeutic contexts. Additionally, this chapter focused on four therapeutic powers of play activated in block and brick play, core techniques, clinical applications, and a case study. At the heart of block and brick play is an ability to sustain focus, to diverge and converge one's thinking to create a structure, and to use imagination to create new solutions. This ability to build, grow, and change offers infinite possibilities for self-expression, leading to growth in confidence and competence. Although blocks and bricks are products of play, it is the process of play that intrigues and helps us to understand its power to effect change. In both block building and play therapy, we cannot fully understand until we take apart, examine, and rebuild with our clients and families. With clear evidence that blocks and bricks hold power for developmental growth in educational settings, perhaps the same exploration holds promise for the play therapy community of practice.

REFERENCES

Bagiati, A., & Evangelou, D. (2016). Practicing engineering while building with blocks: Identifying engineering thinking. *European Early Childhood Education Research Journal, 24*(1), 67–85. https://doi.org/10.1080/1350293X.2015.1120521

Baron-Cohen, S. (2008). Autism, hypersystemizing, and truth. *Quarterly Journal of Experimental Psychology, 61*(1), 64–75. https://doi.org/10.1080/17470210701508749

Barton, E. E., Ledford, J. R., Zimmerman, K. N., & Pokorski, E. A. (2018). Increasing the engagement and complexity of block play in young children. *Education & Treatment of Children, 41*(2), 169–196. https://doi.org/10.1353/etc.2018.0007

Blair, C. (2002). School readiness. Integrating cognition and emotion in a neurobiological conceptualization of children's functioning at school entry. *American Psychologist, 57*(2), 111–127. https://doi.org/10.1037/0003-066X.57.2.111

Bodrova, E., & Leong, D. J. (2005). Self-regulation: A foundation for early learning. *Principal, 85*(1), 30–36.

Cartright, S. (1974). Blocks and learning. *Young Children, 29*(3), 141–146.

Cohen, L., & Uhry, J. (2007). Young children's discourse strategies during block play: A Bakhtinian approach. *Journal of Research in Childhood Education, 21*(3), 302–315. https://doi.org/10.1080/02568540709594596

Gaskill, R. L., & Perry, B. D. (2017). A neurosequential therapeutics approach to guided play, play therapy, and activities for children who won't talk. In C. A. Malchiodi & D. A. Crenshaw (Eds.), *What to do when children clam up in psychotherapy* (pp. 38–68). Guilford Press.

Gil, E. (2006). *Helping abused and traumatized children: Integrating directive and non-directive approaches.* Guilford Press.

Goodyear-Brown, P. (2010). *Play therapy with traumatized children: A prescriptive approach.* John Wiley & Sons.

Hanline, M. F., Milton, S., & Phelps, P. (2001). Young children's block construction activities: Findings from 3 years of observation. *Journal of Early Intervention, 24*(3), 224–237. https://doi.org/10.1177/10538151010240030701

Hewitt, K. (2001). Blocks as a tool for learning: Historical and contemporary perspectives. *Young Children, 56*(1), 6–10.

Hirsch, E. S. (1996). *The block book* (3rd ed.). National Association for the Education of Young Children.

Holliman, R., Myers, C. E., & Blanco, P. J. (2013). Honoring the person within the child: Meeting the needs of children through child-centered play therapy. *The Person-Centered Journal, 20*(1–2), 80–103.

Kaduson, H. (1997). Beat the clock technique. In H. G. Kaduson & C. E. Schaefer (Eds.), *101 favorite play therapy techniques* (pp. 139–141). Jason Aronson.

Kamii, C., Miyakawa, Y., & Kato, Y. (2004). The development of logico-mathematical knowledge in a block-building activity at ages 1–4. *Journal of Research in Childhood Education, 19*(1), 44–57. https://doi.org/10.1080/02568540409595053

Kersh, J., Casey, B. M., & Mercer Young, J. (2008). Research on spatial skills and block building in boys and girls: The relationship to later mathematics learning. In O. N. Saracho & B. Spodek (Eds.), *Contemporary perspectives on mathematics in early childhood* (pp. 233–252). Information Age Publishing.

Kestly, T. A. (2014). *The interpersonal neurobiology of play.* W. W. Norton.

Kottman, T. (2011). *Play therapy: Basics and beyond* (2nd ed.). American Counseling Association.

Kottman, T., & Meany-Walen, K. (2018). *Doing play therapy.* Guilford Press.

Kristiansen, P., & Rasmussen, R. (2014). *Building a better business using the Lego® Serious Play® method.* John Wiley & Sons.

Kronengold, H. (2017). *Stories from child and adolescent psychotherapy: A curious space.* Routledge.

Landreth, G. L. (2012). *Play therapy: The art of the relationship* (3rd ed.). Routledge. https://doi.org/10.4324/9780203835159

The LEGO Group. (2010). LEGO® SERIOUS PLAY®. https://www.lego.com/en-us/seriousplay

LeGoff, D. B. (2004). Use of LEGO as a therapeutic medium for improving social competence. *Journal of Autism and Developmental Disorders, 34*(5), 557–571. https://doi.org/10.1007/s10803-004-2550-0

LeGoff, D. B., Gomez de la Cuesta, G., Kraus, G. W., & Baron Cohen, S. (2014). *LEGO®-based therapy: How to build social competence through LEGO® based clubs for children with autism and related conditions.* Jessica Kingsley Publishers.

LeGoff, D. B., Krauss, G. W., & Levin, S. A. (2010). LEGO®-based play therapy for autistic spectrum children. In A. A. Drewes & C. E. Schaefer (Eds.), *School-based play therapy* (2nd ed., pp. 221–236). John Wiley & Sons. https://doi.org/10.1002/9781118269701.ch11

MacCormack, J. W. H., Hutchinson, L. A., & Matheson, N. L. (2015). An exploration of a LEGO® based social skills program for youth with autism spectrum disorder. *Exceptionality Education International, 25*(3), 13–32.

McGilchrist, I. (2009). *The master and his emissary: The divided brain and the making of the Western world.* Yale University Press.

Ness, D., & Farenga, S. (2007). *Knowledge under construction: The importance of play in developing children's spatial and geometric thinking.* Rowman & Littlefield.

O'Connor, K. (2000). *The play therapy primer* (2nd ed.). John Wiley & Sons.

Ohnogi, A., & Drewes, A. A. (2016). Play therapy to help school-age children deal with natural and human-made disasters. In A. A. Drewes & C. E. Schaefer (Eds.), *Play therapy in middle childhood* (pp. 33–52). American Psychological Association. https://doi.org/10.1037/14776-003

Owens, G., Granader, Y., Humphrey, A., & Baron-Cohen, S. (2008). LEGO therapy and the social use of language programme: An evaluation of two social skills interventions for children with high functioning autism and Asperger Syndrome. *Journal of Autism and Developmental Disorders, 38*(10), 1944–1957. https://doi.org/10.1007/s10803-008-0590-6

Peabody, M. A. (2015). Building with purpose: Using LEGO SERIOUS PLAY in play therapy supervision. *International Journal of Play Therapy, 24*(1), 30–40. https://doi.org/10.1037/a0038607

Pirrone, C., & Di Nuovo, S. (2014). Can playing and imagining aid in learning mathematics? An experimental study of the relationships among building-block play, mental imagery, and arithmetic skills. *Bollettino di Psicologia Applicata, 62*(271), 30–39.

Pollman, M. J. (2010). *Blocks and beyond: Strengthening early math and science skills through spatial learning.* Brookes Publishing.

Ramani, G. B., Zippert, E., Schweitzer, S., & Pan, S. (2014). Preschool children's joint block building during a guided play activity. *Journal of Applied Developmental Psychology, 35*(4), 326–336. https://doi.org/10.1016/j.appdev.2014.05.005

Rogers, D. L. (1985). Relationships between block play and the social development of young children. *Early Child Development and Care, 20*(4), 245–261. https://doi.org/10.1080/0300443850200403

Russ, S., & Wallace, C. (2014). Creative problem solving. In C. E. Schaefer & A. A. Drewes (Eds.), *The therapeutic powers of play: 20 core agents of change* (2nd ed., pp. 213–223). Wiley.

Schaefer, C. E. (2001). Block play therapy. In H. Kaduson & C. E. Schaefer (Eds.), *101 more favorite play therapy techniques* (pp. 277–281). Rowman & Littlefield Publishers.

Schaefer, C. E. (2016). Block play. In C. E. Schaefer & D. Cangelosi (Eds.), *Essential play therapy techniques: Time tested approaches* (pp. 34–37). Guilford Press.

Schaefer, C. E., & Drewes, A. A. (Eds.). (2014). *The therapeutic powers of play: 20 core agents of change* (2nd ed.). John Wiley & Sons.

Schaefer, C. E., & Mattei, D. (2005). Catharsis: Effectiveness in children's aggression. *International Journal of Play Therapy, 14*(2), 103–109. https://doi.org/10.1037/h0088905

Schmitt, S. A., Korucu, I., Napoli, A. R., Bryant, L. M., & Purpura, D. J. (2018). Using block play to enhance preschool children's mathematics and executive functioning: A randomized controlled trial. *Early Childhood Research Quarterly, 44,* 181–191. https://doi.org/10.1016/j.ecresq.2018.04.006

Seo, K., & Ginsburg, H. P. (2004). What is developmentally appropriate in early childhood mathematics education? Lessons from new research. In D. H. Clements & J. Sarama (Eds.), *Engaging young children in mathematics: Standards for early mathematics education* (pp. 91–104). Lawrence Erlbaum Associates.

Sluss, D. J., & Stremmel, A. J. (2004). A sociocultural investigation of the effects of peer interaction on play. *Journal of Research in Childhood Education, 18*(4), 293–305. https://doi.org/10.1080/02568540409595042

Stannard, L. L., Wolfgang, C. H., Jones, I., & Phelps, C. (2001). A longitudinal study of the predictive relations among construction play and mathematical achievement. *Early Child Development and Care, 167*(1), 115–125. https://doi.org/10.1080/0300443011670110

Terr, L. (1990). *Too scared to cry.* Harper & Row.

Thomsen, A. (2018). *Thera-Build® with LEGO®: A playful therapeutic approach for promoting emotional well-being in children.* Jessica Kingsley Publishers.

Tunks, K. W. (2013). Happy 100th birthday, unit blocks! *Young Children, 68*(5), 82–87.

Verdine, B. N., Golinkoff, R. M., Hirsh-Pasek, K., Newcombe, N. S., Filipowicz, A. T., & Chang, A. (2014). Deconstructing building blocks: Preschoolers' spatial assembly performance relates to early mathematical skills. *Child Development, 85*(3), 1062–1076. https://doi.org/10.1111/cdev.12165

Wellhousen, K., & Kieff, J. (2001). *A constructivist approach to block play in early childhood.* Delmar.

Wolfgang, C. H., Stannard, L. L., & Jones, I. (2001). Block play performance among preschoolers as a predictor of later school achievement in mathematics. *Journal of Research in Childhood Education, 15*(2), 173–180. https://doi.org/10.1080/02568540109594958

Wolfgang, C. H., Stannard, L. L., & Jones, I. (2003). Advanced constructional play with LEGOs among preschoolers as a predictor of later school achievement in mathematics. *Early Child Development and Care, 173*(5), 467–475. https://doi.org/10.1080/0300443032000088212

Yelland, N. (2011). Reconceptualizing play and learning in the lives of young children. *Australasian Journal of Early Childhood, 36*(2), 4–12. https://doi.org/10.1177/183693911103600202

4

THE USE OF CHILDREN'S DRAWING IN PLAY THERAPY

NIKOLE R. JIGGETTS

Children often better express their emotions on a nonverbal level through art and play. Children's drawings, for instance, can tell a story about what children are feeling in a way that talking about it does not. As an evidence-based practice, art therapy has played an instrumental part in helping children heal. From the psychoanalytic perspective, Freud reflected on the drawings of his patient "Little Hans" as the start of accepting drawing and painting as part of the child analytic technique (Rubin, 2016). Thereafter, the study of drawings became a popular means to assess the intelligence level and psychological state of the child. As stated by Malchiodi (2012), Freud's work with drawing and dreams was the development and beginning of art therapy. According to the history of art therapy, the developmental approach is based on various perspectives (Rubin, 2016). During the classical period in the 1940s to 1970s, art therapists such as Hanna Kwiatkowska and Margaret Naumburg, who is often referred to as the "mother of art therapy," focused on the theoretical perspectives of psychoanalytic and humanistic approaches when using art with clients. Both perspectives lean toward uncovering buried thoughts and feelings children have and, with assistance, the ability to naturally work through those deep thoughts and feelings through art. Children have been creating art

https://doi.org/10.1037/0000217-005
Play Therapy With Children: Modalities for Change, H. G. Kaduson and C. E. Schaefer (Editors)

using sticks in the sand and dirt for centuries. The impulse to create art is a result of the impulse to play and be creative (Brown, 2009). Brown (2009) further explained that art is a natural part of development and that children possess an innate drive to play and create.

Children's use of a variety of methods through the arts enables them to explore their internal world and discover their own skills and abilities through the healing process. Children referred for therapy need support to find ways to release their emotions.

Art therapy has advanced to help us understand that art expresses feelings, ideas, and self-concept that words cannot (Malchiodi, 2007, p. 2). In other words, children are not always able to talk about what they are feeling. However, art gives them the means to express to others what they are thinking.

This chapter explores how the use of creating art in play therapy as an evidence-based practice has proven to be a beneficial component in the therapeutic healing process. Using drawings as a means of communication brings another aspect to therapy and can enhance the play therapy session. This chapter further explores how working with children who are challenged with the complications of managing their emotions can be problematic for them to focus on the underlying issues. The chapter emphasizes the therapeutic benefits of using drawing in play therapy, as too often children's feelings are too threatening to confront and address verbally. Approaching the subject matter through talk rather than play may cause a child to emotionally and verbally shut down. A case study example explores how having the opportunity to project those emotions onto toys, onto objects, and through art is cathartic. Confidentiality is protected by changes to names and identifying details.

THERAPEUTIC BENEFITS

Landreth (2012) stated that children's feelings are often inaccessible at a verbal level (p. 13). Developmentally, they lack the cognitive verbal facility to express what they feel or to directly connect to those feelings. Because coloring or drawing is one of the ways that children begin to play, it is often used in art therapy. Malchiodi (2007) explained that "drawing from within" (a popular phrase used among art therapists) allows children to explore inner feelings, perceptions, and their own imagination.

Drawing can be a simple task, as paper and pencil or pen are more easily and readily accessible than other art mediums, such as clay, collage, and painting. When asking children to draw what happened, they are free to naturally explore feelings and share their story where words alone would not do justice. Art and play therapy fosters self-expression, catharsis, and the therapeutic relationship and promotes problem solving, which increase the positive mental health of children. These components are part of the core agents called *therapeutic powers of play*, which activate clinical change (Schaefer & Drewes, 2014). The therapeutic powers of play consist of four main elements: Play facilitates communication, fosters emotional wellness, enhances social relationships, and increases personal strengths. Play and expressive arts promote communication through accessing the unconscious and allowing for conscious material to be less frightening. Because verbal communication is difficult, drawing in the therapy session facilitates communication through self-expression. Using the mediums of pencil, crayons, markers, and paint in addition to toys in the playroom allows access to the unconscious. An art and play therapist's "efforts must be made to invite and promote self-expression" when working with children (Gil, 1991, p. 66). Art over time can lead to personal fulfillment and transformation, as the drawings become helpful in communicating what the unconscious is trying to bring into consciousness and gain insight into the underlying issues children are experiencing. For example, a child who is quiet in sessions, has a history of anxiety and/or depression, and usually responds with "I'm fine" or "Nothing is wrong" appears to feel uncomfortable with expressing her inner thoughts. During the therapeutic process where she can use drawing and play instead of verbal expression, her work begins to tell her story. Throughout the sessions, her art is her self-expression, where her unconscious appears in her drawings. With the therapist holding the space, allowing the child to freely express through her art, she then can begin to problem-solve. The art may have color or lack of color. The choice of medium (crayons, pencils, pens, markers) can express feelings through how intense or lightly the child colors and the detail that the child includes; the child can decide to add or leave out things. However, there are times when art can be intimidating and increase anxiety in children, such as when they feel inhibited by their perceived lack of creativity.

Part of the therapeutic powers of play is the enhancement of social relationships, beginning with the therapeutic relationship (Schaefer & Drewes, 2014). Axline (1981) promoted child-centered play therapy and expressed the need for therapists to provide an atmosphere where children feel free to express feelings, as the therapists accept the children as they are. This is where the therapeutic relationship is essential in all therapy sessions. The safety in the therapy room permits children to share their internal thoughts or, even more, share these thoughts through art so the therapist can help children navigate their feelings within the world in which they live. Once the child is comfortable and has a healthy attachment with the therapist, the child can further process emotions in the session. The art begins to help resolve the inner conflicts. It is then that growth and healing can emerge, leading to the component of fostering emotional wellness, addressing the point of catharsis.

Schaefer and Drewes (2014) explained that focusing on affect regulation through the release of feelings can result in mastery when children are initially showing deficits in identifying their emotional state. Over time in the sessions, children continue to feel a sense of improvement in their mental health, and self-regulation, thus increasing personal strengths—the fourth component of the therapeutic powers of play. The therapeutic benefits of drawing assist in expression and release of repressed emotions. To accomplish this, there are two necessary steps: (a) to uncover and discover repressed memories and internal conflicts and (b) to help children gain insight into the meaning of their behavior in terms of these formerly hidden ideas and feelings (Rubin, 2016). This process can strengthen self-esteem and over time increase resiliency.

CORE TECHNIQUES

Art interventions have two approaches in therapy. The therapist can be directive in the session, giving specific instructions on how to create the art, or the therapist can be nondirect, where there is no specific instructions on what to create or how to create the art. With nondirect art, the therapist would provide the materials and may say, "Draw a picture of anything you like." A more directive approach would have instructions such as "Draw a picture of your family doing something together." Directive interventions guide children to create art with specific goals to be addressed. Nondirective interventions allow children the freedom to express their thoughts and feelings how they would like. Both directive and nondirective approaches can engage the flow of creativity from children.

Nondirective Approach

Employing a nondirective approach, such as impromptu drawings or spontaneous art, would be facilitated by a therapist saying, "Draw a picture of whatever you'd like." This approach allows children to draw at will without any preconceived notions of what they are going to make. Children create intuitively and express images of memories, feelings, and even flashbacks during the artistic expression. In addition to "Draw whatever you'd like," spontaneous art such as Scribbles (Malchiodi, 2007, p. 109), a nondirective approach, connects children to when they experienced their first creations—scribbling as children. According to Malchiodi (2012), children as young as

18 months make marks on paper and slowly begin to realize they have control over the marks they make. As they get older, their marks become scribbles and they tell stories about their creations. The following are two drawing interventions using scribbling as spontaneous art (Malchiodi, 2007).

Scribbling With Your Eyes Closed

1. Place a sheet of paper in front of you on a table or a wall. You may want to tape it to the table or the wall so that it doesn't move around while you are scribbling.

2. Pick out one color (oil pastels or crayons). Place the crayon in the center of the paper and begin to scribble around the paper. Do not worry if you go off the page. Create a series of lines for about 30 seconds.

3. You can open your eyes when you feel that your scribble is complete, and look at the drawing. Look at the lines and shapes to see if you can find an image, shape, figure, object, and so on. Try turning your creation around and looking at it from each side.

4. Now using more colors, color the image that you see. Feel free to add any details to the image that you think are necessary. You can outline it as well to make it stand out. Last, give your creation a name or title.

Scribbling With Your Nondominant Hand

To create a scribble with your nondominant hand (i.e., if you normally write with your right hand, use your left hand to create the scribble), you do not need to close your eyes. You can follow the directions just presented and use your nondominant hand. Try scribbling for about 30 seconds. When you complete your scribble, you can add details to make an image with your nondominant hand or dominant hand, whichever feels the most comfortable. Complete your drawing as indicated in the previous exercise.

Serial Drawings

Spontaneous art expressions are believed to be pictures drawn from the unconscious, which has the therapeutic benefit of facilitating communication. The belief is that spontaneous drawings externalize emotions that may be too difficult to speak about. Another example of nondirective art is Serial Drawings (Birch & Carmichael, 2009), a Jungian approach in which drawings are implemented over a period of time to have a better understanding of the children's inner world. The series of pictures are drawn session after session, with the child drawing in the therapist's presence. The therapist has common questions that will allow the healing potential to be activated to facilitate healing. The following directions are for Serial Drawing (Birch & Carmichael, 2009) after the drawings are completed:

1. At the start of each session, provide the child with paper and a variety of art mediums—colored pencils, crayons, markers—and allow the child to draw anything they want.

2. Common questions or statements are: I wonder what it would feel like for you to be in this drawing. Tell me a story that goes with the picture. Give me a moral to go with this picture/or story. What three feeling words go with this picture? Tell what happened before this picture(s). Tell what is going to happen after this picture or this last picture.

3. Through the stages of therapy, the goal of the serial drawings is to move from reflecting the child's inner world and through the troubling emotions. When drawing can be offered in the therapy sessions, difficult experiences can be described in art, and this can encourage steps toward mastery of those troubling feelings (Malchiodi, 2012).

Directive Approach

Directive art interventions can help children connect their feelings to the issues faced in their lives, and thereby create ways to navigate through their problems. Art interventions, such as the Rosebush (Oaklander, 1988), can be an effective tool in helping children with defining their identities while addressing deeper feelings.

The Rosebush
The Rosebush (Oaklander, 1988) is a directive approach that is a guided imagery drawing intervention designed to help children express blocked feelings, wants, and needs. Through guided imagery, children stay in the metaphor to express feelings through the use of the Rosebush (Kaduson & Schaefer, 1997). The therapist asks the child to close her eyes, take a few deep breaths, and imagine that she is a rosebush. The therapist goes on to explain, "You can be any kind of flowering bush, but we will call you a rosebush." From there the therapist asks, "What kind of rosebush are you? Are you very small? Are you large? Are you a full rose bush or skinny? Do you have flowers? If so, what kind? What color are they? Do you have many or just a few? Are you in full bloom or do you have any buds? Do you have any leaves? What do they look like? What are your stems and branches like? What are your roots like? Or maybe you don't have any. If you do, are they long and straight? Are they twisted? Are they deep? Do you have thorns? Where are you: in a yard? in the

park? in the desert? on the moon? You could be anywhere. Are you growing in a pot or in the ground or through cement? What's around you? Are there other rose bushes around, or are you alone? Are there trees? Animals? Birds? People? How do you survive? Who takes care of you? Was the weather like for you right now? Is there a fence or maybe rocks around you?"

As children are sitting comfortably listening to the prompts given, they build an image of themselves as a rosebush with several suggestions and possibilities. Once they are ready, the therapist will instruct them to open their eyes and draw the rosebush. On a piece of 8- × 10-inch white paper, they can use crayons, markers, or colored pencils to create the rosebush using as much or as little color and detail as they wish. When they are finished, the therapist asks them to explain their picture within the context of the questions asked. After their story, the therapist can use notes and other facts shared in previous sessions to talk to children about any correlation between their rosebush and their life. When children have had a trauma or significantly difficult life event that has impacted their perception of the world and created cognitive distortions, the healing benefit of the Rosebush approach can assist in making it easier for children to begin to deal with deeper feelings as they engage in this self-defining activity.

Trauma

In the case of posttraumatic play or art, the child remains static for a period of time in their play and art expression (Gil, 1991, p. 73). The therapist can use directive art interventions, in addition to cognitive restructuring or problem-solving skills, to facilitate posttraumatic growth. Posttraumatic growth is seen when children use the lessons learned from the trauma experienced and focus on their strengths as they display resilience. Another example of a direct intervention—drawing the trauma (trauma narrative)—can also aid children in retelling their own story, being heard, and being validated (Malchiodi, 2008).

Narrative Drawings

Serial Drawings are closely related to Narrative Drawings, but Narrative Drawings are more directive as the therapist asks children to "draw what happened." This intervention can be beneficial for children with posttraumatic stress disorder (PTSD), as children are given time to retell the event that occurred in their life by reexperiencing the event within the safety of therapy. Serial Drawings and Narrative Drawings have therapeutic benefits by helping children gain insight into their problems, reorganize their experiences, and facilitate communication through art. When using drawing techniques to treat children who experienced trauma, prompts should be more direct. The benefit of this intervention being directive is that children who have experienced trauma are reexposed through the memories and experiences during these drawing interventions. Drawing a trauma narrative or telling the story of what happened is done through cognitive reframing in a way to promote safety in the session. It is essential that the intervention is structured to maintain the safety through the process for children to participate in the trauma intervention (Malchiodi, 2012). The therapist could ask the child to draw what happened, or to draw a picture of what the hurt looks like. Drawing provides a symbolic representation of the trauma and allows children to view the large event that had been experienced in a much smaller context. The trauma can be better managed on a smaller scale and slowly assimilated, and this can give children a sense of empowerment over the trauma.

Squiggle Game

Winnicott's (1971) squiggle technique helps children verbalize their feelings through storytelling. Donald Winnicott was a pediatrician who created the Squiggle Game, or the squiggle technique, in which both the child and the therapist participate in the storytelling. The child and therapist alternate drawing squiggly lines and together complete a picture from each other's squiggles. The objective is to allow the child to communicate problems in a safe manner with the therapist's acceptance of the child's imperfect object. To elicit storytelling through the Squiggle Game, the therapist can suggest that the child create a story out of the many pictures they created in the session, individually or collectively. The storytelling aspect allows more insight into the child's presenting problems as they release emotions.

Squiggle Game Instructions. The therapist draws a few simple squiggles with a marker on a blank 8- × 10-inch sheet of white paper. Then the child uses a pencil to create something out of the squiggle. The therapist can instruct the child to turn the page around until the child finds something to create. For example, if the therapist draws a V shape with a purple marker, the child may turn the paper around and use the pencil to make mountains using the upside-down V. Children are directed to use their imagination and turn the squiggles into objects through some type of metaphor to tell a story.

The Egg Drawing and Cave Drawing Techniques

Another directive drawing intervention is the Egg Drawing technique (Malchiodi, 2012) and the Cave Drawing technique, created by Tanaka (1992, 1993, 2001a, 2001b). Both techniques, similar to the Squiggle Game, facilitate storytelling and rely on the therapist's active participation. The therapist initiates the storytelling by drawing an oval and presenting the drawing to the child, implying that it is a picture of an egg or a cave. Once the directive part of the therapist drawing is complete, the child engages in creating their own picture based on the egg or the cave oval and begins the storytelling process.

The Egg Drawing. The therapist starts by drawing an oval shape on an 8- × 10-inch piece of white paper. Then the therapist asks the child what the shape looks like. The therapist guides the child to respond that the drawing is of an egg even though the child may guess many other things. The therapist then explains that something is about to be born and asks the child to add cracks to the drawn egg. While the child draws the cracks, the therapist asks, "What is about to be born?"

If the child guesses a chick, the therapist suggests that they try to think about the egg as a magical egg and imagine anything coming out of it. At this point the child is given a blank piece of paper and directed to draw the magical thing that comes out of the egg along with broken pieces of eggshells. Then the child is directed to finish the drawing by coloring in the pieces.

The Cave Drawing. The Cave Drawing, similar to the Egg Drawing, also begins with the therapist drawing an oval, but this oval should be slightly larger than that in the Egg Drawing. The therapist says that this time it is not an egg. The therapist explains that it is an entrance to a cave. The child is encouraged to think about the following question: "Suppose you live here. What would you see outside?" This intervention's intent is to gain insight into how the world outside is viewed from inside the cave. Once the child understands the directive, they are to create the drawing and color the internal walls of the cave as well.

Technique Use. The two drawings are intended to be used together. Once the two drawings are finished, the child is directed to tell a story about what is happening in both the Egg Drawing and the Cave Drawing that they created. Malchiodi (2012) stated that although post drawing interviews (PDIs) have not been tested, the authors found them useful in engaging children after the drawings were completed. Eliciting storytelling from the children through the use of the PDIs were important for them to tell the story instead of the therapist making clinical assumptions about the drawings. The results of the story also assist the therapist in how to use them within the realm of treatment planning. Malchiodi (2012) used the following questions to assist in storytelling:

- *The Egg Drawing PDI.* Please tell me about your Egg Drawing: What is it that you drew? Does it (he/she) seem to be near or far from you? What makes you feel that way? Suppose it is trying to go somewhere, where do you think it may go? Suppose it were to meet something or someone on the way, who are what would it meet? If it grew up, what would it be like? Does it remind you of anything? What do you think it wants? What do you think it needs? What makes you think that?

- *The Cave Drawing PDI.* Please tell me about your Cave Drawing: What type of place is this and what did you imagine it to be like? Does this cave seem near or far from where you are? Does the cave seem warm or cool inside? What makes you feel that way? Would you want to live in this cave? Tell me about that. What is your favorite part about the drawing? Tell me more about that. What do you like least and why? What is the weather like (sunny, raining, cloudy)? If there is wind blowing, which direction is it coming from (right, left, up, or down)? If someone or something were to come into this cave, who or what might that be? If the person is going out of the cave, where might they go? Do you think this cave needs anything else? Does this drawing remind you of anything? Was there anything that was difficult to draw in here?

When deciding to use directive or nondirective approaches in therapy, the child's developmental age, ability, and readiness are important to consider. The Squiggle Game and Scribbles are great ways to help build rapport and can be used at any age. However, the Rosebush activity is useful once the therapeutic bond is intact and with an older child who is capable of engaging in this process.

CLINICAL APPLICATIONS

Play therapy is an evidence-based practice and is used as a therapeutic approach for a variety of child-related problems (Landreth, 2012). Children often are referred to play therapy because of trauma as a result of physical or sexual abuse or neglect, symptoms associated with PTSD, behaviors stemming from attention-deficit/hyperactivity disorder (ADHD), or difficulty managing emotions from anxiety or depression. When addressing the many childhood disorders in therapy, drawing in play therapy is valuable in the treatment and can give children another language to share feelings, ideas, perceptions, and observations about themselves, others, and their environment (Malchiodi, 2012). Art expression in therapy has been known to help children organize their thoughts and memory of events, help with memory retrieval, and help them tell more about their story that they may not have expressed in a verbal discussion. Judith Herman (1992, p. 1) highlighted that when a person experiences a traumatizing event, there is a concurrent need to articulate the unspeakable and an inability to verbalize or describe what has occurred. Children can retell their experiences through creative expression using art, play, music, and movement to transform suffering and help them recapture health and hope for the future (Malchiodi, 2008).

Research suggests that art therapy combined with additional approaches including play therapy showed a significant decrease in trauma reactions in children (Cohen et al., 2006). Combining art and play therapy when addressing these are traumatic events, has been instrumental in helping children work through their abusive experiences. Since not all children who have been abused will react in the same way, all cases must be carefully evaluated (Malchiodi, 2008). When helping children tell their story through play or drawings (e.g., the Squiggle Game, the Egg and Cave Drawings) in a play therapy session, the child expresses emotions in a safe manner.

When a therapist works with children who display negative behaviors because of an array of diagnoses, the children may experience stagnant or dynamic play or art. An example is posttraumatic play or art, where children get stuck and the play or art expression is repeated over and over but is not moved past that moment. In dynamic play or art, children are able to become more relaxed and expand themes over time. For instance, a client who was stagnant in her art repeatedly drew the same picture at home and in the sessions. Prompted by the therapist to create pictures about specific parts of her story, such as, "Tell me about the time . . .," she was able to add more content to her story and felt safer to move past the moment. Art and play allow children to manage their feelings and make them more bearable and less fearful and chaotic.

Some structured drawing activities used with children who have experienced a trauma are Serial Drawings and Narrative Drawings. "Drawing is one way to provide a link between dissociated memories and their retrieval into consciousness after which the experience can be translated into narrative form and then reintegrated into the child's past, present and future life experiences" (Malchiodi, 2012, p. 165). Malchiodi (2012) further explained that trauma memories for adults and children are stored in our senses rather than solely our cognitions. This is important in relation to art and play, as the therapy helps children process their story or parts of their story through drawing while connecting to the sensations they may feel in their body. Through the drawings, the therapist is able to see how children now view themselves related to the world around them as a result of their trauma. While children are drawing their picture and telling their story, the therapist can ask questions about how they are feeling as they are sharing (i.e., heart racing, feeling shaky or sweaty). Focusing on these themes, the drawing intervention neutralizes the symptoms of the trauma and the senses the children feel when reminded of their past.

One of the most common diagnoses children receive is ADHD. Basic characteristics of ADHD are inattention, impulsivity, and hyperactivity. More specifically, they can experience sudden changes in temper, inability to focus, and inability to stay still for long periods in any setting, and they can be seen as hypersensitive (Kariz, 2003). Art is beneficial to children who have ADHD, as children with impulsivity can express their feelings better through images than they can with words. Because art can be an age-appropriate activity that engages children, it allows them to manipulate images to express boredom, confusion, lack of control in certain situations, and other feelings associated with their impulsivity. The art helps children redirect energy and hyperactivity. Drawing and or play activities provide structure to the therapy, allowing children to become more attentive in the session where inattention is usually a problem. Because art is seen as a relaxing activity, the art-based intervention can help children better experience the activity with ease so they can cope with emotional stress (Kariz, 2003). Group therapy for children diagnosed with ADHD is common. It is also beneficial because children realize that they are not alone and it is not their fault that they cannot control their impulses and activity in many settings. Groups can help them learn that their problems are not an extension of them, and they can learn ways to cope with the feelings and behaviors. Malchiodi (2012) explained that art therapy is an active form of therapy that provides a kinesthetic and visual approach to learning for children with ADHD. In group settings, sharing their thoughts and drawings with peers becomes a method for change and boosts self-worth.

In addition, working with children on the autistic spectrum can be rewarding and challenging. It is important for the therapist to understand the unique learning characteristics and behaviors of children with autism spectrum disorder (ASD). ASD is characterized by impairments in social inter-actions, and language development. They may exhibit severe language deficits, may not connect well to people, often have a desire for repetition, exhibit challenges with attention to detail, and display rigid behaviors (Emery, 2004). Emery (2004) further stated that children often create art and drawings to relate to their world. Children with autism, however, have difficulty relating to others. Drawings can be a bridge toward increased self-awareness and a foundation for relating to others. Art can serve a valuable role to assist children with ASD, as it can help develop important life and communication skills and emotional social awareness.

CASE ILLUSTRATION

Lisa was an 8-year-old girl who was referred to play therapy because of presented symptoms of anxiety and posttraumatic stress. (Permission to use her clinical progress was granted by her aunt.) She was removed from her biological mother at the age of 4 because of founded neglect, and she was placed in the care of her maternal aunt at that time. Lisa began therapy when she turned 6 years of age to process the abuse she had experienced while living in another state with her biological mother and younger brother, who was not removed from her mother's care. She moved into her aunt and uncle's home with their four children. Lisa was still adjusting to her new family and attending a new school.

Lisa had a history of encopresis. Incidences would increase when she was distressed during thoughts about her biological mother or when triggered in school or in the home. Her triggers were not always obvious. She would say rude things or even hit others in school or at home. As a baseline for her art, on Lisa's first day of treatment she was asked to draw a picture of whatever she wanted to. Figure 4.1 shows where Lisa drew a picture of herself inside a ball. She did not describe it in detail, as this was the initial assessment appointment.

This depiction could be assessed as that she had a need to be protected, that she felt isolated from others in her family, or that the ball was her safe place.

When Lisa began sessions, she was often quiet, would talk only about positive aspects of her current life, and would avoid addressing any incidents of her past. At times in the playroom, she would blurt out things about her

FIGURE 4.1. Drawing When Prompted to Draw "Whatever You Would Like": Herself in a Ball

biological mother and brother from when she was living with them. At times she stated that her mother was in jail and asked why her brother could stay but she had to leave. She would revert to baby talk, change the subject, or raise her voice and tone when playing and when mentioning her family of origin. She would quickly change the subject when difficult topics came up in her play. At times Lisa would freeze while playing and divert the play to something different, as though she was going down a difficult path and not ready to address the topic. She experienced stagnant play, and art was integrated increasingly into her play therapy process to promote more emotional release. Lisa's sessions consisted of weekly play therapy sessions in the playroom as well as drawing in the art area. As sessions progressed and rapport was built, Lisa created a multiple art piece that led to expressing her emotions. Simultaneously she became more verbally expressive about her anger toward her birth mother, who could not care for her but continued to care for her little brother. As a result of her neglect she had toileting issues; she could not hold her stool and was receiving medical treatment. She expressed embarrassment and experienced negative social comparison in connection to her peers. Lisa began to use art to express feelings when she reverted to baby talk, as it was apparent that she was not safely able to verbalize her feelings. The toileting issues were heightened when she was anxious or in distress, as shown in Figure 4.2.

As therapy continued, Lisa began to feel more comfortable verbally expressing her feelings about her mother and her current family. In another session,

FIGURE 4.2. Toileting Issues, Encopresis

she was instructed to draw a picture of her past and then her present, as represented in Figure 4.3.

She drew a picture of herself sad and hurt and colored repeatedly over the genital area (possibly because of the encopresis; she did not disclose sexual abuse). In her next drawing, Lisa represented herself as happy in her room playing with dolls. When asked to tell her story, she shared how she had this issue with encopresis when she lived with her mother and that she continues to have the issue but that it is getting better because she has medical treatment. Lisa shared how she is happy where she is. She has toys and a room she can play in. When she would tell these stories, she would indicate that she was also sad about not being with her mother and brother, as shown in Figure 4.4.

Over the course of 2 years, Lisa began to be more expressive in her play, verbalized her anger toward her mother, and began moving closer to accepting her aunt and uncle as her family as seen in Figure 4.5, a picture of herself happy at home.

In another session, Lisa drew her interpretation of the Rosebush activity, which can be seen in Figure 4.6. She shared that she was outside, had roots, and grew in the grass. She was cared for and watered by her mother (aunt);

FIGURE 4.3. Lisa's Past—Encopresis and Her Anxiety About Being Embarrassed in Public

FIGURE 4.4. Lisa's Present—Herself Playing in Her Room

FIGURE 4.5. Happy at Home

FIGURE 4.6. Drawing From the Rosebush Intervention

she was flowering and had leaves. This was toward the end of treatment, when she had made vast improvements with her toileting and anger and maintained positive behavior in the school setting.

EMPIRICAL SUPPORT

Art may assist children to verbally express their fantasies and inner thoughts through storytelling (Malchiodi, 2012). Malchiodi (2012) further stated that the quality of the therapeutic relationship and the progress of the therapy are reflected in the art expression. Play therapy, an evidence-based practice, has demonstrated the reduction of stress and anxiety, improved emotional adjustment of children who have been abused or neglected, and provided better social and emotional adjustment (Landreth, 2012). Although clinicians have agreed that art-making helps clients heal, there is always the need for evidence to support this.

One study on the effectiveness of art therapy for children in treatment sessions for a span of 1 year showed that children identified positive change and growth, and art therapy specifically helped them better cope with feelings (Slayton et al., 2010). More specifically, children being treated for attachment disorders, family issues, grief, and life stressors showed improvement with the use of art in their therapy sessions. Young girls who were sexually abused showed significant reduction on anxiety and PTSD scales (Slayton et al., 2010).

Children can receive therapy in an office, home, or school setting. Incorporating play therapy into school has been a growing interest, as research has shown that one in five children suffers from psychological or behavioral issues that meet criteria for a diagnosable disorder (Blanco et al., 2019). Play therapy includes art and drawings, as well as games, puppets, and other props, to help children express themselves (Malchiodi, 2007). A study conducted in an elementary school setting explored how children's school-based one-to-one art therapy promoted change (Deboys et al., 2017). This study included interviews with 14 children ages 7 to 11 who received art therapy in school within the previous 12 months addressing violence and abuse, anxiety, developmental trauma, parents with mental health concerns, and other emotional regulation difficulties. Through the interviews, the children reported improved mood, confidence, communication, and understanding. The sessions were held in a private and safe place. The study further highlighted the importance of art-making in facilitating children's expression and processing of emotional and social difficulties. Another study of five 10-year-old children with family issues, grief, and other stressors who received art therapy in a school-based setting for 1 year also reported that art therapy specifically helped the children better cope with their feelings (Slayton et al., 2010).

SUMMARY AND CONCLUSION

> Play is the everyday occupation of the child and a kind of practice for his future. . . . In play he practices relationships with people, tries to master play situations (which he creates), finds solutions to problems and reviews all these constantly. (Gondor, 1954)

Gondor (1954) stated that drawing and art allow the child the freedom to express in drawings what cannot be expressed in words. Art and play are explained by Malchiodi (2012) as windows into the child's perceptions of self and the world in which the child lives (p. 190). Even more, allowing children to play and create art in a safe environment is an essential part of the therapeutic relationship, providing progress in their treatment. When art and play are combined with a quality therapeutic relationship, the therapeutic powers of self-expression, emotional wellness, increased personal strength, and enhanced social relationships can be achieved.

REFERENCES

Axline, V. (1981). *Play therapy*. Ballantine Books.
Birch, J., & Carmichael, K. (2009). Using drawings in play therapy: A Jungian approach. *The Alabama Counseling Association Journal, 34*(2), 2–7.
Blanco, P., Holliman, R., Ceballos, P., & Farnam, J. (2019). Exploring the impact of child-centered play therapy on academic achievement of at-risk kindergarten students. *Association for Play Therapy, 28*(3), 133–143.

Brown, S. (2009). *Play: How it shapes the brain, opens the imagination, and invigorates the soul*. Penguin Group.

Cohen, J. A., Mannarino, A. P., & Deblinger, A. P. (2006). *Treating trauma and trauma grief in children and adolescents*. Guilford Press.

Deboys, R., Holttum, S., & Wright, K. (2017). Process of change in school-based art therapy with children. A systematic qualitative study. *International Journal of Art Therapy, 22*(3), 118–131. https://doi.org/10.1080/17454832.2016.1262882

Emery, M. (2004). Art therapy as an intervention for autism. *Art Therapy: Journal of the American Art Therapy Association, 21*(3), 143–147. https://doi.org/10.1080/07421656.2004.10129500

Gil, E. (1991). *The healing power of play, working with abused children*. Guilford Press.

Gondor, E. I. (1954). *Art and play therapy*. Doubleday & Company.

Herman, J. (1992). *Trauma and recovery*. Basic Books.

Kaduson, H. G., & Schaefer, C. E. (Eds.). (1997). *101 play therapy techniques*. Jason Aronson.

Kariz, B. (2003). *Art therapy and ADHD: Diagnostic and therapeutic approaches*. Jessica Kingsley Publishing.

Landreth, G. L. (2012). *Play therapy: The art of the relationship*. Routledge. https://doi.org/10.4324/9780203835159

Malchiodi, C. A. (2007). *The art therapy source book* (2nd ed.). McGraw-Hill.

Malchiodi, C. A. (2008). *Creative interventions with traumatized children*. Guilford Press.

Malchiodi, C. A. (2012). *Handbook of art therapy* (2nd ed.). Guilford Press.

Oaklander, V. (1988). *Windows to our children*. The Gestalt Journal Press.

Rubin, J. (2016). *Approaches to art therapy: Theory and techniques* (3rd ed.). Brunner-Routledge.

Schaefer, C. E., & Drewes, A. A. (2014). *The therapeutic powers of play: 20 core agents of change* (2nd ed.). John Wiley & Sons.

Slayton, S. C., D'Archer, J., & Kaplan, F. (2010). Outcome studies on the efficacy of art therapy: A review of findings. *Art Therapy: Journal of the American Art Therapy Association, 27*(3), 108–118. https://doi.org/10.1080/07421656.2010.10129660

Tanaka, M. (1992). Nagurigaki to momogatari [The Mutual Storytelling and Squiggle Game]. *Studies in Clinical Application Drawings, 7*, 147–165.

Tanaka, M. (1993). Squiggle hou no jissai [Practical method of squiggle drawing game]. *Studies in Clinical Application Drawings, 8*, 19–34.

Tanaka, M. (2001a). Approach to art therapy with gender identity disordered adolescents: The significance of narrative elicited through clinical drawings. *Bulletin of Mejiro University Department of Human and Social Services, 1*, 80–103.

Tanaka, M. (2001b). On squiggle drawing game with delinquent children: Art therapy and psychopathology of expression. *Clinical Psychiatry*, pp. 135–143.

Winnicott, D. W. (1971). *Therapeutic consultations in child psychiatry*. Hogarth Press.

5 USING BIBLIOTHERAPY AS A CATALYST FOR CHANGE

DEANNE (DEEDEE) GINNS-GRUENBERG AND CINDY BRIDGMAN

"Great books help you understand, and they help you feel understood" is a statement attributed to author John Green. This chapter is dedicated to bibliotherapy, the use of books that help increase understanding as well as assist clients in feeling understood. The rationale and history of both bibliotherapy and children's literature serve as a foundation on which to build therapeutic skills. Benefits of bibliotherapy, including communication, emotional wellness, social relationships, and personal strength, are explored. Core techniques that include placement of books, delivery and adaptation of stories, and inclusion of caregivers are provided. Key components of selecting materials and session structure are presented along with a number of common clinical applications. These applications include externalizing and internalizing disorders, social issues, abuse, grief and loss, self-esteem, emotional literacy, and self-control. Case illustrations are offered to assist in a further understanding of the impact that bibliotherapy can have on a client and confidentiality is protected by changes to names and identifying details. Finally, empirical support for the effectiveness of bibliotherapy, a chapter summary, and the conclusion are presented to solidify the usefulness of this methodology.

https://doi.org/10.1037/0000217-006
Play Therapy With Children: Modalities for Change, H. G. Kaduson and C. E. Schaefer (Editors)

The principle of bibliotherapy is the use of books and stories to assist clients in achieving cognitive, emotional, and behavioral changes. Over the years it has been successfully implemented with clients of all ages who are experiencing a myriad of social-emotional issues. Bibliotherapy works well in individual sessions, as well as in groups and classroom settings. It is also helpful for others in the child's life who could benefit from an increased understanding of the issues with which the client is struggling. Gaining insight may lead to a change in both perceptions of the client and their own responses.

The process of bibliotherapy involves more than reading a book. The literature serves to spark the imagination as to what can be. In a review of literature on bibliotherapy, the effectiveness was noted to increase when combined with other play therapy activities (Riordan & Wilson, 1989). Effective implementation of this methodology often uses puppets, dolls, a sandtray, and art to expand upon the concepts presented. Expressive techniques allow clients to experiment with the ideas presented and even personalize the message.

It is the critical role of a trained therapist to maximize the benefit and impact a book has on a client and their caregivers. Facilitating discussion that focuses on the character, not the client, allows an exploration of feelings and issues that do not shame or criticize the client. When joined with the power of play in follow-up activities, whether initiated by the therapist or the client, resolution of problems and issues often take place in an accepting and non-threatening environment.

HISTORY OF BIBLIOTHERAPY

The origins of bibliotherapy date back to ancient Greece, when the Greek historian Diodorus Siculus called the library a house of healing for the soul (Lutz, 1978). It took nearly 2,500 years before Benjamin Rush, a 19th-century physician and signer of the Declaration of Independence, would echo those sentiments when he advocated for the use of literature in hospitals for both the amusement and instruction of patients (McCulliss, 2012).

Using books as therapy began to gain popularity in earnest over the past 100 years. During World War I, the Library War Service stationed librarians in military hospitals, where they dispensed books to patients and developed the emerging "science" of bibliotherapy with hospital physicians. After the war ended, hospital libraries began growing as more health-care professionals began recognizing the health benefits of reading therapy. Many hospital librarians, including E. Kathleen Jones, Sadie Peterson Delaney, and Elizabeth Pomeroy, pioneered the work of bibliotherapy in Veterans Administration hospitals from the 1920s to the 1950s (Beatty, 1962).

In 1950, Carolyn Shrodes developed the first theoretical model for bibliotherapy based on the premise that readers connect with characters in the story (identification), become influenced by the characters and release emotions (catharsis), and achieve a better understanding of their own situations (insight; Shrodes, 1955). In 1966, the Association of Hospital and Institution Libraries, a division of the American Library Association, issued a working definition of bibliotherapy as "the use of selected materials as therapeutic adjuncts in medicine and psychiatry; also guidance in the solution of personal problems through directed reading" (p. 18).

With hospitals taking the lead, bibliotherapy principles and practice began to be recognized for its influence in the United States. In the 1970s, Arleen McCarty Hynes, a patients' librarian at the country's only federal mental hospital, expanded the library to include a "homey" place where patients would read poems, short stories, and essays and discuss their feelings or write responses (Lamb, 2006). She would also bring in objects of nature or clothing to stimulate the senses and give patients relatable experiences. Soon she began training other librarians using her techniques. Her work was the force that established the National Association for Poetry Therapy, a leading creative arts therapy professional organization (Lamb, 2006).

Rhea Rubin (1978), a librarian in the 1970s, is credited with identifying the categories of bibliotherapy that we use today. Developmental bibliotherapy, primarily used in educational settings, is designed to be used as a proactive approach to address behavioral issues or specific situations. Therapeutic (clinical) bibliotherapy is practiced in a clinical setting. Its focus is on emotional and resulting behavioral issues and is usually administered by a psychologist, counselor, or therapist.

At a basic level, bibliotherapy uses guided reading of written materials to gain an understanding or solve problems relevant to a person's therapeutic need (Riordan & Wilson, 1989). Clinical use of both fictional and nonfictional "issues-related" stories allows clients to identify with characters who have experienced similar challenges to those of our clients. Through the thoughtful use of the characters, settings, choices, and pictures, the therapist guides the client to the identification of skills and techniques that lead to the successful resolution of import issues in their lives.

HISTORY OF CHILDREN'S LITERATURE

Worth noting is the history of children's literature. Before the 18th century there was little genuine literature explicitly aimed toward children. The known literature during this era was used for education or religious lessons to convey conduct-related morals, values, and attitudes. Early children's writings present as being void of developmental sensitivities.

There has been a tremendous change in children's literature over the past 100 years. Stories were once told to frighten children into behaving. Today's stories, in contrast, are told to soothe and reassure children. Such literature provides children skills, guidance, and encouragement to help them succeed in a variety of areas. Topics of concern—be they anger, boundaries, divorce, fear, grief and loss, or substance abuse, to name a few—are now issues that are addressed in publications geared for children at various developmental levels of understanding. The advancement of children's literature has expanded the opportunities of effective bibliotherapy.

THERAPEUTIC BENEFITS

For some children, books are an escape into another world. For others, a book offers a new life perspective or an opportunity for self-exploration. In both instances, literature can often have an impact on the reader's life and serve as a nonthreatening opponent. Identification with a story character provides opportunity for reflection on choices and outcomes, of both the character and the client. The empathy or sympathy provided to the character often exceeds that which clients have offered themselves. Distance from their own experiences affords a chance for insights not otherwise available.

Children both need and crave the feeling of safety and predictability. Unfortunately, many children in today's world are void of those basic needs. Bibliotherapy is ideal for people who have experienced traumatic or life-changing events, as well as for those with social, emotional, or behavioral disorders. Literature can provide a learning experience that is palatable and harder to reject because the story is not about them. As with other therapies, the overriding goal of bibliotherapy is to provide hope and empowerment for the client to resolve presenting issues.

Through the use of books in therapy, clients see the world through the eyes of others and realize they are not alone. Books, stories, and characters often serve as a child's guide, in a nondirective and easily embraced manner. They are tools to engage children in the therapeutic powers of play outlined in Schaefer and Drewes's (2014) work.

Facilitating Communication Through Bibliotherapy

In bibliotherapy the writer or character in the book initiates communication. As clients begin to learn about the characters in the story, the clients begin to form a relationship between themselves and the characters. Children start to understand that their situation or experience is not unique and they are not alone. Seeing their own feelings, expressed by others, in print becomes an empowering experience for the clients. This education brings about a normalization of experiences that can disarm defensive and protective factors, thus allowing clients to gain access to their unconscious.

Psychoeducation takes place via indirect teaching through the character as well as self-exploration. Play that follows the bibliotherapy portion of the session should continue the same themes and focus as the written material. Engagement in such activities will facilitate communication—verbal or through nonverbal play—that will pose questions, present scenarios, and seek solutions. An example would be the use of a book addressing fears, such as *Dear Bear* (Harrison, 1994). Play that follows the reading might include a bear puppet, stuffed animal, or plastic figure. Following the child's directed play may provide insight on issues that result in identification or manifestation of their fear, as well as discovery of what is needed to resolve the fear. Other children may wish to dictate a letter to their fear, as in the book. As the clinician serves as the scribe, children verbalize their concerns, behaviors, and hopes for resolution.

Fostering Emotional Wellness Through Bibliotherapy

Catharsis—the process of emotional release or purging—is achieved as the client identifies, understands, and accepts their emotions. Through bibliotherapy, the client is able to safely have a vicarious experience of feelings through the character. As the character is witnessed to solve their issue, the client is able to purge emotional tension related to their own situation. This release leads to insights, which results in positive change in a client's/child's life. With clients who present with issues of racial identity, the book *Violet* (Stehlik, 2009) provides an opportunity for identification, cathartic release, and confidence. An activity that involves mixing paint to create new shades and colors can facilitate a process that builds on the book's presentation and increases understanding and acceptance. These insights and changes of mindset often result in counterconditioning of fears and improved management or inoculation of stress.

Enhancing Social Relationship Through Bibliotherapy

It is common for mental health clients to encase themselves in a self-perception of being different, weird, and not like their peers. Bibliotherapy provides the child with an opportunity to see their feelings and behaviors as normal. As the characters in the book resolve and overcome their problems, the characters also become positive role models who offer suggestions and support. The connection that the client makes with the character gives the client hope of coping with the issue at hand. With the help of a therapist, a reader realizes that just like the character in the story, they have self-control in their situation also. Using the book *My Mouth Is a Volcano* (Cook, 2009) permits children to see that they are not the only ones who struggle with controlling both what and when they say things. Incorporating play with building an exploding volcano, whether with a science experiment kit or a teepee with bean bags or small pillows that can be tossed out of the top, will provide a child with a physical opportunity to experience success controlling themselves. From hopelessness to hopefulness, the client gains self-competency and empathy for themselves and others.

Increasing Personal Strengths Through Bibliotherapy

Equipped with the power of inclusion and belonging, the client's seeds of resiliency that had lain dormant begin to bloom. Hope, safety, understanding, and support allows the client to accelerate their psychological development. Now the client has cleared the ground for exploring new interests, engaging in experiences, choosing friends, and connecting with other people. The use of a book such as *Beautiful Oops!* (Saltzberg, 2010) empowers the reader to view mistakes and messes as opportunities for creativity. Providing clients with paper, paint, glue, and other art materials engage them in altering tears, stains, and crumples into works of art. All of these activities promote self-regulation, moral development, and self-esteem.

CORE TECHNIQUES

Implementing bibliotherapy should be a purposeful and planned part of any therapy session. Consistency in the use of written materials is important, as predictability of the session creates safety for the client. Although the selection of the book is critical, and is addressed later in this chapter, other issues require the therapist's attention if best practice methods are to be implemented.

Placement

Books should not be located in an area where children are allowed to make a selection. In bibliotherapy, a book is an instrument that is to be determined appropriate by the professional trained to use it. Children often select books that are at their eye level or by the attraction of colorful jacket covers or the style of the font. The content of the book is often unknown to children, even if they are able to read the title. Some topics are inappropriate for the developmental level of the child or may provide information that would be premature in the healing journey. Other topics are irrelevant for their clinical presentations and might introduce new issues.

Also relevant to the delivery of the material is the setting in which a book is to be read. Consider an area that is comfortable, allowing personal space and providing escape if the child experiences fear or becomes overwhelmed. Many children find a stuffed animal or puppet to be a comforting companion while being read to. Although it may be difficult, selecting a location where there are few distractions and little noise will assist the child in remaining attentive.

Delivery

Children often ask to read, but in bibliotherapy it is typically not appropriate for them to be the reader. Having the therapist deliver the information provides children the opportunity to contemplate and comment on concepts presented instead of sounding out words. Adolescent clients also enjoy being read to. Sometimes asking them to serve as a consultant to the therapist—asking their thoughts on the material, such as how and to whom it may be helpful—gives them a role that makes children's books acceptable.

Therapists are encouraged to ask the client their thoughts on pictures or meanings of descriptions but always with the focus on the character and not the client—for example, "I wonder what doggy was thinking when they wouldn't let him play." This allows the child to project their own feeling onto the character, trying on the feeling or behavior modeled by the character in the book.

It is important that the child be able to view the book with ease, as illustrations in children's books serve as valuable as the words. They may enjoy the task of turning a page when given a signal from the therapist as to the appropriate time. Also, keeping an eye on the child's affect and level of engagement is key. A child's distracted presentation may be a clue to an area of discomfort or avoidance.

Although the therapist need not be an entertainer, reading with appropriate inflection in one's voice will be helpful in maintaining the client's attention. It behooves the therapist to pause at pertinent places in the book that allow for emphasis and reflection. Repeating phrases with powerful meanings can also assist the client in finding meaning.

Adaptations

Not every word or phrase in a book is appropriate—for example, a therapist in the story "tells" a client what to do, when in your session you invite or ask a child if they wish to participate. Changing the wording in a book can be appropriate. Informing a child who can read that you may be changing or substituting a word in the book can help avoid disruption during the reading.

Word changing is especially necessary if the vocabulary of the book exceeds the client's level of understanding. Do not discard the book but instead change the words to those the client can grasp. Unfamiliar terminology because of culture should also be taken into consideration and changes made that remains true to the delivery of the concept and meaning of the book.

It is also appropriate to invite the client to rewrite the story. Empowering them to change the story in a way that fits their personal situation is a step that has moved many children forward in their healing journey. Others may be motivated to add on a chapter or characters. Still others may choose to create a sandtray following the story.

Keep in mind that a book can be therapeutic for the child even when no discussion follows the reading.

Caregivers

Therapists are encouraged to share with caregivers the books to be used with the children. This not only increases the partnership in treatment but also provides psychoeducation.

During intake sessions, we often share *A Child's First Book of Play Therapy* (Nemiroff & Annunziata, 1990) or *Welcome to Therapy!* (Putt, 2006) with the caregivers to help them understand the purpose and process of each session. Important concepts such as confidentiality are explained in a developmentally appropriate manner. Therapists can request that the adults take the book home and read it aloud to their child. Substituting the therapist's name every time the word "therapist" is written can help the child become familiar with the therapist. Most of all, by reading the book to the child, caregivers are giving the child permission to have confidential conversations in therapy.

In preparation for the initial therapy session with the child, the therapist may send an information-gathering form home with the caregiver to complete with the child. Questions would include the name they prefer to be called; favorite foods, iPad games, TV programs, and singers; and so on. Questions should be adjusted to meet the child's developmental level. Responses from the questionnaire can be integrated into stories adapted from *Once Upon a Time . . . Therapeutic Stories That Teach & Heal* (Davis, 1996). Such activities have been used with success for building relationships and establishing a therapeutic alliance.

Selecting Materials for Bibliotherapy

Garry Landreth's (2012) belief that "toys should be selected, not collected" (p. 156) applies to book selection as well. It is incumbent on the therapist to preview all books prior to introducing them to a child. Important questions to consider in choosing the right book include the following:

- What is the therapeutic value and appropriateness of this book?
- How will this material help my client meet a therapeutic goal or objective?
- Is it relatable and understandable to the client, in both words and illustrations?
- How will it help this child? Are the issues relevant to my client's experience?
- Does it offer positive role models? Emotional support? Hope?
- Does the story present a crisis as surmountable, offering solutions and strategies?

Although it is important to select books that are not written beyond the developmental level of the child, the opposite should not be a concern. Older and more advanced clients can benefit from younger children's books. Sometimes the simplistic presentation of a problem can be the most powerful. Such is the case with *Tough Boris* (Fox, 1994). A book with very few words and vivid illustrations relays a message that it is okay for all persons, even pirates, to cry and to mourn. Many times the metaphors in children's literature speak more clearly to teens and adults.

Some therapists suggest avoiding books with animal characters, professing that children will not be able to identify with an animal. We both have found the opposite to be true. Experience has proven that children readily connect with animal characters. It appears they add an additional layer of safety and psychological distance, making it easier for the child to express their thoughts and feelings.

In general, books of fiction that mirror the reality of a client's struggle are most helpful. Children reading a fictional account can connect with the emotions without feeling personally ashamed or threatened (Gladding, 2005). Although that is true, it is also accurate to say that cognitive behavior workbooks such as *What to Do When You Worry Too Much* (Huebner, 2005) have proven very helpful and are a recognized bibliotherapy tool.

When reviewing materials, the following issues would determine that some books should be avoided:

- Books that do not honor and respect children and adults. Such books place blame on victims; make fun of inappropriate behavior; or portray adult helpers and persons in positions of authority as buffoons, unhelpful, or untrustworthy.

- Books that portray a gender bias or cultural insensitivity. This includes ideas that are contrary to therapeutic best practices of honoring all persons.

- Books that have an unclear or unhealthy message. Literature that increases fears and anxiety is included in this category.

Some books may present with good content but have an exception that might pull them out of contention. Before doing so, take another look at what changes need to take place. If the developmental level exceeds the client, is it possible to reduce it? If the vocabulary is unsuitable, can it be changed? If the book is too wordy or too long, how could it be shortened? If there are inappropriate topics, can those pages be omitted? Or if important information is not included, could it be introduced or pages added?

Therapists are encouraged to consider all books, not just those written for therapeutic purposes. Much of today's children's literature addresses real-life dilemmas that could provide the client with the opportunity to brainstorm for solutions. Other nontherapeutic books provide analogies for the therapeutic process. *Harold and the Purple Crayon* (Johnson, 1955) is such an example. The character draws his way out of every difficulty that comes his way. This book can help clients see obstacles as opportunities and challenge them to problem solving in their own lives.

Bibliotherapy Session Structure

Bibliotherapy is an excellent way to begin each session. It can be done as the child eats a snack or holds a stress ball. Allowing the literature to introduce the topic of the day is often less confrontational than a declaration by the therapist. The process of reading the book can be short, ending at the conclusion of the book, or it could be extended through conversation, consultation, or rewriting. Either way, the information and most likely psychoeducation has been delivered.

At the conclusion of the reading, an activity is often appropriate and necessary. For those children who function best while on the move, kinesthetic activities are helpful to emphasize the topic; the therapist might have buckets with different feeling faces into which children place balls, identifying how they would feel when provided with a scenario. Many children's games can be adapted to serve as a therapeutic tool. For older or more sedentary clients, a table game that uses colors to represent different feelings might serve the same purpose.

Once children become accustomed to identifying emotions of presented scenarios, they have a natural tendency to apply feelings to their own experiences. This application can be done through puppet or dollhouse play. It is helpful to have characters available that are similar to those in the literature just read or similar to the clients and their own family makeup. Sandtray work is often used for children to depict and work through their personal experiences, hopes, or fears. Older children may prefer to draw, create poetry, or write a rap song.

Building the therapy session to incorporate all of the learning styles—auditory, visual, and kinesthetic—will provide the greatest opportunity for the client to grasp the concepts presented. Although most people think of a book as primarily auditory and/or visual, telling the story through the use of toys can be most effective. This process also allows for the child to be an active participant.

To emphasize the idea stated earlier, including the caregiver in the therapeutic process is key for permanent change to take place. Inviting the client to share their session experience with the caregiver can be a good beginning. At times it may be appropriate to include the caregiver in the play of the session, provided the adult is given information and preparation to ensure their success. Handouts or reading lists can also be provided for informational purposes as well as implementation suggestions.

CLINICAL APPLICATIONS

Bibliotherapy can be appropriately incorporated in most therapeutic treatment theories and methodologies. Many books have psychoeducational components with activities for client participation. Dawn Huebner has authored a series of *What to Do When . . .* books on worry, anxiety, bad habits, and other issues common to children. Although the focus of this chapter has been on individual treatment, it is easily adaptable to use in group therapy, school counseling, or classroom teaching. A vehicle for psychoeducation, exploration, and modification, bibliotherapy truly is a catalyst for change.

Externalizing Disorders

Specific issues lend themselves well to the use of bibliotherapy—externalizing disorders such as attention-deficit/hyperactivity disorder, aggression, or conduct disorder. Because of its indirect approach through story characters, bibliotherapy offers the psychological distance that children need to achieve change without the pressure and/or condemnation. *The Worst Day of My Life Ever* (Cook, 2011) and *It's Hard to Be a Verb* (Cook, 2008) are books that offer the client insight into behaviors they may be exhibiting as well as solutions. The role of nonthreatening opponent challenges the client and allows the clinician to join with them, teaming up against the issue that is the source of the child's problems.

Internalizing Disorders

Those individuals who struggle with internalized disorders, including anxiety, loneliness, and depression, can also greatly benefit from bibliotherapy. The normalization of often unspoken experiences empowers verbalization, acknowledgment, and acceptance of the problem. Psychoeducation provided through characters can reduce complex issues to an understandable level of development. Such is the case in the books *When I Couldn't Get Over It, I Learned to Start Acting Differently* (Smith, 2018) and *You've Got Dragons* (Cave, 2003). Observing skills and success through books provides a path of hope and achievability.

Social Issues

Bibliotherapy is particularly helpful in addressing social issues. School violence, foster care, adoption, incarceration, and homelessness are just a few concerns that overwhelm both children and adults. Because of the lack of under-standing, power, and control, these issues often leave all involved feeling weak and ineffective. Books such as *Elliot* (Pearson, 2016); *Far Apart, Close in Heart* (Birtha, 2017); and *You Weren't With Me* (Ippen, 2019) provide insights and understanding to complex situations. Well-written materials, presented in a childlike manner, help to regain focus and identify effective coping strategies.

Abuse

Healing from abuse, particularly sexual abuse, is particularly well suited for bibliotherapy. Sexual abuse is a crime, perpetrated on children, that thrives in secrecy, isolation, and shame. Its victims are often too naive, appropriately so, to be able to understand what has happened to them. What they do know is often too difficult and embarrassing to describe. They experience unwarranted guilt and fear that someone will find out—all the while hoping to be rescued. These children often feel different from everyone else around them, but books such as *Not in Room 204* (Riggs, 2007) and *Tears of Joy* (Behm, 1999) help to remove the isolation.

Bibliotherapy offers acceptance to children who have been abused. They are not the only ones to whom this has happened, as described in *The Kid Trapper* (Cook, 2010). Their thoughts, feelings, and fears are normalized by the characters in the story, such as Maggie in *Some Secrets Hurt* (Garner, 2009). Their confusion is often cleared up through books appropriately written on the subject, as seen in Jessie's (1991) story *Please Tell!* Most of all, bibliotherapy offers hope and healing for victims and their caregivers.

Grief and Loss

Grief and loss is another area in which bibliotherapy provides significant help. For any child, the experience of death can be an emotionally stressful time and a traumatic event. Grief and loss may lead to feelings of isolation, confusion, and fear. A loved one who suicided or died from a drug overdose is often stigmatizing to survivors. Clients often have difficulty expressing and verbalizing their thoughts and feelings after a loss. Making sense of death is hard for all but even more so for children.

The use of bibliotherapy can lead the client to express their understanding of the loss and their own grief experience. *When Dinosaurs Die* (L. Brown & Brown, 1996) is an example of a book that reduces advanced concepts to a child's level. Beliefs and understandings that are contrary to reality and emotionally harmful can then be corrected, again through grief and loss literature. Books on the subject, such as *Lifetimes* (Mellonie & Ingpen, 1983), can also provide comfort and ultimately a healing context. Through bibliotherapy, clients share memories, continue bonds with the person they lost, and work through their grief and fear (Berns, 2004).

Self-Esteem

Bibliotherapy is a positive approach for clients who lack self-esteem. Many children have a fragmented view of self. The characters in stories such as *Zero* (Otoshi, 2010) and *Giraffes Can't Dance* (Andreae, 1999) persevere in spite of their flaws and circumstances. They serve as great role models for clients who struggle with perfectionism.

Bibliotherapy teaches clients to recognize their own positive attributes and strong points, not focusing on their weaknesses or history. However, helping children realize their strengths takes more than books; once again, incorporation of caregivers can hasten the healing process. Realistic expectations are that a single story may not be transformational, but together with other activities and incorporation of support systems, bibliotherapy can help to make a real impact in developing a healthy sense of self-esteem.

Emotional Literacy

Much of what is done in therapy is to improve the child's and caregiver's emotional literacy. This begins with identifying their own feelings through books such as *The Way I Feel* (Cain, 2000) and *In My Heart* (Witek, 2014). The next goal is to increase understanding of the emotion and its source. *My Cold*

Plum Lemon Pie Bluesy Mood (T. F. Brown, 2013) and *I'm Happy Sad Together* (Britain, 2012) are a few books that assist in making this connection. Building on these foundational blocks, self-regulation—often referred to as behavior management—can be achieved.

This area of personal development is often underdeveloped in children and adults. When asked to identify an intense feeling, many people are unable to respond with accuracy. This confusion often leads to increased frustration and the inability to self-regulate. Bibliotherapy not only provides education on the subject but focuses on application. Books such as *Anh's Anger* (Silver, 2009), *Andrew's Angry Words* (Lachner, 1995), and *When Sophie Gets Angry— Really, Really Angry* (Bang, 1999) allow the client to observe, consider, and try on responses to intense feelings without personally experiencing the intensity. Distinguishing one feeling from another and taking ownership of that emotion replaces guilt and embarrassment with empowerment and self-control.

CASE ILLUSTRATION

Carla was an 8-year-old biracial girl in the second grade. Her presenting problem was fear and avoidance of social situations at school and in the community. Her second-grade teacher reported that Carla was "timid around children" and spoke in an "overly soft voice that was difficult to hear," especially when asked to speak in front of her peers.

When she was alone with her teacher, Carla was more talkative. She was a good student but lacked confidence. Her teacher believed she was embarrassed or worried about being negatively evaluated. She mentioned in passing that every student in the class was Caucasian. She wondered if Carla's anxiety stemmed from feeling "different" from her classmates. Carla started making frequent trips to the school nurse, complaining of stomachaches.

Carla is an only child being raised by a single parent father. Her mother died when she was 4 years old. According to her father, Carla was outgoing at home but "shy in restaurants and around other children." Counseling was recommended after a medical evaluation showed no physiological basis for her stomachaches.

Early in treatment, the book *Hector's Favorite Place* (Rooks, 2018) was read to help normalize the client's worries. The story is about an adorable hedgehog who used to love spending time with friends but had recently convinced himself that his favorite spot was at home where he felt comfy and safe. "He knew deep down his worries were stopping him from participating in activities" (p. 13).

Hector models positive or possible self-talk, saying to himself, "You can do this." This phrase was repeated several times throughout sessions with Carla in hopes that the repetition of the affirmations implanted in the text would speak directly to her. At the conclusion of the reading of the story, the question of why Hector didn't want to join his friends was posed. Carla was silent and then whispered, "Maybe he knows they don't really like him." She did not elaborate.

Moving to the sandtray, Carla created a scene with a variety of friendly-looking animals in a forest. She titled it "The Friends" but chose not to talk about her creation. It wasn't until after she had left the session that the therapist (DG) noticed that one of the monkeys was facing away from all the other animals. In that moment, the therapist recalled the teacher's hypothesis that Carla felt "different" from her classmates.

In the next session, the book *Violet* (Stehlik, 2009) was read to Carla. This is the story of a little girl who worries that the kids won't like her. The day turns out to be wonderful, and after school her friends comment that she and her dad are not the same color. At home an upset Violet is taught that her color derives from the mixing of her red mom and blue dad. Her mom then assures Violet that there are many mixed children, resulting in a whole rainbow of colors. She continues by explaining that people should like her for who she is and not the color of her skin. Violet is able to proudly proclaim that her mom is red and her dad is blue, and she is Violet!

Carla hesitated prior to turning several pages, as she appeared engaged by the illustrations. There was a visible change in her affect as the story was read. Her smile was memorable as she looked up after the conclusion of the book. *Violet* was a metaphor for this client's life experience. Without direction or explanation from the therapist, Carla headed straight for the paints. She painted a red person and then covered the red with blue. Proudly and emphatically she stated, "So I'm purple!"

Fear of being different from her peers was divulged while reading the story. Carla experienced a breakthrough toward social-emotional compe-tence building and developing a sense of self.

Bibliotherapy was an important part of Carla's play therapy treatment. Follow-up activities provided opportunity for her to make personal applica-tions. A month into therapy, Carla announced that she was going to read *Violet* (Stehlik, 2009) to her class. For this child, bibliotherapy was a catalyst for change and healing.

EMPIRICAL SUPPORT

Although there has been limited research using bibliotherapy, a series of empirical studies with adolescent students conclude that effectiveness of this method. Using three conditions—bibliotherapy, helping methodologies, and a control no-treatment group—bibliotherapy was measured as more effective than the helping methods in reducing aggression and increased empathy, and no change was noted in the control group of children where bibliotherapy was not used (Shechtman, 2006). Similar findings of the use of bibliotherapy leading to improved outcomes in areas of insight and therapeutic change have been noted (Hill & O'Brien, 1999; Prochaska, 1999). Possibly the most prominent study, conducted by the National Institute for Trauma and Loss, demonstrated a statistically significant reduction of posttraumatic stress disorder symptoms in students who participated in I Feel Better Now!, a sensory-based intervention program using bibliotherapy (Steele et al., 2009).

SUMMARY AND CONCLUSION

Bibliotherapy provides a voice for the fears, concerns, behaviors, and hopes of the clients served. Through the process, noninvasive entry into the child's world can take place, and the child is encouraged to take the lead. Psychoeducation and empowerment take place in a nonthreatening way. Partnership between the therapist and client is formed through exploration and identification of issues, strengths, and future goals.

The selection of books is crucial, and the therapist should thoughtfully consider each choice. Changes in wording or selection of pages should be contemplated prior to a child's session. Partnering various play therapy techniques with the selected literature is key. Choosing activities to engage all learning styles—auditory, visual, and kinesthetic—will increase the effectiveness of a session that begins with bibliotherapy.

Bibliotherapy provides insight, psychoeducation, skills, guidance, and hope to live a life without the problems that brought the client into counseling in the first place. As change is the goal for all therapeutic encounters, bibliotherapy is truly an effective catalyst for that change.

REFERENCES

Andreae, G. (1999). *Giraffes can't dance*. Orchard Books.
Association of Hospital and Institution Libraries. (1966, Summer). *AHL Quarterly*, 18.
Bang, M. (1999). *When Sophie gets angry—Really, really angry*. Scholastic Corporation.
Beatty, W. (1962). Historical review of bibliotherapy. *Library Trends, 11*(1), 106–117.
Behm, B. (1999). *Tears of joy*. WayWord Publishing.
Berns, C. (2004). Bibliotherapy: Using books to help bereaved children. *Omega: Journal of Death and Dying, 48*(4), 321–336. https://doi.org/10.2190/361D-JHD8-RNJT-RYJV
Birtha, B. (2017). *Far apart, close in heart*. Albert Whitman & Company.

Britain, L. (2012). *I'm happy sad together.* CreateSpace Independent Publishing.

Brown, L., & Brown, M. (1996). *When dinosaurs die.* Little, Brown and Company.

Brown, T. F. (2013). *My cold plum lemon pie bluesy mood.* Viking Press.

Cain, J. (2000). *The way I feel.* Parenting Press.

Cave, K. (2003). *You've got dragons.* Peachtree Publishers.

Cook, J. (2008). *It's hard to be a verb.* National Center for Youth Issues.

Cook, J. (2009). *My mouth is a volcano.* National Center for Youth Issues.

Cook, J. (2010). *The kid trapper.* National Center for Youth Issues.

Cook, J. (2011). *The worst day of my life ever.* Boys Town Press.

Davis, N. (1996). *Once upon a time . . . Therapeutic stories that teach and heal.* Nancy Davis Publishing.

Fox, M. (1994). *Tough Boris.* HMH Books for Young Readers.

Garner, L. (2009). *Some secrets hurt.* Shadow Mountain.

Gladding, S. (2005). *Counseling as an art: The creative arts in counseling* (4th ed.). American Counseling Association.

Harrison, D. (1994). *Dear bear.* Carolrhoda Books.

Hill, C. E., & O'Brien, K. M. (1999). *Helping skills: Facilitating, exploration, insight, and action.* American Psychological Association.

Huebner, D. (2005). *What to do when you worry too much.* Magination Press.

Ippen, C. G. (2019). *You weren't with me.* Piplo Productions.

Jessie. (1991). *Please tell! A child's story about sexual abuse.* Hazelden Foundation. Available at https://www.hazelden.org/store/item/1797?Please-Tell

Johnson, C. (1955). *Harold and the purple crayon.* Harper Collins.

Lachner, D. (1995). *Andrew's angry words.* NorthSouth.

Lamb, Y. (2006, September 15). Arleen Hynes, 90: Bibliotherapy pioneer. *The Washington Post,* B07.

Landreth, G. (2012). *Play therapy: The art of the relationship* (3rd ed.). Taylor & Francis. https://doi.org/10.4324/9780203835159

Lutz, C. (1978). The oldest library motto: ψῦχῆς ἰατρεῖον. *The Library Quarterly: Information, Community, Policy, 48*(1), 36–39. https://doi.org/10.1086/629993

McCulliss, D. (2012). Bibliotherapy: Historical and research perspectives. *Journal of Poetry Therapy, 25*(1), 23–38. https://doi.org/10.1080/08893675.2012.654944

Mellonie, B., & Ingpen, R. (1983). *Lifetimes.* Bantam Books.

Nemiroff, M., & Annunziata, J. (1990). *A child's first book of play therapy.* Magination Press.

Otoshi, K. (2010). *Zero.* KO Kids Books.

Pearson, J. (2016). *Elliot.* Pajama Press.

Prochaska, J. O. (1999). *How do people change, and how can we change to help many more people?* American Psychological Association. https://doi.org/10.1037/11132-007

Putt, C. (2006). *Welcome to therapy!* Author House.

Riggs, S. (2007). *Not in room 204.* Albert Whitman & Company.

Riordan, R., & Wilson, L. (1989). Bibliotherapy: Does it work? *Journal of Counseling and Development, 67*(9), 506–508. https://doi.org/10.1002/j.1556-6676.1989.tb02131.x

Rooks, J. (2018). *Hector's favorite place.* Magination Press.

Rubin, R. (1978). *Using bibliotherapy: A guide to theory and practice.* Oryx Press.

Saltzberg, B. (2010). *Beautiful oops!* Workman Publishing Company.

Schaefer, C. E., & Drewes, A. A. (2014). *The therapeutic powers of play: 20 core agents of change* (2nd ed.). Wiley.

Shechtman, Z. (2006). The contribution of bibliotherapy to the reduction of childhood aggression. *Psychotherapy Research, 16,* 645–651. https://doi.org/10.1080/10503300600591312

Shrodes, C. (1955). Bibliotherapy. *The Reading Teacher, 9,* 24–30.

Silver, G. (2009). *Anh's anger.* Plum Blossom Books.

Smith, B. (2018). *When I couldn't get over it, I learned to start acting differently.* Boys Town Press.

Steele, W., Kuban, C., & Raider, M. (2009). Connections, continuity, dignity, opportunities model: Follow-up of children who completed the I Feel Better Now! trauma intervention program. *School Social Work Journal, 33*(2), 98–111.

Stehlik, T. (2009). *Violet.* Second Story Press.

Witek, J. (2014). *In my heart.* Abrams Books.

6

THE THERAPEUTIC USE OF STORIES IN PLAY THERAPY

SONIA MURRAY

Like play, stories and the use of stories have been part of humans' everyday existence since the beginning of humankind. There is historical evidence of stories being used in 4000 BC and during ancient Egyptian times (Myers et al., 2012). As noted by Davis (1990), "Long before the invention of written language, fairy tales, legends and stores existed to transfer knowledge from one generation to another" (p. 1). Stories have been used to educate, prepare for adulthood, pass on information, and create social and cultural connections. Lahad (2017) proposed that "story-making, storytelling, and artistic expression to be a basic human need of survival" (p. 19).

Stories connect on multiple levels. By connecting physiologically, neurobiologically, and socially, stories provide a holistic experience for both the listener and the storyteller. Physiologically, stories can bring us to tears, make us laugh, and evoke fear-based responses such as increased heart rate and shallow breathing. From a neurobiological perspective, play and stories connect and communicate to the autonomic nervous system, the limbic system, and the prefrontal cortex. Socially, stories provide a common ground to connect. Using stories in the context of play therapy therefore seems a

https://doi.org/10.1037/0000217-007
Play Therapy With Children: Modalities for Change, H. G. Kaduson and C. E. Schaefer (Editors)

natural and logical combination. The play facilitates the story, the story facilitates the play, and the interconnection facilitates change.

For the purpose of this chapter, the therapeutic use of stories in play therapy is based in a humanistic, prescriptive, developmental perspective that integrates the impact of trauma, attachment theory, and neurobiology. Incorporating these perspectives within Axline's (1947) nondirective principles while using the therapeutic powers of play within the context of the therapeutic relationship and environment creates an ideal space for stories to develop. The therapeutic change agents that enable children to process their experiences and develop different internal working models are identified. Case vignettes are used to illustrate these concepts, and for the purpose of anonymity, case material and the stories have been changed. The terminology of story/narrative is used, but it does not refer only to the verbalization of a story; it encompasses stories created in play, nonverbally, art mediums, and enactments.

Stories have been used in psychotherapy as far back as 1895 (Freud & Breuer, 1895) with the case study of Anna O, who would use storytelling while in a hypnotic state; Breuer noticed that the stories were comparable to Hans Christian Andersen's narratives and were regularly depictive of her own experiences. Furthermore, as suggested by Jones (1977), Freud's "free association" method had been influenced by Börne's (1823) essay titled "The Art of Becoming an Original Writer in Three Days." Börne's concept was that individuals should just write whatever comes into their head and not to censor it. This, in turn, may have predisposed the use of stories in psychotherapy along with the human drive to create meaning and understanding. More recently, authors such as Gersie (1990), Cattanach (1994, 1997, 2002, 2007), Jennings (2005b), Lahad (2017), and Taylor de Faoite (2011) have influenced the use of stories, particularly in the field of play therapy.

To understand the different "story" terminology in play therapy, it is useful to define the terms: narrative, story, therapeutic narrative, narrative play therapy, bibliotherapy, and meta-storying (see Chapter 9, this volume). First, a *narrative* is "a spoken or written account of connected events" (Oxford University Press, n.d.-a) and a *story* is "an account of imaginary or real people and events told for entertainment" (Oxford University Press, n.d.-b). McLeod and Balamoutsou (1996) described a *therapeutic narrative* as "an attempt by the client to 'narrativize' a problematic experience through creating a series of stories, connected by linking passages and therapist interventions" (p. 65). *Narrative play therapy* "is a form of play therapy that supports the child through playing and stories to reach a satisfactory understanding of their situation. This understanding is negotiated through the co-construction of stories" (Taylor de Faoite, 2011, p. 9). *Bibliotherapy* involves the reading of books or specific narratives in therapy. For a greater understanding of bibliotherapy, please refer to Chapter 5 in this volume. Finally, *meta-storying* is a story created from a collation of stories or play in the play therapy context (Taylor de Faoite, 2011).

It is worth noting that sometimes children who attend play therapy have an underdeveloped ability to form a narrative, which frequently correlates to their underdeveloped play skills. Typically developing children by the age of 2 are beginning to story-make. However, children who have experienced developmental interpersonal trauma needed to use their energies to survive in their 1st few years of life and therefore may not have developed the play or language skills required to begin story-making. These children will be playing at the embodiment stage of play (Jennings, 2005a) or at the early projective play stage (Jennings, 2005a) where they set up the toys, but they are then unable to create a story or undertake in fighting role play with little or no identified characters or narrative.

Stories in play therapy can be used in many ways and provide a vast amount of information about the child to the play therapist. The therapist can gain knowledge of the child's developmental stage, their language ability, their play skills, their attachment style, and their understanding of their life experiences. Stories can be created individually by the child or the therapist, or they can be cocreated. Additionally, the stories can be developed through the mediums that the play therapy environment provides, including sensory materials, music, toys, puppets, and role-play materials.

When children create a story by using the humanistic approach of following their own lead, the children can form a story in any way that they chose (without influence from the therapist). In most other settings, children are directed in some way to create a story, as it is often linked to a topic in school or they are given a story starter sentence. Rarely do they have the opportunity to create truly their own story. Play therapy is one place where a story can be created without direction.

A story created by the therapist generally emerges out of their observations and connections with the child. Often, reoccurring themes arise from the sessions, but the theme feels stuck and with little resolution, so a well-timed therapist-created story can provide a new understanding and pathway. As Morgenstern (2012) stated,

> You may tell a tale that takes up residence in someone's soul, becomes their blood and self and purpose. That tale will move them and drive them and who knows what they might do because of it, because of your words. That is your role, your gift. (p. 5)

As with any interjection, consideration needs to be given to whose need it is fulfilling. If it is to speed up the process or bring resolution for the therapist, it may not be useful to the child. Furthermore, the play therapist needs to be aware of their own personal, social, and cultural bias that might influence the story. For one child, the therapist created a story about a young kangaroo whose body had learned to be hypervigilant because of his early life experiences. Unfortunately, his hypervigilant body responses were presenting a number of challenges in his school setting. The story was developed to enable the child to understand how and why his own body was reacting currently and to understand his early life experiences. The story incorporated some therapeutic life story elements. Using the kangaroo provided a symbolic safety and distance from the child's own experiences for him to be able to hear it. This story also provided a greater understanding to his parents and his key school staff.

Therapeutic life stories may be incorporated as per the example just presented or evolve out of children's need to understand their life experiences. Having ascertained the child's history, the therapist of one child enacted the child's life experiences using two families of cat figures in the sandtray. The child selected which cat represented each family member, and she was then able to visually see the sequence of her life experiences within the safety of the story and the play.

Cocreated stories involve both the child and the therapist adding their own elements to create a story, again using any medium as just described. The stories can be developed by the child asking the therapist to join or by the developmental stage of cooperative social pretend play emerging (Howes & Matheson, 1992). The stories become cooperatively developed. For example, if a client assigns the therapist the role of a fashion show commentator, the therapist might have to invent impromptu commentary as each model (the client) walks down the catwalk.

THERAPEUTIC BENEFITS

The use of stories is practiced differently depending on the theoretical orientation of the play therapist. For example, in Adlerian play therapy, the therapist may use the mutual storytelling technique (Kottman & Stiles, 1990). Mutual storytelling technique involves the child creating a story and the therapist analyzing the metaphoric content to provide psychological meaning for the child (Kottman & Stiles, 1990). Regardless of the orientation, the therapeutic use of stories can facilitate all core change agents of the therapeutic powers of play (Schaefer & Drewes, 2014). However, for the purpose of this chapter, the following therapeutic change agents are discussed: self-expression, access to the unconscious, direct/indirect teaching, creative problem solving, resiliency, self-esteem, self-regulation, catharsis and counterconditioning fears, and the therapeutic relationship.

Self-Expression

Stories facilitate communication on numerous levels. Stories develop the child's nonverbal and verbal expression, including language formation, but also provide a way for the child to communicate their experiences and emotions. The child choosing and directing the story facilitates the therapeutic change agent of self-expression (Morrison Bennett, 2014). It can be nonverbal play, a two-sentence long narrative, or a sandtray story spread over several sessions; whatever form it takes, it is the child's self-expression.

Access to the Unconscious

Through the creation or the hearing of the story, unconscious material is made accessible to the conscious mind (Crenshaw & Tillman, 2014). As the unconscious is often a driver for behavioral responses, bringing it safely through the medium of story/play into the conscious mind assists change. Bettelheim (1976) stated, "The child fits unconscious content into conscious fantasies, which then enable him to deal with the content" (p. 7).

Direct/Indirect Teaching

Stories naturally provide the core agents of change: direct teaching (Fraser, 2014) and indirect teaching (Taylor de Foaite, 2014). Whether the story is created individually by the child or the therapist or cocreated, it will regularly portray some aspect of learning to both the storyteller and the listener. This can be the direct aspect by providing a different conclusion or way of solving the problem. Alternatively, for some children, they are unable to access and are resistant to the therapist approaching the issues directly, so using the play and the metaphor provide an opportunity to bypass the child's fear-driven safety mechanisms of avoidance and not wanting to "talk" about it. Sometimes it is too scary, too exposing, and too cognitive—and of course, too complex to look at it directly. Storytelling is a way to give those children a structure or form to bring the story to life. An example of this is illustrated later in this chapter.

Creative Problem Solving and Resiliency

The modality of using stories therapeutically in play therapy provides children with opportunities to create different solutions to the complexities they are experiencing, using the change agent of creative problem solving (Russ & Wallace, 2014). They can rework the story again and again until they find a resolution that works for them, thus building up the essential skill of being able to problem solve. With an increased ability to problem solve comes an enhanced resiliency (Seymour, 2014). The greater the ability to creatively think through solutions, the greater the ability to bounce back from life's trials and tribulations. Furthermore, the telling and hearing of stories within the therapeutic relationship in play therapy meets Grotberg's (1997) three domains for resilience: external support and resources, inner personal strengths, and social and interpersonal skills. The external support of the therapist hearing and accepting the child's story helps expand their external supports and resources while being wholly connected socially and interpersonally. The deeply felt connection and inherent pleasure of someone wholly listening to your story, hearing you word for word, seeing you play for play, and then reading it back to you are so emotionally powerful.

Self-Esteem

With regard to inner personal strengths, creating a story—whether through play, pictures, or words—develops a sense of mastery and enhancing self-esteem (Frey, 2014). Many children come to play therapy disaffected about creating stories because the term *story* is often linked to writing in schools. However, the play therapy environment allows the child to develop/restore their self-belief and self-confidence in their story-making capabilities. When the toys play the story, this bypasses the child's perception of creating a story. If asked to make a story, the child may repeatedly say, "I can't make stories"; however, they are able to make stories through the play, assisting with their psychological development (S. Prendiville, 2014). Children have been shocked, thrilled, and amazed when their stories are read back to them. They often say, "Did I really say that?" or "Wow, I can make a story."

Self-Regulation

A story can be a container for children learning to regulate their emotions and behavioral responses. Regulation occurs within the presence and scaffolding of another. Therefore, the use of stories in the therapeutic relationship can replicate healthy regulatory experiences. As noted earlier, learning to regulate can be through the teaching therapeutic power of play with the story of Dracco (Compton, 1997) or through the organization, structure, planning, and enacting of a story. The Dracco story is about a young male dragon who struggles to manage his feelings and sometimes lets out his fire inappropriately.

Following an incident, his family decides to never use fire again to help Dracco learn to control his fire. The story follows him into adulthood, where he discovers that there are times when a dragon may need to use his fire. Regularly, when children are referred for play therapy, their stories are disjointed and rushed and have little coherence. The process of the therapist reflectively responding, being curious, and clarifying the story/play enables the child to process and to regulate their thoughts and actions. A child can process consciously while developing internal impulse control and regulating behavioral responses. As a child narrates their story, often they will speak faster than the therapist can write. The therapist can repeat the child's words while writing, which naturally slows the child, enabling the child to keep in mind what has happened so far in the story and providing a moment for the child to plan the next part. The child thus develops the executive functioning skills of planning, sequencing, and organization. Additionally, an attuned synchronization can occur; the child internally knows when to pause and to start again even if they cannot see the writing.

Catharsis and Counterconditioning Fears

Many children who are referred for play therapy have experienced traumatic and emotionally overwhelming experiences without the consistent support of a caring other, thus leaving them in a confused and troubled state. Stories amid play therapy provide opportunities for the change agent of catharsis (Drewes & Schaefer, 2014) to occur. The stories offer a cathartic safety for the child to explore these experiences and to understand, process, and release the strong emotions connected to the experiences. For example, if a client uses Playmobil® figures to create stories to portray their experiences of domestic violence and victimization by other residents in their community, that client can process experiences of feeling helpless and of not being helped. The client can move between the story/play and other activities such as sensory materials, when the story/play becomes too overwhelming, and can experience the fear memories through the story/play.

Stories/play have the ability to trigger a fear memory safely but also provide some elements that are incompatible to the original fear memory. Therefore, the counterconditioning fear (Van Hollander, 2014) change agent can be used to process the fear and learn to overcome it (Lang, 1977). The "incompatible" elements are the play and its sensory aspect, the therapeutic relationship, the therapist's reflections, and the therapeutic environment. Foa and Kozak (1986) and Lahad (2017) therefore posited that creating the narrative of the memory enables the brain to gain control of the fear. The narrative memory can come in the form and safety of a story for the client. Additionally, the story/play can promote the opportunity to experience positive emotions, which would counteract the fear and terror (Kottman, 2014). As noted by Garland et al. (2010), "evidence from behavioral and brain sciences suggests that repeated activation of even mild emotional states may ultimately alter emotional traits, a transformational process that we speculate is undergirded by sustained changes in brain function and structure" (p. 860). Additionally, stories can decrease stress responses by releasing oxytocin and changing the listener's cortisol level (Zak, 2012).

Therapeutic Relationship

Stories have been used for centuries to build and maintain social relationships. Long before the written word, stories connected people and communities. Stories can be the bridge between the child and therapist. Through the safety of the change agent of the therapeutic relationship (Stewart & Echterling, 2014), stories can flourish. Within the context of play therapy and using Axline's (1947) principle of acceptance, there are no judgments made by the therapist about the child's vocabulary, grammar, spelling, or sentence formation or about "how good it is." Therefore, it provides the child with a safe place from which to explore and take the risk to create a story. The therapeutic relationship has similar features to a secure parent–child attachment—predictability, emotional stability, attunement, and being connected emotionally (Divecha, 2017). Therefore, stories created within the therapeutic relationship can bring about changes in the neural pathways in the brain (Cozolino, 2010). Stories bring brains together (Stephens et al., 2010). Stories can enhance the links between the lower limbic brain and the more complex region of the prefrontal cortex. The imaginative element of stories links the right hemisphere of the brain to the language aspect of left hemisphere (Taylor de Faoite et al., 2016).

CORE TECHNIQUES

As previously discussed, stories in play therapy can be created in a variety of ways; however, the fundamental element for any technique is the play therapist and their ability to create an environment to hear the child's stories/play wholly. A few examples of techniques follow.

One technique is creating a Play Story. The play therapist writes the child's story as it evolves in the play. After obtaining permission from the child, the play therapist writes the child's verbal narrative as they are playing. It is necessary to write word for word what the child says. This is not a time to teach grammar or sentence formation; it is a time to hear and accept the child completely. Once the child completes the narrative, the play therapist reads it back, checking to see if the child wants to add, amend, or remove elements. Following this, the play therapist can type it up and create a book for the child, incorporating photos of the objects used, the images created, or the story being enacted. The book is brought to the following session and read to the child if the child wants to.

The BASIC Ph Six Part Story Making method (Lahad et al., 2013) provides an ideal opportunity to gain a greater understanding of the child and could be undertaken at the assessment stage. The technique involves the child's creating a story using the method's six questions. The play therapist then uses the scoring system to evaluate the narrative and ascertain the child's coping strategies. From this, the play therapist can determine the most appropriate way of working with the child. For example, if the child has little or no emotional affect in their story, then it is important to not work directly with feelings initially, as the child will not be able to connect. However, emotional language can be modeled by the play therapist to develop this. For example, if the client creates a story without emotional language but the play therapist wonders about what the characters are physically doing, it is possible that the hidden emotional content can be articulated through a physical action in the play, such as the car is in a puddle of tears and is crying. Thereby, the therapist is able to model emotional language about the car being sad and crying.

Cocreated stories can evolve in a variety of ways, from the child asking for the therapist's input into the play/story to the play/story emerging from a game. Resources such as storytelling cards or Rory's Story Cubes can be used in a similar way to objects in taking turns to create a story. In this way, the play therapist can interject different elements that may be useful for the child into the story on their turn (direct/indirect teaching). Storytelling cards can provide a safe structure for some clients. For clients with underdeveloped imaginations and narrative abilities, the repeated use of the cards, plus the modeling from the play therapist, enables them to learn to use magical and imaginative elements in their stories. Additionally, the stories produce laughter and connection. Thus, the cocreated stories accelerated their psychological development and induced positive emotions.

CLINICAL APPLICATIONS

Stories can be used to address most childhood challenges, including trauma, fear, anxiety, and attachment. There is always a story that can be created. Stories, whether they are developed by the child and/or therapist or previously written, can be the symbolic pathway to exploring the past, the present, and the future. Stories can provide an opportunity to release previously repressed emotions (abreaction) created by traumatic experiences through the reliving of the experience within the safety of the story (E. Prendiville, 2014) or offer opportunities to develop different ways of responding in relationships for children who have experienced attachment challenges. Stories enable fears and anxiety to be understood and processed such that children gain mastery over them. Stories provide symbolic messages of different ways to regulate and react (please refer to the Dracco story; Compton, 1997).

CASE ILLUSTRATION

This case illustration follows a child's use of stories to process and rework her early life experiences. Lucy, at 8 years old, was referred for play therapy by her teacher, as she was displaying her distress with anger, aggression, and challenging behaviors toward her peers and school staff. She was the oldest child of three. At the time of the play therapy she was experiencing significant neglect and abuse. During the play therapy, her parents abandoned her, and she went to live with a foster family. She was cautious about the play therapy and the play therapist. Plus, she had learned to use avoidant attachment strategies to survive in her birth family. Initially, her story creating was limited, and she was working at the projective play level. Her first story was developed in the sandtray and involved some animals living in a volcano land. In the story, the unicorn, horse, tiger, frog, and gorilla were subjected to boiling-hot lava every day. However, it was "okay," as three of them were made of lava and the other two were just used to it. The story concluded there, and she went to paint. The therapist can only surmise that the story reflected her experience of her world, as there was no verbalization to corroborate this. The story did not need interpreting; it just needed to be heard. As Bettelheim (1976), concluded, "It is always intrusive to interpret a person's unconscious thoughts" (p. 18). She did not refer to this story again. Over time, her stories developed to incorporate role play and she played having a birthday party. She would create the story first, and it involved a little girl experiencing a birthday party where everyone was excited and happy for her. However, invariably during the story, something or someone would come along and ruin the party. (This was a lived experience for the child.) This was replayed repeatedly, but with the therapist reflecting how awful and sad it was for the little girl that her party was spoiled, the story began to evolve. Different characters began to block the things trying to spoil the party. Initially they could not, but they kept trying. Eventually, they were able to block the saboteurs and the little girl in the story was able to experience a wonderful birthday party where everyone was there to celebrate her. Lucy was able to reexperience and rework the safety of the story and play her experiences of not being wanted, nurtured, and accepted. The story acted as a container of the experience.

EMPIRICAL SUPPORT

The roles of stories and storytelling have been studied and continue to be studied around the world. However, there is limited empirical support about the benefits of using stories therapeutically in play therapy. Therefore, it is useful to consider how stories are beneficial in society generally. Stephens et al. (2010) researched the brain wave synchronization (neural entrainment) that occurs between the storyteller and the listener. They found that the brain waves become synchronized with only a slight delay in the listener. They become attuned. This corroborates the power of stories. Stories have been found to significantly increase empathy toward others. (Johnson et al., 2014) Additionally, stories provide an understanding of others, as a story "uniquely engages the psychological processes needed to gain access to characters' subjective experiences" (Kidd & Castano, 2013, p. 378) Therefore, with these studies in mind, it may be useful to suggest that stories in the play therapy context provide similar benefits.

SUMMARY AND CONCLUSION

Using stories in play therapy provides a medium for the optimal social–emotional environment to be developed, allowing for growth to occur. Stories are the containers of pain, distress, fear, excitement, happiness, joy, and hope. Through them, different solutions can be explored and acted upon. Stories enable children to organize, process, verbalize, and understand their experiences. They offer a symbolic distance to reexperience. Stories provide a foundation for growth; therefore, one of the essential requirements for play therapists is to be a good storyteller. Additionally, they need to be a good story listener, not only verbally but also through the play and its symbolism.

REFERENCES

Axline, V. (1947). *Play therapy*. Ballantine Books.
Bettelheim, B. (1976). *The uses of enchantment: The meaning and importance of fairy tales*. Penguin Books.

Börne, L. (1823). The art of becoming an original writer in three days. *Harvard Review*, *31*, 63–70.

Cattanach, A. (1994). *Play therapy: Where the sky meets the underworld*. Jessica Kingsley Publishers.

Cattanach, A. (1997). *Children's stories in play therapy*. Jessica Kingsley Publishers.

Cattanach, A. (2002). *The story so far: Play therapy narratives*. Jessica Kingsley Publishers.

Cattanach, A. (2007). *Narrative approach in play with children*. Jessica Kingsley Publishers.

Compton, S. (1997). Stories used in educational settings. In K. N. Dwivedi (Ed.), *The therapeutic use of stories* (pp. 157–170). Routledge.

Cozolino, L. (2010). *The neuroscience of psychotherapy: Healing the social brain* (2nd ed.). W. W. Norton & Company.

Crenshaw, D., & Tillman, K. (2014). Access to the unconscious. In C. E. Schaefer & A. A. Drewes (Eds.), *Therapeutic powers of play: 20 core agents of change* (2nd ed., pp. 25–38). John Wiley & Sons.

Davis, N. (1990). *Once upon a time*. Psychological Associates of Oxon Hill.

Divecha, D. (2017). What is a secure attachment? And why doesn't "attachment parenting" get you there? *Developmental Science*. https://www.developmental-science.com/blog/2017/3/31/what-is-a-secure-attachmentand-why-doesnt-attachment-parenting-get-you-there

Drewes, A. A., & Schaefer, C. E. (2014). Catharsis. In C. E. Schaefer & A. A. Drewes (Eds.), *The therapeutic powers of play: 20 core agents of change* (2nd ed., pp. 71–81). John Wiley & Sons.

Foa, E. B., & Kozak, M. J. (1986). Emotional processing of fear: Exposure to corrective information. *Psychological Bulletin*, *99*(1), 20–35. https://doi.org/10.1037/0033-2909.99.1.20

Fraser, T. (2014). Direct teaching. In C. E. Schaefer & A. A. Drewes (Eds.), *The therapeutic powers of play: 20 core agents of change* (2nd ed., pp. 39–50). John Wiley & Sons.

Freud, S., & Breuer, J. (1895). *Studies on hysteria*. Franz Deuticke.

Frey, D. (2014). Self esteem. In C. E. Schaefer & A. A. Drewes (Eds.), *The therapeutic powers of play: 20 core agents of change* (2nd ed., pp. 295–348). John Wiley & Sons.

Garland, E. L., Fredrickson, B., Kring, A. M., Johnson, D. P., Meyer, P. S., & Penn, D. L. (2010). Upward spirals of positive emotions counter downward spirals of negativity: Insights from the broaden-and-build theory and affective neuroscience on the treatment of emotion dysfunctions and deficits in psychopathology. *Clinical Psychology Review*, *30*(7), 849–864. https://doi.org/10.1016/j.cpr.2010.03.002

Gersie, A. (1990). *Storymaking in education and therapy*. Jessica Kingsley Publishers.

Grotberg, E. H. (1997). The International Resilience Project: Findings from the research and the effectiveness of interventions. In B. E. Bain (Ed.), *Psychology and education in the 21st century: Proceedings of the 54th Annual Convention. International Council of Psychologists* (pp. 118–128). ICP Press.

Howes, C., & Matheson, C. (1992). Sequences in the development of competent play with peers: Social and social pretend play. *Developmental Psychology*, *28*(5), 961–974. https://doi.org/10.1037/0012-1649.28.5.961

Jennings, S. (2005a). *Creative play with children at risk*. Speechmark.

Jennings, S. (2005b). *Creative storytelling with children at risk*. Routledge.

Johnson, D. R., Huffman, B. L., & Jasper, D. M. (2014). Changing race boundary perception by reading narrative fiction. *Basic and Applied Social Psychology, 36*(1), 83–90. https://doi.org/10.1080/01973533.2013.856791

Jones, E. (1977). *The life and work of Sigmund Freud.* Penguin Books.

Kidd, D. C., & Castano, E. (2013). Reading literary fiction improves theory of mind. *Science, 342*(6156), 377–380. https://doi.org/10.1126/science.1239918

Kottman, T. (2014). Positive emotions. In C. E. Schaefer & A. A. Drewes (Eds.), *The therapeutic powers of play: 20 core agents of change* (2nd ed., pp. 103–120). John Wiley & Sons.

Kottman, T., & Stiles, K. (1990). The mutual storytelling technique: An Adlerian application in child therapy. *Individual Psychology: The Journal of Adlerian Theory, Research & Practice, 46*(2), 148–156.

Lahad, M. (2017). *The lonely ape that told himself stories—The necessity of stories for human survival.* Nova Science Publishers.

Lahad, M., Shacham, M., & Ayalon, O. (Eds.). (2013). *The "BASIC Ph" model of coping and resiliency: Theory, research and cross-cultural application.* Jessica Kingsley Publishers.

Lang, P. J. (1977). Imagery in therapy: An information processing analysis of fear. *Behavior Therapy, 8*(5), 862–886. https://doi.org/10.1016/S0005-7894(77)80157-3

McLeod, J., & Balamoutsou, S. (1996). Representing narrative process in therapy: Qualitative analysis of a single case. *Counselling Psychology Quarterly, 9*(1), 61–76. https://doi.org/10.1080/09515079608256353

Morgenstern, E. (2012). *The night circus.* Vintage Books.

Morrison Bennett, M. (2014). Self-expression. In C. E. Schaefer & A. A. Drewes (Eds.), *The therapeutic powers of play: 20 core agents of change* (2nd ed., pp. 11–24). John Wiley & Sons.

Myers, C. E., Tollurd, T. R., & Jeon, M. (2012). *The power of personal storytelling in counselor education* (Vol. 1). Vistas.

Oxford University Press. (n.d.-a). Narrative. In *Oxford online dictionary.*

Oxford University Press. (n.d.-b). Story. In *Oxford online dictionary.*

Prendiville, E. (2014). Abreaction. In C. E. Schaefer & A. A. Drewes (Eds.), *The therapeutic powers of play: 20 core agents of change* (2nd ed., pp. 83–102). John Wiley & Sons.

Prendiville, S. (2014). Accelerated psychological development. In C. E. Schaefer & A. A. Drewes (Eds.), *The therapeutic powers of play: 20 core agents of change* (2nd ed., pp. 257–268). John Wiley & Sons.

Russ, S. W., & Wallace, C. E. (2014). Creative problem solving. In C. E. Schaefer & A. A. Drewes (Eds.), *The therapeutic powers of play: 20 core agents of change* (2nd ed., pp. 213–223). John Wiley & Sons.

Schaefer, C. E., & Drewes, A. A. (Eds.). (2014). *The therapeutic powers of play: 20 core agents of change* (2nd ed.). John Wiley & Sons.

Seymour, J. (2014). Resiliency. In C. E. Schaefer & A. A. Drewes (Eds.), *The therapeutic powers of play: 20 core agents of change* (2nd ed., pp. 225–242). John Wiley & Sons.

Stephens, G. J., Silbert, L. J., & Hasson, U. (2010). Speaker-listener neural coupling underlies successful communication. *Proceedings of the National Academy of Sciences of the United States of America, 107*(32), 14425–14430. https://doi.org/10.1073/pnas.1008662107

Stewart, A. L., & Echterling, L. G. (2014). Therapeutic relationship. In C. E. Schaefer & A. A. Drewes (Eds.), *The therapeutic powers of play: 20 core agents of change* (2nd ed., pp. 157–169). John Wiley & Sons.

Taylor de Faoite, A. (Ed.). (2011). *Narrative play therapy: Theory and practice.* Jessica Kingsley Publishers.

Taylor de Foaite, A. (2014). Indirect teaching. In C. E. Schaefer & A. A. Drewes (Eds.), *The therapeutic powers of play: 20 core agents of change* (2nd ed., pp. 51–67). John Wiley & Sons.

Taylor de Faoite, A., Prendiville, E., & Fraser, T. (2016). Telling tales; Weaving new neural networks. In E. Prendiville & J. Howard (Eds.), *Creative psychotherapy: Applying the principles of neurobiology to play and expressive arts-based practice* (pp. 171–184). Routledge.

Van Hollander, T. (2014). Counterconditioning fears. In C. E. Schaefer & A. A. Drewes (Eds.), *The therapeutic powers of play: 20 core agents of change* (2nd ed., pp. 121–130). John Wiley & Sons.

Zak, P. J. (2012). *The moral molecule.* Plum Book.

7

PUPPET PLAY THERAPY

ELIZABETH KJELLSTRAND HARTWIG

Most likely, puppets have influenced our lives in one way or another. Some of the most renowned puppets include *Mister Rogers' Neighborhood*'s King Friday XIII and Lady Elaine Fairchilde, *Sesame Street*'s Bert and Ernie, and Muppets Kermit the Frog and Miss Piggy. These puppets engaged children by meeting them at their developmental level with colorful bodies, musical voices, realistic movement, captivating interactions with others, and applicable topics for children. As developmentally appealing toys, puppets can also engage children in the process of play therapy. Puppet play therapy is the therapeutic use of puppets in play therapy to promote psychological well-being in children. Puppets are often used by children as a tool in symbolic play. Both Piaget (1951) and Vygotsky (1976) asserted that the process of symbolic play is an important component of child development. In symbolic puppet play, children use puppets to represent people, objects, thoughts, and behaviors through play. This type of play can help children develop social and emotional skills as well as promote healthy coping skills. Puppets are used in varied contexts of play therapy including child, adolescent, group, and family therapy settings. This chapter explores the history, therapeutic

https://doi.org/10.1037/0000217-008
Play Therapy With Children: Modalities for Change, H. G. Kaduson and C. E. Schaefer (Editors)

benefits, core techniques, clinical applications, and empirical support for puppet play therapy. A case illustration of a puppet play therapy technique is also provided.

HISTORICAL ROOTS AND SETTINGS

In one form or another, puppets have been present in almost every culture throughout the history of mankind (Blumenthal, 2005). The origin of puppetry began as a form of theater in which a puppeteer used inanimate objects (i.e., what became "puppets") that represented some type of human or animal character in a performance. The first documented therapeutic use of puppets was by Bender and Woltmann (1936). In their study, Bender and Woltmann used puppet shows with children in a psychiatric ward. In these puppet shows, the puppets would act out a story and the children were encouraged to help the puppets make choices. Bender and Woltmann's intent was for children to identify with the puppet characters and consider their behavior and expression of feelings. This study demonstrated how puppets could be used in a therapeutic way to help children explore self-expression and behavioral choices.

Puppets have been used in diverse settings to promote well-being in children. These include educational settings (Aminimanesh et al., 2019; James & Meyer, 1987; M. D. Salmon & Sainato, 2005), hospital settings (Leite et al., 2019; Linn et al., 1986; Pélicand et al., 2006; Shapiro, 1995), research and assessment settings (Epstein et al., 2008; Irwin, 1985; Ringoot et al., 2013; K. Salmon, 2006), and group settings (Butler et al., 2009; Gallo-Lopez, 2006; Ludlow & Williams, 2006). In addition to these settings, the literature recommends the use of puppets in play therapy settings. Schaefer and Drewes (2018) asserted, "Puppets are the quintessential childhood toy whose power to stimulate the imagination cannot be replicated by modern electronic toys that flash and beep" (p. 3).

THEORETICAL APPLICATIONS

Within play therapy settings, authors have expounded on how to integrate puppets using different theoretical approaches. Hartwig (2014, 2018) described the use of facilitative skills with puppets in child-centered play therapy. Hartwig (2018) applied nine advanced play therapy skills (Ray, 2011) to puppet play: tracking behavior, reflecting content, reflecting feeling, facilitating decision making and returning responsibility, facilitating creativity, esteem-building, facilitating relationship, reflecting larger meaning, and limit-setting. Practitioners can use all of these skills in nondirective puppet play to promote the therapeutic alliance and the ability of the child to lead their own healing process.

Crenshaw and Kelly (2018) described how puppets can be used in psychodynamic play therapy as vessels to explore underlying feelings or issues that present as maladaptive behaviors in children. These authors discuss how puppets can participate in the beginning, middle, and end stages of treatment to help the child express their inner world through symbolic puppet play.

For Adlerian play therapy, Meany-Walen (2018) provided examples of how puppets can be involved in its four phases: (a) building an egalitarian relationship, (b) exploring the child's lifestyle, (c) helping the child to gain insight, and (d) reorienting and reeducating the child. Through these four phases, the puppet used by the practitioner can serve as an alter ego, a wise wizard, or even a character that has challenges that are similar to the client. The interaction of puppet play between the client's puppet(s) and the practitioner's puppet allows practitioners to guide clients through the four phases in a creative and responsive way.

In solution-focused play therapy (SFPT), puppets can be valuable tools for helping children identify internal and external resources and explore ways in which they can work toward self-healing. Nims (2007) described how puppets can be used to facilitate several SFPT techniques, including goal-setting, the miracle question, finding exceptions, scaling, and a summary solution message. The case illustration later in this chapter provides an example of puppet play using SFPT.

Puppets can be used in cognitive behavioral play therapy to teach cognitive restructuring strategies such as developing positive self-statements and confronting negative thought patterns (Knell & Dasari, 2011). These cognitive behavioral play therapy authors suggest that a practitioner can use puppets in role-plays with children, in which the practitioner gives one of the puppets a problem that is similar to the child's problem (e.g., "This puppet gets sad when she's dropped off at her dad's house. Sometimes she cries and doesn't want to leave her mom's car"). This type of role-play gives children the opportunity to explore a similar presenting problem with the psychological distance provided by puppets.

In prescriptive play therapy, practitioners can customize interventions to address specific presenting problems. Newman (2020) recommended the use of puppets through the prescriptive modality in the treatment of depression in children. With a combination of cognitive behavior therapy and internal family systems, Newman uses puppets to represent various "parts" within the child that need to be heard and validated. Children then can begin to accept these parts of themselves through their interaction with the puppets in order to achieve more healthy functioning.

CURATING PUPPETS FOR PLAY THERAPY

Puppets should be carefully chosen, or curated, rather than gathered randomly. It is advantageous for practitioners to have a variety of puppets that allow children to express a range of emotions. The selection of puppets should also represent symbols, roles, or characters to which the child can relate. Irwin (2002) recommended having 15 to 20 puppets; however, Sori (2018) suggested having up to 30 puppets for more variety. Some puppet literature has presented the use of finger puppets or life-sized puppets for clinical work, however Schaefer and Drewes (2018) asserted that hand puppets are the most beneficial type of puppet used in play therapy because hand puppets typically fit on a child's hand, are colorful, and are easy to manipulate (R. B. Carter & Mason, 1998).

Four primary categories of puppets are used in puppet play therapy. The following list provides examples of 30 puppets that can be curated for puppet play.

- Animals: dog, turtle, bird, kangaroo with joey (for parent/child play), llama, snake, lion, tiger, shark

- Fantasy: fairy, queen, king, unicorn, witch, wizard, dragon, two monsters with googly eyes

- People: family set of four puppets (two parents and two children), two additional males, and two additional females; the additional males and females could be characters, such as a female scientist, or puppets with no designated character

- Special roles: doctor, judge, police officer, military member

It is vital that a practitioner's puppet collection have puppets with varying skin tones and different sexes and ages. The puppets should also represent the cultures and characters associated with common presenting issues of clients whom the practitioner serves. As an example, for practitioners working in a hospital setting, it would be helpful to have doctor and nurse puppets, and perhaps even a dog, if therapy dogs visit the hospital. Puppets should be displayed openly on a puppet tree, shelves, or a shoe rack so that children can easily access puppets when they would like to play with them. Children are less likely to choose toys that are kept in drawers, are in a closet, or are hard to reach.

THERAPEUTIC BENEFITS

Play therapy can have a powerful influence on children's abilities to communicate, regulate, build relationships, and develop strengths. Schaefer and Drewes (2014) presented 20 therapeutic powers of play that serve as agents of change in play therapy. These powers of play include powers for facilitating communication (e.g., self-expression, access to the unconscious, direct and indirect teaching), fostering emotional wellness (e.g., catharsis, abreaction, position emotions, counterconditioning fears, stress inoculation, stress management), enhancing social relationships (e.g., therapeutic relationship, attachment, social competence, empathy), and increasing personal strengths (e.g., creative problem solving, resiliency, moral development, accelerated psychological development, self-regulation, self-esteem). In *Puppet Play Therapy*, Schaefer and Drewes (2018) extended these powers of play by introducing 10 therapeutic powers of puppet play. These powers represent the primary means through which puppet play can foster therapeutic change in clients.

1. *Self-expression*: Puppets provide psychological distance so that child clients can use puppets to express difficult thoughts, feelings, and behaviors. Hartwig (2018) suggested that clients may choose a puppet that embodies personal qualities they already have (e.g., a monkey for playfulness) or a puppet that exemplifies qualities they would like to have (e.g., a tiger for power).

2. *Access to the unconscious*: In puppet play, children can project their own feelings and needs; symbolize real-life people or experiences; and displace frustrations, feelings, or impulses onto puppets. In these roles, puppets serve as less threatening objects with which children can play through these issues.

3. *Catharsis*: Clients can release strong or inhibited emotions through puppets. For example, a client may express anger at her mom for getting a divorce by using a princess puppet to scream at a queen puppet who just made the king puppet move out of the castle. This client may not have been able to express her anger verbally and directly to her mother but is able to use puppets to express this feeling.

4. *Direct teaching*: Puppets can be used to teach skills, such as emotional regulation and social skills. A school counselor might use a puppet in a classroom guidance lesson to demonstrate to children how to make wise choices about interacting with peers. The counselor could present a challenging scenario in school, such as bullying, with puppets. Then the children watching the scenario can make choices about right and wrong ways to respond in that scenario.

5. *Abreaction*: Children can use puppets to relive challenging or traumatic experiences. Through this process, clients can gain emotional release of repressed emotions and the opportunity to practice curative actions to develop a sense of mastery over the distressing experience.

6. *Awareness of feelings*: Children can learn about feelings by watching puppets, such as in a classroom guidance lesson, or by using puppets to express their own emotions. As practitioners reflect the child's feelings, children learn how to acknowledge and connect feelings to thoughts and behaviors.

7. *Rapport*: Through puppet play, child clients and practitioners can develop rapport. Practitioners can respond to puppets that children use in empathic and affirming ways, which allows children to feel affirmed for what they choose to express. Playing with puppets can be fun and engaging for both children and practitioners.

8. *Problem solving*: Both child clients and practitioners can use puppets and puppet play to discover ways of solving problems and working through concerns. For example, a 7-year-old child may use a bunny puppet to express how lonely he feels when he comes home and is by himself for a couple of hours after school. The practitioner can use a unicorn puppet to explore things the bunny puppet could do to feel less lonely (e.g., call his mom, tell his mom about his fears, go to a friend's house).

9. *Behavioral rehearsal*: Practitioners can use puppets to practice procedures or events that could be stressful, such as going to the dentist or taking a test.

10. *Assess family dynamics*: By using puppet play in family play therapy, practitioners can learn more about family communication patterns, roles, and relationships. The Family Puppet Interview (FPI; Gil, 2015) is a technique that helps practitioners to assess family dynamics during family play therapy sessions.

Practitioners can employ several or all of these therapeutic powers of play with puppets in the playroom.

CORE TECHNIQUES

Puppets can be used in both nondirective and prescriptive play approaches. This section presents three puppet techniques: nondirective puppet play, the Choose a Puppet technique, and the FPI.

Nondirective Puppet Play

A nondirective approach to puppet play involves the practitioner allowing the child to choose or not choose to play with puppets. If a child chooses to play with puppets, the practitioner can use facilitative skills, rather than directive prompts, to support the child in the play while allowing the child to guide the content of the play. Here is a brief example of nondirective puppet play:

Jimmy, a 5-year-old client, picks up a dragon puppet.

JIMMY: Wow—I found a cool dragon!

PRACTITIONER: [Reflecting feeling] You're excited you found that dragon!

The dragon breathes fire on all the animal figurines on the shelf. The dragon makes a loud breathing sound.

DRAGON: You're all melting.

PRACTITIONER: [Reflecting content] They're melting because of your hot breath.

DRAGON: Yeah, it's fire breath. My fire breath makes the bad guys melt.

PRACTITIONER: [Reflecting content] The bad guys melt when you use your fire breath.

The dragon moves over to the dollhouse.

PRACTITIONER: [Acknowledging nonverbal behavior] Now you're moving over there.

DRAGON: What should I do here?

PRACTITIONER: [Facilitating decision making] You can choose what you want to do.

In this illustration, readers may notice that when Jimmy begins to interact as the dragon, the practitioner responds directly to the dragon, not to Jimmy. This action of staying in the metaphor is an important component of puppet play. This scenario gives a brief example of how to employ nondirective skills with puppets. Hartwig (2014, 2018) has provided more in-depth applications of child-centered puppet play.

Choose a Puppet

Directive puppet play therapy interventions allow children to use puppets to express themselves with intentional and theoretically grounded prompts from the practitioner. The Choose a Puppet technique is a directive technique that I developed and adapted from Leggett's (2017) *Selected Toy* process as an SFPT technique for describing the presenting problem and establishing goals. Describing the problem is an important step in SFPT because it helps the practitioner to learn more about the child and allows the child to express their feelings, challenges, and a preferred future. This technique is a good fit for children 7 years of age and older who have the developmental capacity to be engaged in more verbal and directive play therapy techniques. In this technique, the practitioner asks the child to choose a puppet that represents some aspect of the child's thoughts, feelings, self-concept, and strengths. The following statements are prompts that practitioners can use for this technique:

- Choose a puppet that shows how you are feeling right now.
- Choose a puppet that you think is most like you.
- Choose a puppet that seems most like your [family member, friend, loved one who died].
- Choose a puppet that shows what you're like when you're very [angry, sad, happy, scared] or not [angry, sad, happy, scared] at all.
- Choose a puppet that has skills or abilities that you would most like to have.

Once a child has chosen a puppet, the practitioner can also use these processing questions:

- What are some words to describe your puppet?
- How is your puppet like [you, your family member, friend, loved one who died]?
- What strengths does your puppet have?
- What challenges does your puppet have?
- How would you like to be different from this puppet?
- If you could choose another puppet that shows how you'd like to feel, what one would you choose?

It's important for practitioners to remember to reflect what the child has shared before asking another question so that the child feels heard. For example, if 9-year-old Patty shared that her grandma was "bright, colorful, and smart" like the pink flamingo puppet she chose, the practitioner should reflect something similar to this statement: "You chose the flamingo because it's colorful and smart, just like your grandma."

The Choose a Puppet technique can even be used with teenagers. Some teens may not choose to play with puppets on their own but may be willing to choose a puppet that represents part of their narrative. The following four prompts could be used with teens:

- Choose a puppet that represents your ex-boyfriend.
- Choose a puppet that resembles how you would feel if all of your problems were solved. (This prompt is similar to the miracle question in SFPT.)
- Choose a puppet that characterizes each of your friends.
- Choose a puppet that best illustrates the qualities that you like most about yourself.

The Choose a Puppet technique can be used as a stand-alone therapeutic activity or as an introduction to further puppet play, such as role playing. The Choose a Puppet technique can also be used in groups, families, and play therapy supervision.

Family Puppet Interview

The FPI is a family play therapy technique that was originally developed by Irwin and Malloy (1994) and then further developed by Gil (2015). The FPI is a beneficial technique in family play therapy because it has the capacity to involve young children in families, who are often excluded from talk therapy family sessions. The FPI is also kinetic, visual, interactive, and engaging. Gil described how to facilitate the FPI. Practitioners can provide a prompt similar to the following example:

> Today we're going to do an activity with puppets. You all are going to create a story together—one that has not been created before, such as Beauty and the Beast. Your story should have a beginning, middle, and end. I'm going to give you some time to create your story and choose the puppet characters. Then when you're ready, you will perform your story for me. After you're done, I may ask your puppet characters or even each of you about your story.

The practitioner can then give the family some time to create the story. This author typically gives families about 15 minutes to create their story, 10 to 15 minutes to present their story, and reserves another 15 minutes to process the narrative with the family. During the time that the family is developing their story, the practitioner should pay attention to how the family communicates, who leads and follows, the involvement of the children, what characters they choose, and the process they use to develop their narrative. During the performance, the practitioner can notice the plot of the story, how the characters interact, if there is conflict or support between the characters, and how the story ends.

Several authors have provided helpful guidelines for processing the FPI (Gil, 2015; Gil & Smelser, 2018; Sori, 2018). After the family has performed their story, the practitioner—or a puppet character that the practitioner chooses—can "interview" the family. The interview questions largely depend on the process of the story creation and the performance. It is helpful to start by interviewing the puppet characters first so as to stay in the metaphor, and then later talking with family members. The following are examples of processing questions for this technique:

- Ally the Alligator, I noticed that you scared your friends in the story. How did it feel to scare them?

- Simon the Sloth, you didn't seem to mind that Ally scared you. What were you thinking when Ally was trying to scare her friends?

- Mr. Frog, as Ally's teacher, what things could Ally do differently to help her make more friends?

- [To one or each character] If the story could end the way you would like it to end, what would happen?

After interviewing the story characters, the practitioner can ask questions directly to the family members, such as "What was it like to do this activity with your family?" and "If you could choose another puppet to help other characters in the story, what would it be?" Practitioners should be mindful that young children may not be as engaged during verbal processing. For this reason, the practitioner may ask puppet characters to enact new parts or reenact certain parts of the story to keep the processing time more engaging, or the processing time may need to be shortened. This technique can also be used with groups, in which groups are asked to create a story with a beginning, middle, and end using puppets. Gil (2015) and Sori (2018) provided applied examples of the FPI.

CLINICAL APPLICATIONS

Practitioners and authors have described the employment of puppets for an array of presenting issues in play therapy with children. Carlson-Sabelli (1998) and Desmond et al. (2015) noted the benefits of puppets with children who have experienced trauma. Carlson-Sabelli provided an account of therapeutic puppet groups with children who were struggling with psychiatric issues in a hospital setting. In therapeutic puppet groups, children cocreated stories with puppets that provided access to their inner world. This approach offers a method for practitioners to assess children's feelings and behaviors associated with the trauma they have experienced while providing children with a wide range of expression. Desmond et al. asserted that children who have experienced trauma may struggle with verbal and emotional forms of expression. These authors suggested that puppets offer children a safer way to express their trauma story and often reveal children's coping skills.

Some practitioners have explored the use of puppets in individual case studies. Carter (1987) used a nondirective approach with an 8-year-old boy working through traumatic grief after the tragic death of his father. The boy chose puppets as a medium for working through his anger and grief. Barrows (2004) described using puppets with a child with autism to explore the theme of aggression. According to Barrows, the puppet play allowed the child to acknowledge and own his feelings of aggression through nonverbal play.

Puppets have also been applied in settings where practitioners work with children who have experienced sexual abuse. Johnston (1997) asserted that puppets are beneficial in accessing a child's symbolic world and facilitating the child's exploration of traumatic experiences. In support of puppet play through the lens of cognitive behavior therapy, Drewes (2018) recommended three techniques for supporting children in working through the trauma of sexual abuse. One technique presented by Drewes is the three-headed dragon technique, in which one head of the dragon represents thoughts, one is feelings, and one is actions. The goal of this technique is to help one of the heads calm down, such as the "thoughts" head, so that the other two heads can regulate and be heard. Puppets can be utilized in a variety of ways to support children in clinical settings.

CASE ILLUSTRATION

This case illustration demonstrates puppet play therapy from the theoretical lens of SFPT (Hartwig, in press), using a composite sketch and not an actual client. Seven-year-old Judy was referred to play therapy by her mother, Kim, because of symptoms of anxiety that began after Judy and Kim experienced a hurricane that hit their neighborhood 4 months prior. Amy, the play therapist, asked Kim, who was a single mother, to meet for a caregiver consultation prior to starting play therapy with Judy. At the beginning of the caregiver consultation, Amy discussed the process of play therapy, gave Kim a tour of the playroom, and reviewed informed consent. During the caregiver consultation, Kim explained that both she and Judy were safe in their home during the hurricane, but the heavy winds were loud and damaged their home. Kim and Judy had to move out of their home for 2 months so contractors could fix the roof and windows, but they are back in their home now. Amy inquired about Kim's primary concerns about Judy. Kim shared that Judy used to be a happy and vibrant child, but after the hurricane she stays near her mom most of the day and night, doesn't sleep well at night, turns down playdates with friends, and is anxious about attending school every day.

Amy then asked Kim about Judy's strengths. Kim shared that Judy loves music and has set up her bedroom so that she can perform songs for her stuffed animals. Kim also noted that, even though Judy was reluctant to go to school, she was getting good grades in school. To identify potential goals, Amy asked Kim what she would like to see Judy do differently that would let Kim know that Judy is making progress in play therapy. Kim said she would like to see Judy express her feelings of anxiety more openly and play with her friends after school. Amy asked if Kim could identify one small change that would let Kim know that Judy was starting to make some progress. Kim stated that she would know Judy was making progress if Judy was able to have some playtime by herself or with a friend in her room. Amy summarized Kim's primary concerns about Judy, Judy's strengths, and the potential goals that Kim had for Judy. Amy thanked Kim for her time and told her she looked forward to meeting Judy at the next session.

This section describes Judy's first session. At first Judy was hesitant to go to the playroom without her mom, Kim. When she saw that Kim would be sitting in the waiting room just outside the playroom, she was willing to go into the playroom with Amy. SFPT skills and techniques are provided in brackets in this case example.

AMY:	(*Introducing the playroom*) Judy, this is the playroom. In here you can play with toys, be creative, and find solutions to problems in a lot of different ways.
JUDY:	*Walks around the playroom. Notices a puppet tree with 20 different puppets and a shelf with several more puppets. She chooses a cat puppet and puts it on her hand.*
AMY:	[Reflecting behavior] You found one and decided to put it on.
JUDY:	(*Meows and says,*) I'm Callie the Cat.
AMY:	(*Chooses a llama puppet and says to the cat puppet,*) Hi, Callie! I'm Lexy the Llama.
CALLIE THE CAT:	Nice to meet you, Lexy. What do you want to play with?
LEXY THE LLAMA:	[Returning focus to the client] You can choose, Callie.

CALLIE:	Let's play with the dollhouse.
LEXY:	OK.
CALLIE:	(*Looks at the dollhouse*) This house doesn't look right.
LEXY:	[Reflecting content] You want it a different way.
CALLIE:	I'm going to make it really messy.

Judy uses her Callie puppet to turn over people and furniture in the dollhouse. Callie even pushes several pieces of furniture out of the house and onto the floor.

CALLIE:	There! Now it's right.
LEXY:	[Amplifying solution talk] Wow, Callie! You got it just the way you wanted it. How were you able to get it right?
CALLIE:	I became a strong wind and made it move.
LEXY:	[Complimenting] You used your strength to get it just how you wanted it.
CALLIE:	Yeah.
LEXY:	[Open-ended questions] Callie, how would you feel if you were in that house?
CALLIE:	I would be scared!
LEXY:	[Reflecting feeling] You would feel scared in that messy house.
CALLIE:	Yeah—I don't want to go in there.
LEXY:	[Finding exceptions] Callie, sometimes we feel scared and sometimes we don't. Are there times when you don't feel scared?
CALLIE:	I don't feel scared when I'm with my big momma cat. (*Judy goes to get a tiger puppet and puts it in front of the house.*)
LEXY:	[Reflecting content] When you're with your momma cat you feel safe.
CALLIE:	(*Nods the cat puppet's head*)
LEXY:	[Miracle question] Let's pretend a miracle happened and the house didn't get messed up. What would be different for you?

CALLIE: I wouldn't be so scared.

LEXY: [Goal-setting] Maybe we could play together to help you feel less scared. What do you think?

CALLIE: OK. (*Judy takes the cat puppet off and walks over to the sandbox to play in the sand.*)

This case illustration represents several SFPT basic skills, including reflecting behavior, content, and feeling; complimenting; amplifying solution talk; returning focus to the client; and open-ended questions. This case example also showcased three SFPT techniques: finding exceptions, the miracle question, and goal-setting. In future sessions, Amy could incorporate the Choose a Puppet technique with scaling, to explore on a scale of 0 to 10 how scared Judy/Callie feels and what helps her feel less scared. Using puppets in SFPT provides a playful and strength-based expressive modality for children to identify internal strengths and abilities and external resources to work toward clinical goals.

EMPIRICAL SUPPORT

A few outcome studies compare puppet play therapy with other tools used in play therapy. Rather, studies involving puppets as a clinical tool describe how puppets have influenced psychological and behavioral outcomes in children. Pitre et al. (2007) assessed the effects of puppet plays in reducing stigmatizing attitudes of elementary-school–aged children. The results indicated that the children who viewed the puppet plays had significant reductions in three of the six factors of the Opinions About Mental Illness Scale (Cohen & Struening, 1962): Separatism, Restrictiveness, and Stigmatization. Several studies have illustrated that puppets are effective in reducing anxiety and increasing communication for hospitalized children or children undergoing stressful medical procedures (Cassell, 1965; Shapiro, 1995; Sposito et al., 2016). These studies indicate that puppets can be helpful tools for teaching, modeling behavior, and exploring perspectives with children.

Much self-report research with young children involves measures that are completed by caregivers, teachers, or other adults in a child's life. The Berkeley Puppet Interview (BPI) was originally developed by Measelle et al. (1998) to elicit children's perspectives related to self-concept. The BPI currently has 25 scales that measure social well-being, emotional and behavioral concerns, academic functioning, and family environment (Ablow et al., 2003; Measelle & Ablow, 2018). During the interview, two dog puppets (Iggy and Ziggy) operated by research assistants, are presented to a child. After an initial introduction, each puppet states opposing statements, such as "I am a lonely kid" and "I am not a lonely kid. How about you?" (Ringoot et al., 2013, pp. 3–4). The child has the opportunity to answer however they want. The interviews are recorded and later coded by research assistants who are independent of the interviewers. Using a 50-item BPI, Ringoot et al. sought to explore the psychometric properties of the BPI using a large sample (*N* = 6,375) of socioeconomically diverse children ages 5 to 7. The findings from the study identified that children are capable of providing valid and multifaceted information about emotional, social, and behavior issues through the use of the BPI.

SUMMARY AND CONCLUSION

Puppet play therapy is an interactive approach to engaging with children in the playroom. Puppets can be employed using different theories and in both nondirective and directive ways. This chapter summarized the history, clinical applications, and empirical support for puppet play therapy. The author also presented three techniques: nondirective puppet play, the Choose a Puppet technique, and the FPI. A case illustration using SFPT was also provided as an applied example of how a practitioner could facilitate puppet play with a child client. Puppets are a beneficial resource in the playroom because they can be utilized with children, teens, groups, and families.

REFERENCES

Ablow, J. C., Measelle, J. R., & the MacArthur Working Group on Outcome Assessment. (2003). *Manual for the Berkeley Puppet Interview: Symptomatology, social, and academic modules* (BPI 1.0). University of Pittsburgh.

Aminimanesh, A., Ghazavi, Z., & Mehrabi, T. (2019). Effectiveness of the puppet show and storytelling methods on children's behavioral problems. *Iranian Journal of Nursing and Midwifery Research, 24*(1), 61–65. https://doi.org/10.4103/ijnmr.IJNMR_115_15

Barrows, P. (2004). "Playful" therapy: Working with autism and trauma. *International Forum of Psychoanalysis, 13*(3), 175–186. https://doi.org/10.1080/08037060410024005

Bender, L., & Woltmann, A. G. (1936). The use of puppet shows as a psychotherapeutic method for behavior problems in children. *American Journal of Orthopsychiatry, 6*(3), 341–354. https://doi.org/10.1111/j.1939-0025.1936.tb05242.x

Blumenthal, E. (2005). *Puppetry and puppets: An illustrated world survey.* Thames & Hudson.

Butler, S., Guterman, J. T., & Rudes, J. (2009). Using puppets with children in narrative therapy to externalize the problem. *Journal of Mental Health Counseling, 31*(3), 225–233. https://doi.org/10.17744/mehc.31.3.f255m86472577522

Carlson-Sabelli, L. (1998). Children's therapeutic puppet theatre: Action, interaction, and cocreation. *The International Journal of Action Methods, 51*(3), 91–112.

Carter, R. B., & Mason, P. S. (1998). The selection and use of puppets in counseling. *Professional School Counseling, 1*(5), 50–53.

Carter, S. R. (1987). Use of puppets to treat traumatic grief: A case study. *Elementary School Guidance & Counseling, 21*(3), 210–215.

Cassell, S. (1965). Effect of brief puppet therapy upon the emotional responses of children undergoing cardiac catheterization. *Journal of Consulting Psychology, 29*(1), 1–8. https://doi.org/10.1037/h0021670

Cohen, J., & Struening, E. L. (1962). Opinions about mental illness in the personnel of two large mental hospitals. *Journal of Abnormal and Social Psychology, 64*(5), 349–360. https://doi.org/10.1037/h0045526

Crenshaw, D. A., & Kelly, J. E. (2018). The use of puppets in psychodynamic child therapy. In C. E. Schaefer & A. A. Drewes (Eds.), *Puppet play therapy: A practical guidebook* (pp. 86–97). Routledge/Taylor & Francis Group.

Desmond, K. J., Kindsvatter, A., Stahl, S., & Smith, H. (2015). Using creative techniques with children who have experienced trauma. *Journal of Creativity in Mental Health, 10*(4), 439–455. https://doi.org/10.1080/15401383.2015.1040938

Drewes, A. A. (2018). Play therapy puppet techniques for childhood sexual abuse trauma. In A. A. Drewes & C. E. Schaefer (Eds.), *Puppet play therapy: A practical guidebook* (pp. 155–161). Routledge/Taylor & Francis Group.

Epstein, I., Stevens, B., McKeever, P., Baruchel, S., & Jones, H. (2008). Using puppetry to elicit children's talk for research. *Nursing Inquiry, 15*(1), 49–56. https://doi.org/10.1111/j.1440-1800.2008.00395.x

Gallo-Lopez, L. (2006). A creative play therapy approach to the group treatment of young sexually abused children. In H. G. Kaduson (Ed.), *Short-term play therapy for children* (2nd ed., pp. 245–270). Guilford Press.

Gil, E. (2015). *Play in family therapy* (2nd ed.). Guilford Press.

Gil, E., & Smelser, Q. K. (2018). Puppets in family therapy with a case of trauma and sexual abuse. In A. A. Drewes & C. E. Schaefer (Eds.), *Puppet play therapy: A practical guidebook* (pp. 165–173). Routledge/Taylor & Francis Group.

Hartwig, E. K. (2014). Puppets in the playroom: Utilizing puppets and child-centered facilitative skills as a metaphor for healing. *International Journal of Play Therapy, 23*(4), 204–216. https://doi.org/10.1037/a0038054

Hartwig, E. K. (2018). The child-centered approach to puppet play with children. In C. E. Schaefer & A. A. Drewes (Eds.), *Puppet play therapy: A practical guidebook* (pp. 77–85). Taylor & Francis.

Hartwig, E. K. (in press). *Solution-focused play therapy: A strengths-based clinical approach to play therapy*. Routledge.

Irwin, E. C. (1985). Puppets in therapy: An assessment procedure. *American Journal of Psychotherapy, 39*(3), 389–400. https://doi.org/10.1176/appi.psychotherapy.1985.39.3.389

Irwin, E. C. (2002). Using puppets for assessment. In C. E. Schaefer & D. Cangelosi (Eds.), *Play therapy techniques* (2nd ed., pp. 101–113). Jason Aronson.

Irwin, E. C., & Malloy, E. S. (1994). Family puppet interview. In C. E. Schaefer & L. Carey (Eds.), *Family play therapy* (pp. 21–33). Jason Aronson.

James, R. K., & Meyer, R. (1987). Puppets: The elementary school counselor's right or left arm. *Elementary School Guidance & Counseling, 21*(4), 292–299.

Johnston, S. S. M. (1997). The use of art and play therapy with victims of sexual abuse: A review of the literature. *Family Therapy: The Journal of the California Graduate School of Family Psychology, 24*(2), 101–113.

Knell, S. M., & Dasari, M. (2011). Cognitive-behavioral play therapy. In S. W. Russ & L. N. Niec (Eds.), *Play in clinical practice: Evidence-based approaches* (pp. 236–263). Guilford Press.

Leggett, E. S. (2017). Solution-focused play therapy. In E. S. Leggett & J. N. Boswell (Eds.), *Directive play therapy: Theories and techniques* (pp. 59–79). Springer Publishing Company.

Leite, A. C. A. B., Alvarenga, W. A., Machado, J. R., Luchetta, L. F., Banca, R. O., Sparapani, V. C., Neris, R. R., Cartagena-Ramos, D., Fuentealba-Torres, M., & Nascimento, L. C. (2019). Children in outpatient follow-up: Perspectives of care identified in interviews with puppet. *Revista Gaúcha de Enfermagem, 40*, Article e20180103. https://doi.org/10.1590/1983-1447.2019.20180103

Linn, S., Beardslee, W., & Patenaude, A. F. (1986). Puppet therapy with pediatric bone marrow transplant patients. *Journal of Pediatric Psychology, 11*(1), 37–46. https://doi.org/10.1093/jpepsy/11.1.37

Ludlow, W., & Williams, M. K. (2006). Short-term group play therapy for children whose parents are divorcing. In H. G. Kaduson (Ed.), *Short-term play therapy for children* (2nd ed., pp. 245–270). Guilford Press.

Meany-Walen, K. K. (2018). Puppet play in Adlerian therapy. In A. A. Drewes & C. E. Schaefer (Eds.), *Puppet play therapy: A practical guidebook* (pp. 98–107). Routledge/Taylor & Francis Group.

Measelle, J., & Ablow, J. C. (2018). The Berkeley Puppet Interview for Child Assessment. In A. A. Drewes & C. E. Schaefer (Eds.), *Puppet play therapy: A practical guidebook* (pp. 29–47). Routledge/Taylor & Francis Group.

Measelle, J. R., Ablow, J. C., Cowan, P. A., & Cowan, C. P. (1998). Assessing young children's views of their academic, social, and emotional lives: An evaluation of the self-perception scales of the Berkeley Puppet Interview. *Child Development, 69*(6), 1556–1576. https://doi.org/10.1111/j.1467-8624.1998.tb06177.x

Newman, E. (2020). Play therapy for children with depression. In H. G. Kaduson, D. Cangelosi, & C. E. Schaefer (Eds.), *Prescriptive play therapy: Tailoring interventions for specific childhood problems* (pp. 35–53). Guilford Press.

Nims, D. R. (2007). Integrating play therapy techniques into solution-focused brief therapy. *International Journal of Play Therapy, 16*(1), 54–68. https://doi.org/10.1037/1555-6824.16.1.54

Pélicand, J., Gagnayre, R., Sandrin-Berthon, B., & Aujoulat, I. (2006). A therapeutic education programme for diabetic children: Recreational, creative methods, and use of puppets. *Patient Education and Counseling, 60*(2), 152–163. https://doi.org/10.1016/j.pec.2004.12.007

Piaget, J. (1951). *The psychology of intelligence*. Routledge and Kegan Paul.

Pitre, N., Stewart, S., Adams, S., Bedard, T., & Landry, S. (2007). The use of puppets with elementary school children in reducing stigmatizing attitudes towards mental illness. *Journal of Mental Health, 16*(3), 415–429. https://doi.org/10.1080/09638230701299160

Ray, D. C. (2011). *Advanced play therapy: Essential conditions, knowledge, and skills for child practice*. Routledge/Taylor & Francis Group. https://doi.org/10.4324/9780203837269

Ringoot, A. P., Jansen, P. W., Steenweg-de Graaff, J., Measelle, J. R., van der Ende, J., Raat, H., Jaddoe, V. W., Hofman, A., Verhulst, F. C., & Tiemeier, H. (2013). Young children's self-reported emotional, behavioral, and peer problems: The Berkeley Puppet Interview. *Psychological Assessment, 25*(4), 1–13. https://doi.org/10.1037/a0033976

Salmon, K. (2006). Toys in clinical interviews with children: Review and implications for practice. *Clinical Psychologist, 10*(2), 54–59. https://doi.org/10.1080/13284200600681601

Salmon, M. D., & Sainato, D. M. (2005). Beyond Pinocchio: Puppets as teaching tools in inclusive early childhood classrooms. *Young Exceptional Children, 8*(3), 12–19. https://doi.org/10.1177/109625060500800303

Schaefer, C. E., & Drewes, A. A. (Eds.). (2014). *The therapeutic powers of play: 20 core agents of change* (2nd ed.). John Wiley & Sons.

Schaefer, C. E., & Drewes, A. A. (2018). Fundamental concepts and practices of puppet play therapy. In A. A. Drewes & C. E. Schaefer (Eds.), *Puppet play therapy: A practical guidebook* (pp. 3–16). Routledge/Taylor & Francis Group.

Shapiro, D. E. (1995). Puppet modeling technique for children undergoing stressful medical procedures: Tips for clinicians. *International Journal of Play Therapy, 4*(2), 31–39. https://doi.org/10.1037/h0089146

Sori, C. F. (2018). The Family Puppet Interview. In A. A. Drewes & C. E. Schaefer (Eds.), *Puppet play therapy: A practical guidebook* (pp. 48–58). Routledge/Taylor & Francis Group.

Sposito, A. M. P., de Montigny, F., Sparapani, V. de C., Lima, R. A., Silva-Rodrigues, F. M., Pfeifer, L. I., & Nascimento, L. C. (2016). Puppets as a strategy for communication with Brazilian children with cancer. *Nursing & Health Sciences, 18*(1), 30–37. https://doi.org/10.1111/nhs.12222

Vygotsky, L. (1976). Play and its role in the mental development of the child. In J. Bruner, A. Jolly, & K. Sylva (Eds.), *Play: Its role in development and evolution* (pp. 537–554). Basic Books.

8

GUIDED IMAGERY

CLAIR MELLENTHIN

Guided imagery has been defined as "a mind–body intervention that uses the power of the imagination to bring about change in physical, emotional, or spiritual dimensions" (Fitzgerald & Langevin, 2010, p. 63). In psychotherapy, guided imagery involves the blending of relaxation techniques alongside the evocation of mental images that also incorporate the senses of sight, sound, touch, taste, and smell. It is used to deliberately evoke specific images to influence physiological and emotional states through the client's imagination (La Roche et al., 2006). In this chapter, the use of guided imagery in the play therapy process is described in depth, as well as various ways it can be incorporated in contemporary psychotherapy practice, using case studies, research, and practical interventions and techniques.

Imagine you are walking through a beautiful meadow. The sun is shining in the midmorning day. Through your hair, you feel a gentle breeze blowing that is not too cold and not too hot; it just feels pleasant. Butterflies are flying about the many wildflowers. You stop for a moment to enjoy the beauty of the world around you and count your favorite colors and shapes within the flowers. The fragrance of wildflowers is mild but ever present. As you continue

https://doi.org/10.1037/0000217-009
Play Therapy With Children: Modalities for Change, H. G. Kaduson and C. E. Schaefer (Editors)

walking, you can hear the swish of the tall grass. The grasses feel soft and are not scratchy or itchy; they remind you of the velvet curtains that hung in your grandmother's living room. As you are moving through the tall velvety grasses, you come to a small door hidden in the field. You recognize this as the door to a magical place your heart has been dreaming of. You reach for the golden handle, twist the knob, and walk inside. What is around you? What do you see? Who is with you in this magical place, or are you alone? What does it feel like to be here? Spend some time enjoying this space, and when you are ready, open your eyes, come back to this book, and we will learn how guided imagery can enhance your play therapy practice.

Through guided imagery, the client is directed to engage in a series of relaxation cues and is then asked to imagine different scenarios or fantasies. It can be used alone as a powerful therapeutic tool or in conjunction with expressive arts and/or sandtray. As with other expressive therapies, guided imagery allows the unconscious to become conscious. The use of imagery has been considered to be a healing tool in virtually all cultures around the world, including Native American and indigenous traditions, Hinduism, Judeo–Christian, and other religions (Utay & Miller, 2006; Veena & Alvi, 2016).

Guided imagery has long been used as a creative tool in psychotherapy, beginning in the early 20th century. Early psychoanalysts such as Freud, Kretschmer, and Desoille used imagery to make sense and meaning out of dreams, daydreams, and fantasies (Utay & Miller, 2006). Winnicott (1971) believed that imagery and fantasy "brought the inner world alive" and was a critical therapeutic function to make meaning in the client's life (Porat & Sadeh, 2013). Leuner was one of the first psychotherapists to induce images as a therapeutic tool. This therapeutic intervention is now known as *guided imagery*. In contemporary psychotherapy, guided imagery is used in most theoretical models (Porat & Sadeh, 2013), as it has been shown to help clients make meaning of their inner worlds, improve performance, increase empathy and resiliency, and manage distressing symptoms of mental and physical health disorders.

Within the field of play therapy, Violet Oaklander was one of the first play therapists who blended the power of guided imagery and play therapy using gestalt play therapy. Oaklander's approach allowed for high levels of imagery, creativity, storytelling, and problem solving throughout her many interventions using guided imagery. She would often take her clients on a guided imagery exercise and then ask them to draw what they saw or how they felt. This type of intervention often elicits strong feelings on behalf of the client and a deeper awakening of and connection to the *self* (Oaklander, 1978).

THERAPEUTIC BENEFITS

There are many known therapeutic benefits to using guided imagery in play therapy to access the therapeutic powers of play. Schaefer and Drewes (2014) wrote, "Play, the natural language of the child, is often the easiest way for children to express troubling thoughts and feelings that are both conscious and unconscious" (p. 9). Harnessing and creating meaning of the child's internal world through guided imagery can allow for feelings of calm, healing, and resolution. In the following sections, specific therapeutic powers of play are identified in relation to using guided imagery in play therapy.

Self-Expression

Guided imagery helps imagination blossom in both children and adults. Imagination is an important aspect of child development. A child makes sense of their world through play and fantasy, often using imagination as a vehicle as they play out different scenarios and feelings. We witness the power of imagination each day in our play therapy rooms, as a child battles a dragon and learns to face her fears or holds a baby doll so tenderly, acting out their deepest wishes and hopes for attachment and nurture. Imagination is what facilitates growth and understanding through sandtray, creative arts, and play interventions. Through joining in play and imagination with children, their self-expression deepens, and self-confidence grows, as the play therapist joins in their play, seeking out *their* direction and leadership, allowing them to be experts in their own stories. As we lead our clients down a fantastical path, inviting them to imagine what is around them, to explore their imagined sensory experience, we help them to explore both the familiar and unfamiliar, aiding them in developing an understanding of self, others, and their experiences (Bennett & Eberts, 2014).

This deeper connection to the self is a critical component in psychodynamic play therapy, as is the *access to the unconscious*—another important therapeutic power of play. Play and fantasy create the safe emotional experience and climate that allow a child permission to access and experience a wider range of internal experiences that are typically outside their conscious awareness (Crenshaw & Tillman, 2014). Once a child's unconscious material comes to the conscious, change and healing can begin, as there is a new understanding of self and others. This is a crucial element of the therapeutic powers of play, as attachments can be identified, strengthened, and repaired and an identity can be developed for this child to attach to the concept of their core self.

Oaklander (1978) wrote of her child client's astonishment and wonderment that they could *find themselves* in their guided imagery, or to make meaning and connection to the images the client saw as they drew their fantasies and feelings after a guided imagery intervention. She would often ask the client to identify where they saw themselves in their fantasy or how they would like to see themselves instead. She believed that through the use of fantasy and imagination, a child's world came into focus, as their life and the hidden, as well as overt themes, came to life. This insight helps a child form a connection to their personal thoughts, feelings, and experiences. As a child is able to do this, the sense of self more fully develops.

Attachment

As the child develops an internal working model of self—I am loved and I am loveable—their ability to create attachments in other relationships throughout their world increases. Secure attachment is created through consistency, kindness, and nurture. As Stewart and Echterling (2014) stated, "Children feel safe when adults interact with them in developmentally appropriate and contextually compatible, that is, expected and predictable ways" (p. 158). A child experiences these important elements each time they enter the playroom and as they engage in a safe therapeutic relationship with the play therapist. For some children, this may be the one secure relationship they experience in their life, and in this instance, the therapist becomes the surrogate attachment figure (Whelan & Stewart, 2014). For other children, the therapeutic relationship become the leaping-off point from which they can repair, rebuild, and create secure attachments with their caregiver and/or family members (Mellenthin, 2019).

Direct and Indirect Teaching

Guided imagery can entail indirect teaching and direct teaching skills as well. Guided imagery can be applied in teaching social skills and managing anxiety, depressive, or trauma symptoms as well as enhancing relationships and deepening attachments within family relationships. Indirect teaching takes place as the integration of explicit and implicit cognition develops as the child absorbs the storytelling used within the imagery experience and then imagines themselves applying their newfound knowledge in their clinical work or everyday life (Taylor de Faoite, 2014). Levy (2011) proposed that as children learn and use their imagination, they develop new cognitions and behaviors, which promotes an integration of neural networks that creates therapeutic change.

CORE TECHNIQUES

It is important for the play therapist to ascertain which images or sensory experiences are relaxing and comforting to their client prior to beginning a guided imagery intervention. Well-meaning clinicians can unintentionally cause harm when they project their own views or images of comfort and safety onto their child clients. Much like in the introductory guided imagery at the beginning of this chapter, the reference to the grandmother's velvet curtains can be emotionally triggering both positively and negatively depending on the nature of this relationship and experience of the individual. For example, if a child was victimized in a room with velvet curtains, it could be highly traumatizing for them to visualize this out of context. It would also be highly confusing to receive the indirect message they *should* feel a certain way, or the opposite of what their emotional experience was with the triggering stimuli.

Enns (2001) cautioned therapists to be mindful of applying guided imagery for facilitating the resolution of past trauma, as it can be disconcerting and confusing for the client. Clients may spontaneously develop memory confusions and misconceptions, particularly when there is a history of trauma or large gaps of memory. Guided imagery should not be used to "recover" lost memories or gaps. However, it has been shown to be a highly effective tool in helping the client learn how to relax, engage mentally within their body, and to begin to create a sense of safety within the therapeutic relationship (Enns, 2001). It is important for the clinician to be trauma informed and trained in the treatment of complex trauma to use guided imagery for trauma work.

When working with young children or clients who have difficulties in closing their eyes and focusing, fear of closing their eyes because of loss of control, or other clinical issues, teaching them to use an open-eyed imagery is a playful way to begin establishing safety and trust with the play therapist in order to move toward a closed-eyed process. Richard de Mille's (1955) classic *Put Your Mother on the Ceiling* is full of wonderful and playful imagination "games" or guided visualization techniques that can help to enhance imagination as well as offer a regulatory experience for the anxious child. One of my favorite visualizations from de Mille's work is called Animals. To facilitate this open-eye guided imagery exercise, the therapist should invite the child to sit comfortably on a chair or on the floor and follow the script, pausing a few seconds after each sentence. The child can verbalize their responses or mentalize them.

> This game is called Animals. We are going to start with one little mouse and see what we can do. Let us imagine that there is a little mouse somewhere in the room. Where would you like to put him? / All right, have him sit up and wave to you. / Have him turn green. / Change his color again. / Change it again. /

Have him stand on his hands. / Have him run over to the wall. / Have him run up the wall. / Have him sit upside down on the ceiling. / Turn him right side up and put him in a corner up there. / Put another mouse in another corner up there. / Put a mouse in each of the other two corners up there. / Put other mice in the four corners down below. / Are they all there? / Turn them all yellow. / Have them all say "Hello" at the same time. / Have them all say, "How are you?" / Have them all promise to stay in their corners and watch the rest of the game. (de Mille, 1955, pp. 57–58)

Often in my play therapy practice, young children will wave goodbye to their mice friends at the end of each session and start the next week's play therapy session by making sure their mice are waiting for them in their respective corners. They may also want to name their mice friends who are waiting for them on the ceiling. This intervention allows the child to begin developing a secure attachment and connection to not just the play therapist but also the play therapy room itself. A child has to not only *feel* safe within the play therapy room but also *believe* that they are safe within it. The play therapy room acts as a container for all of the child's unconscious and conscious affect and experience. The play that happens within this room and within the play therapy process promotes the integration of the past, present, conscious, imagined, and unconscious material a child experiences.

When a therapist begins to implement closed-eyed guided imagery in play therapy, a few steps need to be taken with care. Reznick (2009) developed a five-phase model of guided imagery consisting of relaxation, induction, the main imagery experience, the return, and the processing. The first step in implementing guided imagery is to teach relaxation techniques and deep-belly-breathing skills to the child client. You can use several playful interventions to teach this to a child. A child can place a stuffed animal or soft toy on their stomach while laying down on their back. As they breathe in and out, their belly will move up and down. This is diaphragmatic breathing, which promotes long, slow, deep breaths critical for mindfulness and relaxation. Another playful technique is the Cooking Breathing Game by Lowenstein (2016). The child imagines that they can smell fresh baked cookies and breathe the scent of the cookies in deeply and cools down the hot cookie with the exhaled breath. This promotes deep, slow breathing practiced in a fun, playful manner.

A child needs to be able to sit still, regulate their affect, and experience a sense of relaxation during the guided imagery experience for it to be truly effective. Teaching the child how to regulate their body and quiet their internal chaos is an important therapeutic technique as well as a benefit to the child. Incorporating mindfulness into the relaxation script is valuable. Guiding the child to be mindful and aware of how their body feels, what they taste in their mouths, how their feet feel on the floor, and what their breath feels like during the inhale and exhale is important so that the client learns organize their internal experience.

The next phase in this model is the induction phase. As the child learns to calm and regulate their body and breathing, they are now ready to experience calming their minds and engaging in guided imagery. The therapist will invite the child to find their special place, using guided imagery to help them find a calm, peaceful, happy place in their imagination. The child is asked to close their eyes if they feel comfortable doing so; if not, the child can leave their eyes open. The child is invited to begin doing their belly breathing to quiet their body and mind, and the therapist will begin to read the guided imagery script they have prepared or created for this therapy session. The therapist's voice should be calm and quiet. It is important for the therapist to sit still while engaging in guided imagery in order for the client to feel safe and secure, not wondering what the walking or rustling sounds may be.

To find their special place, a child is asked to imagine or create a calm, peaceful, beautiful, or magical space. The child is invited to imagine this special place, whether it is an indoor or outdoor space, if there are people or animals there, or if they are alone. Reznick (2009) wrote the following in her script:

> This is your Special Place, where you can feel good about yourself. You deserve a peaceful place of your own. Here you are safe. You can play, study, rest, talk with whomever you wish, or do absolutely nothing. Surround yourself with everything and everyone that brings you joy. Invite people or animals you'd like to be with you. Whenever anyone walks through the door, they love and accept you just the way you are. (p. 26)

Oaklander's (1978) Cave Fantasy is another wonderful script and resource for therapist's new to guided imagery to use to facilitate finding the client's special place.

This exercise leads to the third phase of the model of the main imagery experience. As the child is able explore this special place, Reznick (2009) invites them to meet either an animal friend/guide or a wizard to help them problem solve and manage their emotional experiences. Depending upon the child's presenting treatment issue or current emotional struggle, Reznick tends to offer very prescriptive scripts to her clients. These scripts are designed to help them to identify their emotional experiences, as well as pinpoint ways to manage their affect, experience empowerment, and learn to problem-solve.

The return phase helps the child to come back to a space of conscious awareness and alertness. It is common for a child to feel sleepy or to become engrossed in their imagery. The child may not want to come back to real life or face the reality of their everyday world and experience. Giving the child a cue or time to awaken from the imagery is important. For some children, quietly and slowly counting to five can be a safe way to awaken their conscious and come out of the imagery calmly and in a regulated manner. Others may benefit from hearing a verbal cue such as a small chime from a bell or the rustle of paper being placed in front of them to be able to create a visual representation of their experience. The phase of processing is important for the client to remember their experience, make meaning of their feelings, and then express and let go of any uncomfortable or difficult emotions they may have felt or are currently experiencing. Using any of the expressive arts can be a powerful way for a child to process their experience. Making a Sandtray representing their journey or drawing a picture can help deepen their processing.

CLINICAL APPLICATIONS

Guided imagery has been shown to be effective in treating a range of presenting treatment issues, across environments from clinical outpatient settings to hospitals to education centers (Utay & Miller, 2006). When working with children in play therapy, it is common for themes revolving around stress, anxiety, fear, safety, and relationship struggles to manifest in their play. Guided imagery can help the child make sense of their world and give meaning to their experience. As noted earlier in the chapter, these interventions promote a child's sense of self, belonging to and connecting with the story of their life. These interventions can be used in individual, family, and group therapy. Most scripts can be adapted for therapeutic application across ages and stages.

For the purpose of this chapter, the application of guided imagery for the treatment of anxiety is discussed. Worry and fear are normal parts of child development. It is common for young children to suddenly worry about the monster under their bed or if something "bad" will happen, as their imagination begins to blossom in a period of dramatic brain development. It is when the worries or fears begin to become overwhelming to the child or impede their daily functioning that professional intervention needs to occur.

Anxiety has been defined as the presence of significant worry, nervousness, and fear (Mellenthin, 2018). When a child experiences heightened levels of anxiety, these symptoms impact their daily functioning across environments and relationships. It is common for a child with anxiety symptoms to also experience somatic symptoms such as headaches, stomachaches, and other aches and pains. Difficulty sleeping, changes in eating habits, crying spells, and clingy behaviors are also common. The child may also begin withdrawing from social activities, missing school, playdates, and family functions (Reznick, 2009). A child's imagination often will go into overdrive, as their anxiety fuels their deepest fears and worries.

Teaching children the therapeutic skills of visualization, relaxation, and deep breathing are beneficial coping skills in and of themselves. They learn the skills needed to relax and begin using their imagination to find peace, quiet, and calm instead of chaos and worry, which helps to regulate their emotions and affect as well as teach them how to quiet their mind when under stress and worry. One of the positive impacts of digital technology is the multitude of apps, YouTube videos, and social media platforms that are dedicated to guided imagery and relaxation for both children and adults. The digital intervention of nighttime guided imagery is a positive addition to a child's therapy; children can do this in their bed, with or without their parents, as they ready themselves to sleep. This can be particularly useful for children with nighttime fears and worries.

In the current situation of the COVID-19 pandemic that is affecting children and families across the globe, the ability to use technology for therapy purposes is also increasing. Guided imagery can be an incredibly useful play therapy that is easily adapted for telehealth services. Through online play therapy sessions, therapists can offer their child clients—as well as the parents of their clients—internal resources to decrease their fears, anxiety, and apprehension of the world using guided imagery techniques. These powerful approaches help to provide the child internal resources needed to find a calm, peaceful imaginary place away from the stressors of the current world. Kaduson (2018) wrote, "Stress that is prolonged and managed poorly can result in negative physical, mental, and cognitive outcomes for children and youth" (p. 79). Connecting with children who have been quarantined or facing restrictive social isolation measures to combat this global disease is especially important for play therapists to keep in mind. Experiencing a sense of control when you feel helpless to change the situation around you is important and critical for mental health. Researchers (George & Sam, 2017) have determined that experiencing a sense of being in control is, in and of itself, therapeutic and can help us to feel better and do better. "Feeling in control is associated with higher optimism, self-esteem, and ability to tolerate pain, ambiguity and stress" (George & Sam, 2017, p. 81). Guided imagery provides an emotional experience of feeling in control of both body and mind. Therapists can use guided imagery for stress reduction and relaxation, imagining a positive future, and development of insight and problem solving (Utay & Miller, 2006). In the current world climate, this may be especially powerful work to do with anxious and scared children and parents.

Lemon Squeezies (Mellenthin, 2018) can be a powerful guided imagery intervention for use with anxious children. In this full-body relaxation technique, a playful guided imagery is used to help the child's brain and body regulate, relax, and calm. The child is initially directed to imagine that they are squeezing a lemon in each hand, tightening the hand into a fist, and then releasing to a relaxed state. Next they are guided to imagine that they have turned into a variety of animals, where they stretch, release, and tense different parts of their body from kitten stretches to a turtle hiding in the shell. At the end of the visualization exercise, the child is asked to draw on a blank puzzle pictures of their lemon squeezies to help them remember how to use them in their home environment.

Unzipping Me From OCD (Mellenthin, 2018) is a guided imagery technique developed to help a child manage the distressing thoughts and compulsions that accompany obsessive-compulsive disorder (OCD) or whose anxiety presents with similar symptomatology. The goal of this intervention is to help the child begin to differentiate the OCD thoughts and behaviors from normal, healthy thoughts, as well as to separate the child's sense of self from their disordered symptoms. The child is asked to get as comfortable as possible. They can choose to keep their eyes open or closed, depending on their comfort level. They are instructed to begin breathing deeply, inhaling through the nose and exhaling through the mouth. The child can answer verbally or choose to remain silent. The script is as follows:

> Please breathe in deeply and slowly for five breaths. I want you to think of your OCD and listen for its voice. What does it sound like? Is it a male or female voice? Does it whisper or yell or talk normally? What color is the voice? If the voice could be some type of shape or object, what does it look like? What is its name? When you feel ready to come back into the playroom, please open your eyes and draw your creature. (p. 91)

The child is then asked to draw a picture of their OCD, using the colors and shapes of their imagery. They are asked to write the name of their creature on the picture, further separating their OCD from their true self.

CASE ILLUSTRATION

The client described here is a composite of several children seen by the author, and confidentiality is protected by changes to the name and identifying details. Owen was 8 years old when he was referred to play therapy for increasingly disturbing obsessive–compulsive symptoms. His parents reported that they had first noticed some compulsive behaviors beginning when Owen had entered kindergarten but had just assumed it was a phase and he would grow out of it. As the years had progressed, Owen's behaviors and emotional response had grown increasingly volatile and annoying to those around him. When he would enter a room, he would look under the furniture and then smack his hands twice on the floor and twice on the walls. Owen would then lick his hand and wipe it along the surface of the furniture. This entire ritual needed to take place before Owen could sit on the floor or enter a room without an emotional outburst. When he could complete the ritual, Owen would then appear calm and easily engage with those around him. If teachers or adults thwarted his finishing this compulsion, particularly the licking and wiping part, Owen would rage, scream, and cry, often yelling that people would get hurt and there were germs and bad guys in the room.

In play therapy, Owen engaged in minimal sensory-seeking play, which was somewhat surprising given the nature of his sensory-seeking compulsions. He preferred to draw pictures with crayons and markers or play with the dollhouse, and he was engaging and pleasant with the play therapist. As the therapeutic relationship developed, Owen was taught different strategies to manage his distressing symptoms, including teaching relaxation and mindfulness. He was taught distress tolerance and how to recognize when a compulsion "tricked" his brain into thinking there was danger present or worry of harm happening to self and others.

One of the most powerful moments in Owen's therapy journey occurred through the implementation of guided imagery and emotive imagery techniques. As Owen learned how to calm his mind and his body, he was able to begin engaging in the various guided imagery interventions. He was able to visualize himself walking into a room without engaging in his compulsion and how this would feel in his body, as well as squishing his fears into a tiny box that he could hold in his hands and open when he felt ready to look at them. Through the guided imagery intervention Unzipping Me From OCD (Mellenthin, 2018), Owen was able to separate his symptoms from his *self* and learn to listen to his "thinking brain" and not the fear his OCD brought to him. He was able to create an imagery about his OCD and make it into a separate person named Mr. Giggles, with a voice, body, color, and mannerisms.

Using the imagery of Mr. Giggles, Owen began to identify the anxiety, obsessions, impulses, and compulsions he experienced as a symptom instead of a pressing reality or necessity. He was able to visualize himself as more powerful and knowledgeable than Mr. Giggles and could practice squishing Mr. Giggles like a ball of slime or shrinking him down to the size of an ant and telling him he couldn't trick his brain anymore. His parents began engaging in the play therapy process and helped Owen manage his fears and symptoms better as they learned new parenting strategies to help their child, as well as new ways to connect with their child in an attachment-promoting engagement through play.

EMPIRICAL SUPPORT

Surprisingly, there has been very little research on the use and efficacy of guided imagery within the field of play therapy. This fact was especially astonishing to this author, as guided imagery has been used in psychotherapy for decades and has been shown to be a highly effective tool in managing stress, anxiety, eating disordered behaviors, sleep disturbance, and many more treatment issues that are commonly seen in child and adolescent clientele (Utay & Miller, 2006). Guided imagery has been shown to help with executive functioning such as planning and rehearsing goals, coping with negative or intrusive thoughts, increasing confidence, developing prosocial skills, increasing self-soothing, managing stress, overcoming fear, and gaining control over painful emotions (Arbuthnott et al., 2001; Enns, 2001; Hernández-Guzmán et al., 2002; Levy, 2011; Taylor de Faoite, 2014).

Within the medical field and health psychology, guided imagery has been used to decrease pain (Vagnoli et al., 2019), depression, and anxiety symptoms (Beizaee et al., 2018) with patients who undergo various cancer treatments and surgeries and who have chronic medical conditions (Carpenter et al., 2017). Research has found that by incorporating guided imagery with medical patients both before and after medical interventions, the patient's pain levels are significantly lowered as well as their symptoms of anxiety and depression. Within pediatric populations, this has been especially beneficial for children and adolescents with chronic medical conditions, as the hospital can already feel like a frightening place and many children experience multiple painful medical procedures (George & Sam, 2017).

As the clinician, it is important to be mindful to use culturally significant and familiar images, smells, tastes, tactile sensitivity, sounds, and music within the guided imagery. As Bennett and Eberts (2014) stated, "Discounting the culture of clients as unimportant can limit children's self-expression" (p. 17). Increasing one's awareness of bias, stereotypes, and assumptions is important in developing cultural sensitivity and is essential in facilitating self-expression of our clients. It is also critical for the clinician to be culturally sensitive in their work with clients and to use a guided imagery approach that allows for familiarity and cultural responsiveness. For example, La Roche et al. (2006)

found that when working within the Latino community, using relationship-based images or allocentric self-orientation was much more impactful than incorporating the traditional individualistic/idiocentric-guided imagery scripts. An example of this would be guiding the client with thoughts and images such as *think about someone you feel connected to in a positive way* versus the more traditional imagery of *imagine yourself standing in a meadow*.

Other researchers found that when working to enhance social skills and performance, offering guided imagery techniques that allowed for the visualization of relationship building and enhancing was more powerful than using images of positive social skills. They found that this increased the child's ability for long-term positive success in making and keeping friends (Hernández-Guzmán et al., 2002). The application of attachment theory and guided imagery could be a significant area for future research in play therapy, as the understanding of the importance of creating relationships across cultures and populations grows, particularly in Western industrialized cultures, as children and families have become increasingly isolated and fragmented.

SUMMARY AND CONCLUSION

Guided imagery can be a powerful tool for use in play therapy. It can help the child client improve social skills, quiet fears and anxieties, and learn healthy coping strategies for use across environments. This type of intervention is powerful for use with individuals, families, and group therapy. It is important for the play therapy community to begin to research the effectiveness of these interventions as an empirically validated play therapy intervention, as it has been shown to be effective in treating multiple mental health and physical health issues across disciplines and practice settings.

REFERENCES

Arbuthnott, K. D., Arbuthnott, D. W., & Rossiter, L. (2001). Guided imagery and memory: Implications for psychotherapists. *Journal of Counseling Psychology*, *48*(2), 123–132. https://doi.org/10.1037/0022-0167.48.2.123

Beizaee, Y., Rejeh, N., Heravi-Karimooi, M., Tadrisi, S. D., Griffiths, P., & Vaismoradi, M. (2018). The effect of guided imagery on anxiety, depression and vital signs in patients on hemodialysis. *Complementary Therapies in Clinical Practice, 33*, 184–190. https://doi.org/10.1016/j.ctcp.2018.10.008

Bennett, M. M., & Eberts, S. (2014). Self-expression. In C. E. Schaefer & A. A. Drewes (Eds.), *The therapeutic powers of play: 20 core agents of change* (2nd ed., pp. 11–24). John Wiley & Sons.

Carpenter, J. J., Hines, S. H., & Lan, V. M. (2017). Guided imagery for pain management in postoperative orthopedic patients: An integrative literature review. *Journal of Holistic Nursing, 35*(4), 342–351. https://doi.org/10.1177/0898010116675462

Crenshaw, D., & Tillman, K. (2014). Access to the unconscious. In C. E. Schaefer & A. A. Drewes (Eds.), *The therapeutic powers of play: 20 core agents of change* (2nd ed., pp. 25–38). John Wiley & Sons.

de Mille, R. (1955). *Put your mother on the ceiling*. Ross-Erickson Publishers.

Enns, C. Z. (2001). Some reflections on imagery and psychotherapy implications. *Journal of Counseling Psychology, 48*(2), 136–139. https://doi.org/10.1037/0022-0167.48.2.136

Fitzgerald, M., & Langevin, M. (2010). Imagery. In M. Snyder & R. Lindquist (Eds.), *Complementary and alternative therapists in nursing* (6th ed., pp. 63–89). Springer Publishing Company.

George, R. J., & Sam, S. T. (2017). Guided imagery: Child + guided imagery = reduced pain, stress and anxiety. Let your child get healed without pain and expenses. *Asian Journal of Nursing Education and Research, 7*(1), 79–85. https://doi.org/10.5958/2349-2996.2017.00017.9

Hernández-Guzmán, L., Gonzáles, S., & López, F. (2002). Effect of guided imagery on children's social performance. *Behavioural and Cognitive Psychotherapy, 30*(4), 471–483. https://doi.org/10.1017/S1352465802004083

Kaduson, H. G. (2018). Release play therapy for children who have experienced stressful life events. In A. A. Drewes & C. E. Schaefer (Eds.), *Play-based interventions for childhood anxieties, fears, and phobias* (pp. 78–103). Guilford Press.

La Roche, M. J., D'Angelo, E., Gualdron, L., & Leavell, J. (2006). Culturally sensitive guided imagery for allocentric Latinos: A pilot study. *Psychotherapy, 43*(4), 555–560. https://doi.org/10.1037/0033-3204.43.4.555

Levy, A. J. (2011). Neurobiology and the therapeutic action of psychoanalytic play therapy with children. *Clinical Social Work Journal, 39*(1), 50–60. https://doi.org/10.1007/s10615-009-0229-x

Lowenstein, L. (2016). *Creative CBT interventions for children with anxiety*. Champion Press.

Mellenthin, C. (2018). *Play therapy: Engaging and powerful techniques for the treatment of childhood disorders*. Pesi Publishing.

Mellenthin, C. (2019). *Attachment centered play therapy*. Routledge. https://doi.org/10.4324/9781315229348

Oaklander, V. (1978). *Windows to our children*. The Gestalt Journal Press.

Porat, J., & Sadeh, A. (2013). Imagination-based interventions with children. In M. Taylor (Ed.), *The Oxford handbook of the development of imagination* (pp. 529–538). Oxford University Press. https://doi.org/10.1093/oxfordhb/9780195395761.013.0034

Reznick, C. (2009). *The power of your child's imagination*. Penguin Group.

Schaefer, C. E., & Drewes, A. A. (2014). *The therapeutic powers of play*. John Wiley & Sons.

Stewart, A. L., & Echterling, L. G. (2014). Therapeutic relationship. In C. E. Schaefer & A. A. Drewes (Eds.), *The therapeutic powers of play: 20 core agents of change* (2nd ed., pp. 157–169). John Wiley & Sons.

Taylor de Faoite, A. (2014). Indirect teaching. In C. E. Schaefer & A. A. Drewes (Eds.), *The therapeutic powers of play: 20 core agents of change* (pp. 51–67). John Wiley & Sons.

Utay, J., & Miller, M. (2006). Guided imagery as an effective therapeutic technique: A brief review of its history and efficacy research. *Journal of Instructional Psychology*, *33*(1), 40–43.

Vagnoli, L., Bettini, A., Amore, E., De Masi, S., & Messeri, A. (2019). Relaxation-guided imagery reduces perioperative anxiety and pain in children: A randomized study. *European Journal of Pediatrics*, *178*(6), 913–921. https://doi.org/10.1007/s00431-019-03376-x

Veena, D., & Alvi, S. (2016). Guided imagery intervention for anxiety reduction. *Indian Journal of Health and Wellbeing*, *7*(2), 198–203.

Whelan, W. F., & Stewart, A. L. (2014). Attachment. In C. E. Schaefer & A. A. Drewes (Eds.), *The therapeutic powers of play: 20 core agents of change* (2nd ed., pp. 171–182). John Wiley & Sons.

Winnicott, D. W. (1971). *Therapeutic consultations in child psychiatry*. Basic Books.

9

DRAMATIC PLAY THERAPY

ELIANA GIL AND TERESA DIAS

The finalization of this chapter occurred during the global pandemic of COVID-19 (coronavirus) and the changes forced upon our daily lives. In the midst of fear and anxiety, grief and loss, sickness and recovery, and a staggering number of deaths across the United States and the world at large, messages of hope and solidarity arrived robust and consistent. The expressive arts soared in popularity, emerging and growing spontaneously during this period of intense crisis. Social media is replete with artists or amateur performers who are generously sharing their music, art, yoga, mindful practices, and performance art. In fact, many of the components of drama therapy are on full display, including improvisation, comedy, songwriting, storytelling, dance and movement, imagination, and creative expression. In times of despair, the human spirit moves toward self-expression as a gesture of connection, generosity, or unity; expression and release can combat and decrease feelings of isolation and despair. Jones (1996) considered that "participating in drama and theater allows connections to unconscious and emotional processes to be made," thus "satisfying human needs to play and to create" (p. 7). American drama therapist pioneer and author Dr. Renée Emunah (1994) supplied the

https://doi.org/10.1037/0000217-010
Play Therapy With Children: Modalities for Change, H. G. Kaduson and C. E. Schaefer (Editors)

following definition: "Drama therapy is the intentional use of drama/theatre processes to achieve psychological growth and change" (as cited in Jones, 1996, p. 8).

McNiff (1981) stated two significant facts about expressive therapies: (a) The arts have consistently been part of life as well as healing throughout history, and (b) they introduce action into traditional psychotherapy. This action seems consistent with contemporary views on neuroscience, which seek to target under- or overdeveloped parts of the brain, which clearly impact personal neuroception—the process that individuals use to gauge when there is danger and when there is safety. Obviously, safety is a critical necessity for positive treatment outcomes. Drama therapy provides purposeful methods for engaging clients in top-down and bottom-up activities to improve overall functioning (Godsal, 2017; Perry & Szalavitz, 2006).

This chapter provides readers with a deeper understanding of the intersections between drama and play therapies, how the fields are compatible and frequently integrated by practitioners conversant with both fields of study. The authors also present examples of core drama therapy techniques and include a case illustration that highlights the application of drama and play therapies to target specific treatment goals. In our clinical experience, children who play are almost always engaged in some form of dramatic interaction, be it storytelling, pretend play, or relational enactments. It's actually challenging to tease out when drama therapy is occurring without play and when play therapy is occurring without some type of dramatic involvement. Many play therapy approaches involve some type of drama therapy techniques, such as role-playing, symbolic or verbal trauma narratives, family sculpting, and others. Drama therapy techniques are heavily borrowed and integrated into other approaches and modalities; in fact, it is often referred to as an integrated or multimodal approach that lends itself to ample use. Notable examples are Internal Family Systems (Schwartz, 2011) and Theraplay (Booth & Jernberg, 2010).

THERAPEUTIC BENEFITS

The World Alliance of Drama Therapy website highlights a quote from Dr. Renée Emunah, director of the California Institute of Integral Studies in San Francisco, California:

> Under the guise of play and pretend, we can—for once—act in new ways. The bit of distance from real life afforded by drama enables us to gain perspective on our real-life roles and patterns and actions, and to experiment actively with alternatives. (https://www.worldallianceofdramatherapy.com)

This resonates with the "safe-enough distance," considered one of the important variables in play therapy. Jones (1996) proposed nine core therapeutic factors that he believed would apply across all the varied types of drama therapies: dramatic projection, drama therapeutic empathy and distancing, role-playing and personification, interactive audience and witnessing, embodiment, playing, here and now, life–drama connection, and transformation. Cassidy et al. (2014) named two metaprocesses worth mentioning: (a) working in the here and now *alongside* clients and (b) helping to establish safety by offering clients experiences of control and choice (like leading and following) and encouraging active participation in the therapy (Cassidy et al., 2017). There is a consensus that drama therapy provides a new language for communication, increasing self-agency (Fong, 2007), self-concept (Orkibi et al., 2017), and mental health issues, including experiences of trauma (D. Feldman et al., 2015).

Drewes and Schaefer's (2014) study of the therapeutic factors of play therapy identified 20 important change agents present in play therapy and, as a result, encouraged the practice of transtheoretical play therapy that "entails selecting and adding to your repertoire the best change agents from among all the major theories of play therapy" (p. 4). Dramatic play therapy is a transtheoretical approach that seeks to promote therapy goals by applying specific change agents viable within both practices. Thus, when comparing and contrasting Schaefer and Drewes's 20 common change agents, play therapy and drama therapy coincide in many areas but most especially in creative problem solving, resiliency, psychological development, self-esteem, catharsis and abreaction, the emergence of positive emotions, stress management/inoculation, and empathy. Drama therapy encourages individuals to express their own emotions verbally and nonverbally, amplifying their expressive repertoire to include embodied expression. Often when individuals achieve communication through dramatic means, it can increase their sense of mastery and self-esteem and elicit a shift in perspective. In addition, resonating with others' emotions might feel safer and thus allow for greater personal insight. Drama play can also tap into alternatives to stuck thinking and feeling and thus may open up optimistic views that lead to resiliency and a belief that positive change is possible. Sometimes, it is only in pretending and role-playing that abstract ideas become clarified and more immediately available; these views often include the ability to problem-solve in new and creative ways. Finally, drama play can provide legitimate opportunities for release, either through cathartic or abreaction experiences alone or with others. In so doing, unconscious thoughts can be brought forward with an "as if" quality that encourages insight and subsequent action. Any and all of these experiences occurring with unconditional acceptance and support from a therapeutic witness create a context for reparative personal and relational experiences. In fact, drama therapy research has focused on many of the core agents mentioned here and includes research on psychodrama and more general integrated drama therapy.

CORE TECHNIQUES

To approach a discussion of drama therapy techniques, it is important to note that the field is limitless in direction, technique, and purpose. In that context, the term *core techniques* refers to commonly used, popular techniques. The term *drama therapy* often includes traditional drama therapy, psychodrama, and Playback Theater. Even the most casual review of Jones's (1996) core agents, discussed earlier, will be familiar to and resonate with play therapists. As Jones stated, "the everyday, usual ways of experiencing the self and events are altered by the use of dramatic language . . . the dramatic language can transform the experience as it opens up new possibilities of expression, feeling and association" (p. 121). One of the basics of the practice of play therapy is the safe-enough distance aspect of play, a process that often includes projection, role-playing, and problem solving. For some children, play can result in an experience of insight in which they make a life-drama (or life-play) connection, sometimes guided by trusted clinicians, depending on their orientation. Play therapy clients also use impersonation and empathy-building as they tell verbal or puppet stories, create and narrate their sandtrays, and seek interaction with clinicians, who serve the role of witness. Drama therapists single out play as an essential process for drama therapists and note that drama therapy "is involvement in drama with a healing intention," specifying that clients make use of "the content of drama activities, the process of creating enactments, and the relationships formed between those taking part in the work within a therapeutic framework" (Jones, 1996, p. 8).

A number of highly popular techniques have been borrowed from drama therapy, and many directive therapies have incorporated movement, dramatic storytelling, and energetic physical activities when working with children, especially boys, and their families (Haen, 2011). Drama therapists encourage clients to embody feelings, express themselves verbally and nonverbally, engage in pretend play to deepen their understanding of the human condition in self and others, achieve insight, and most important, participate actively in problem solving and visualizing alternative action-oriented behaviors. The following core techniques are used regularly by drama therapists.

Warm-Up Exercises

Drama therapists almost always begin sessions by inviting clients to participate in a series of warm-up exercises designed to increases reconnection to the physical self. Nash and Haen (2005) stated that "energies that have been frozen, rigified, and turned inward begin to come to life again"(p. 123), thus increasing client receptivity to engage in focused role-playing, movement, and play. As the name implies, warm-up exercises allow clients to develop a sense of comfort and relaxation.

Mirroring/Trading Leadership

The clinician begins to slowly stretch and move, narrating as the child copies exactly what the therapist does. At times, the clinician encourages the child to focus his observation by saying, "See how my hands are balled up?" or "See how straight my arms can be." After a while, leadership changes and the child leads and therapist follows. The clinician will get some indication of the child's attachment style—that is, how comfortable he is with eye contact, how well he attunes to another, how well he tolerates someone attuning to him, how easy it is to lead or follow, and how easily he follows directives.

Yoga Ball Toss With Mirroring

In this exercise, child and clinician take turns throwing the ball in a specific way (e.g., twist throw, bounce pass), calling out the kind of toss being used. The other person then mirrors by returning the ball in the same fashion. This activity has a leader/follower component while requiring that the client use internal controls to choose and then signal the catcher as to what kind of toss will be used. This activity will increase impulse control and model respect and reciprocity.

Freeze Dance With Bell, Bowl, or Drum

The clinician creates a steady beat, or song, and then cues a freeze moment. In doing so, the therapist takes a leadership role, establishes a rhythm, and then stops the movement by freezing in place. Clients learn to synchronize their own movements to the therapist and create connectivity through rhythm. This activity also includes a leader/follower component, especially useful to children who must take cues from others, follow rules, and learn to work harmoniously with others.

Other Drama Therapy Interventions

Once warm-up is completed, drama therapists proceed to therapeutic focus on the issues that have been identified as presenting problems. This phase of addressing the problem directly is called *working through*, and specific drama therapy techniques are chosen that will promote and advance treatment goals (Weber, 2005). The following examples of drama therapy interventions address affective identification and expression, role-playing, and attachment-based work.

Charades With Emotion Cards

The child and clinician identify six relevant emotions and then act them out by taking turns acting out or guessing the emotions. When these emotions are acted out, the observer notices how the body looks, what parts of the body are different, and then points it out. The clinician might also ask the child to differentiate between two emotions that might look the same, such as anger and frustration, teasing out any subtleties in how each might be expressed. In addition, the clinician directs the child to identify how different emotions are felt in the body—for example, "What is your body doing when you're angry?" "Where do you feel anger the most in your body?" Eventually, clinicians can reframe these body feelings as "cues" that their anger has been ignited, and the cues can help them pause and figure out what to do instead of escalating feelings of anger (until the dam breaks or the kettle blows its top or whatever other metaphor might fit). The clinician might ask about the last time the child felt a particular feeling and what the child did with it when they had it.

Gross Motor Play With Cool-Down Sessions

Physical activities such as sword fights, soccer, jumping on a trampoline, and playing "horse" are particularly useful with young boys, who tend to find engaging in expressive language more challenging (Haen, 2011). It is important to start these activities with a few minutes of calming the body with deep breaths or visualization. As the games get going, the clinician finds times to signal "cool down" so that client and child can notice their heart rate, breathing, and other body sensations, such as feeling warm, moist (sweating), or unable to sit still. The clinician explains how the body is "activated" or turned on by running and jumping, just as it's activated when it feels strong emotions such as anger. The clinician leads the child in taking three deep cleansing breaths and encourages the child to notice what is happening in his body and how his breathing, heart rate, and temperature might have changed. Eventually, the clinician suggests a "life-drama connection" by directing the child to identify a time or situation that could benefit from a cooldown in real life.

Developmental Transformations

Developed by David Read Johnson (2009), developmental transformations (DvT) are "a form of embodied improvisation with individuals and groups . . . that has been used for over thirty years in a variety of settings" (Reynolds, 2011, p. 297). Reynolds described the components of what constitutes DvT as threefold: the play must be mutual, discrepant, and absent of harm (p. 300). The activities are small cocreated improvised scenes in which the therapist subtly generates creative material that can be meaningful or significant to the child and his problem behavior. The activity includes free play (or "improv"), which remains in the here and now and begins to get close to the presenting concern or the target goal.

The Weather Report

The Weather Report is a Theraplay activity (Booth & Jernberg, 2010) that includes a brief massage, or nurturing touch, as people stand back to back. This type of activity is designed to establish or enhance attachment between family members whose attachment may be compromised. Incorporating safe touch within a therapy session conveys the importance of kind, attuned, sensitive interactions that promote safety and emotional connection.

Family Band

The Family Band is a large oval piece of stretchable material, often used in dance and movement, that drama and play therapists find compelling in a number of ways. In particular, these therapists have found some utility in working with families that are formed through adoption or families whose members have entered, exited, and returned (as in foster care). The band is sturdy and can hold family members who lean into it. The trick is that in order for everyone to be safe, achieving balance is of the utmost importance. It takes some negotiating for everyone to feel reliably supported in the band, and it takes some work to achieve joint movement within the band, such as rocking sideways or holding the smaller people in place (see the Case Illustration section). For sure, the band can be used to allow parents to rock a child as if the child were in a hammock, and to play tug of war—both activities that families can initiate. The therapeutic goal of this technique is to convey that the family is an emotionally connected (or attached) unit: a family system in which the movement of one affects all.

CLINICAL APPLICATIONS

Drama therapy can be easily incorporated when working with children and adolescents with an array of problems, including depression, anxiety, low self-esteem, and affective and behavioral dysregulation. Drama play therapy can be initiated in dyads (therapist and client) by either the young client or the therapist. More common, however, is for drama therapy techniques to be used with groups or families, as there are increased benefits of performance art (being observed by others), as well as having the support of others (through applause and encouragement). In addition, there are forms of psychodrama in which the client and/or clinician will invite group or family members to speak for the client, act out assigned roles, or create alternative outcomes to a particular story. Both directive and nondirective play therapists have encountered children whose primary mode of interaction in sessions is to invite active physical play (running, ball, or sword games) or, for those who prefer to stay in storytelling (pretend) mode, to assign traits and voices to puppets or toys in the room. Thus, play therapists are often engaged in dramatic play without knowing the full impact of using this modality more purposefully in recognition of its full potential.

CASE ILLUSTRATION

The following case illustration is a composite of clients we have seen, and confidentiality is protected by changes to names and identifying details. Mr. and Mrs. Saeger came into the intake appointment looking fatigued and feeling frustrated and near despair. Mr. Saeger arrived 20 minutes late, and Mrs. Saeger insisted on not waiting, noting that her husband was always running late. She began by saying that their son Brad, who is 11 years old, has been challenging from the beginning: "Even before he was born he was wreaking havoc. . . . He was not a planned baby, our kids were already starting college, and I was incredibly sick with this pregnancy." She went on to say that she and her husband did not feel they could terminate the pregnancy even though neither of them was ready to "start again" with more children. They had a set of twins (now in college)—boy and girl—who had been wonderful children. "At first we were worried about having two kids, but we quickly learned they took care of each other. Everything was easy with them." Mother was teary as she talked about Brad and was trying to manage her time: "I have so much to tell you. I will focus on where we are right now." She noted that Brad had started having problems almost immediately after birth: He was colicky, didn't sleep through the night for almost the first year, seemed to need to be held all the time, and got into everything. Mother noticed that her experience with Brad was the polar opposite from the twins. Brad's father arrived halfway through our time, and he seemed stressed out and kept checking his phone. I asked Mother to give a brief summary to Father of what we had discussed so far, and she did so, very rapidly. Father stated that his wife was the primary caretaker and that his job kept him away from home for months at a time. Even when he was at home, he worked in his office and they had a strict division of labor: He was the breadwinner; she was the caretaker.

The parents described a child who was controlling, mean, sullen, and potentially threatening; they said they felt he was "holding us hostage." Mother felt she had made every effort she could to manage Brad's "impossible" behavior and now needed someone's help. She asserted that Brad's contrasting behaviors in private and public caused her a great deal of anger and resentment, and during the intake, the clinician described these two behaviors, paradoxically, as a hopeful sign: *If* the child could regulate in public, it suggested that he had internal controls that were firmly in place. The job of the clinician would be to explore how to encourage Brad to better apply his internal controls and understand the nature of the family dynamics that seemed to be contributing to his acting-out behaviors.

Upon further inquiry, Mother stated that she had taken Brad to a therapist when he was 4, and Brad was a perfect "angel" with the therapist but "a holy terror" at home. Mother said that the therapist told her that Brad did not need to be in therapy and terminated therapy after 3 months. This had made Mother feel worse, and unfortunately her perception that Brad was "out to get her" grew. Mother even confided in an email that "maybe he senses that he was unwanted. . . . That's why he hates me so!" When the clinician asked what it was like when mother and son got along well at home, Mother commented, "The only time he leaves me alone is when he's got screen time, but now even that is getting to be a problem because he wants to be playing games all the time." Mother added with disdain in her voice, "Personally, I wouldn't care if he was on it 24/7 as long as he left me alone." Mother could not find anything positive to say about her son except that he was "a good con artist."

After a few meetings with Brad, the clinician discussed therapy goals with parents and Brad. The goals included (a) establishing a therapy relationship and familiarity with clinician and setting, (b) decreasing dysregulation (temper tantrums) from daily to three times weekly, and (c) exploring attachment styles and family relationships that might contribute to Brad's dysregulation at home.

First and Subsequent Early Meetings With Brad

Mother's description had been very accurate: Brad made a great first impression. He was polite, extended his arm for a strong handshake, and appeared sweet and friendly. He displayed great enthusiasm during his first session and seemed receptive and agreeable. He sat on the couch when the clinician asked what his mom had told him about coming to therapy. He said that Mom said he needed help with his temper. When the clinician asked if he agreed with this, he nodded his head affirmatively. When asked if he had anything that he would like to show or tell in therapy, he shook his head *No.* When asked if he could say a little more about his temper problems, he said he just gets mad a lot but was not sure why. He announced that he was "very good" at darts and proceeded to show off his excellent skills. He did not ask the clinician to participate and seemed to soak in the focused attention. He also had good math skills and added up his points with accuracy. He seemed content to leave the room when it was time to leave and said, "See you next time." He also said, "I'm gonna get me some darts like that" and asked his mom to get them as soon as he walked out to the waiting room. His tone of voice changed when addressing his mother, and it was noticeable to the therapist. The positive behaviors with the clinician persisted for the first 2 months, and his play was rather repetitive, including playing darts, playing the UNO card game, and looking around for other things he was good at. He was consistently nonverbal, volunteering very little personal information about himself and speaking usually in command form.

In the early sessions, the clinician opted to do child-centered play therapy to allow the child to establish comfort with the setting and the clinician. The child was participating in a fashion, and yet none of the behavioral problems emerged in the therapy sessions; in fact, Brad seemed to be invested in the clinician's liking him. For a child who was brought to therapy for misbehavior, he was quite committed to looking good, as parents had stated during intake. The clinician felt there was a superficial engagement on Brad's part, as if he were going through the motions without real investment.

Adding Drama Therapy Activities

The clinician opted to introduce drama therapy techniques to engage the child in more active participation in therapy and, she hoped, to initiate novelty and to increase his receptivity to addressing the presenting problem. The clinician believed that working with the child physically, giving him less familiar sit-down tasks, and introducing the possibility of more relational work might loosen him up and decrease his defenses. Brad offered little resistance other than saying, "Are you sure you don't want to do this?" and stating, "So after we do some of that, I can pick what to do." Even though Brad was not eager to give up control of the session, he established a structure by which he would get to choose whatever he wanted after the drama therapy session.

The clinician used several of the techniques described previously. To get a sense of Brad's attachment style and how well he attunes to others, the clinician used the Mirroring/Trading Leadership warm-up exercise. Brad seemed to enjoy these exercises, trying to come up with more and more challenging movements for the therapist to follow, and the clinician noticed how Brad usually placed himself side by side, seemingly uneasy with direct face-to-face contact. Brad did seem to enjoy being more active in the room and on occasion asked to do "the drama stuff."

He seemed to enjoy Yoga Ball Toss with Mirroring, in which a ball is thrown in specific ways, calling out the kind of toss being used. Brad had a hard time staying regulated during this exercise, throwing the ball harder and harder. When the clinician was in the leader position, she tossed the ball "slow motion," and Brad always seemed to add a little variation to escalate speed. When he was in the leader position, his dysregulation was visible and limits needed to be implemented. After assessing that his impulsivity was easily engaged, the clinician established a throwing and catching rhythm with the child to help with coregulation.

With coregulation as a focal point, the clinician used a drumming exercise and Brad was able to lead and follow successfully beating on the drum and then putting his hand on the drum face to keep it from humming. Likewise, he also appreciated the humming bowls and thoroughly enjoyed making the pitch lower and higher and counting how long the bowl would sing. Trading leadership roles went more smoothly with this activity, although Brad was excited to beat out his therapist in the bowl-humming department. It became clear that being better at something was very important to Brad, and this came as no surprise to his parents, who viewed him as "intensely perfectionistic and competitive." At the same time, his frustration tolerance was low, and when he could not master something immediately, he tended to withdraw his efforts rather than try again and fail. Brad was more fully engaged in the session, and the therapy relationship grew more comfortable.

Brad became more interactive in therapy once drama therapy activities were introduced and quickly developed his favorites, asking for those freely. The therapist incorporated his suggestions and always came prepared to introduce drama therapy interventions that promoted the overall goals.

To deepen the focus on the presenting problem—specifically, what emotions led to his dysregulation—the therapist introduced a new game in which emotions would be acted out, an activity we called *emotional charades*. The clinician and Brad identified a wide range of emotions, and the therapist was sensitive to including some of the emotions that Brad avoided, such as frustration, resentment, and anger, in addition to emotions Brad found important, such as confidence and pride. When these emotions were acted out, the observer noticed how the body looks and what parts of the body are different, and took some guesses about the emotion being acted out. Because anger was central to his temper tantrums, the clinician asked, if she were a fly on the wall at school (and later at his home) and he were angry, what would she see and notice? Brad was perfectly capable of showing a muted response in school and an agitated one at home. This brought Brad and the therapist close to the core of the problem, learning how the two environments were different and how he responded differently depending on where he was.

When the clinician gave feedback to Brad about how different the same emotion looked in these two settings, Brad shrugged his shoulders and wanted to move on. It was clear that a nerve was struck, and the clinician said that she would move on right then but sometime soon would love to understand more about how the same feeling could look so different in two places and what was *so* different about the two settings. The clinician also mentioned that Brad was able to keep himself more calm and in control at school and stated that, because Brad was such a good actor, maybe someday he could act out the two scenarios.

Given that self-soothing was directly identified as a skill, the clinician introduced a specific activity designed to "cool down" by noticing the body's breathing and other physical sensations, introducing small changes to interrupt the agitation. The clinician then invited Brad to see if he could do a successful cooldown at home, as she was confident he could do a perfect one at school. (The clinician also made a mental note that it would be useful to have a family therapy session in which Brad could direct his parents to learn about activating and deactivating the body.)

Because Brad was now actively engaged in exploring his emotions and times he got dysregulated or times he was able to cool down, the therapist introduced improvised free pretend play informed by DvT and asked Brad to participate in a scene in which one or the other of them got mad "for no apparent reason." Little by little, pretending he was mad and pretending to cool down began to have a positive impact on Brad's temper tantrums at home, and the parents called to inform the clinician that the tantrums were getting much better, much to their delight.

The clinician told the parents that she too was pleased with Brad's increased investment in his therapy, acknowledgment of the problem behaviors, and perspective taking. At the same time, it became obvious that Brad needed family interventions so that the systemic dynamics that were contributing to his emotional and behavioral problems could be addressed. The clinician thus invited the family to join Brad's sessions, and Brad made a list of the activities he wanted to share with his parents. He thoroughly enjoyed teaching them about mirroring/trading leadership. The parents were more receptive to leading than following. The clinician noted that the mother in particular became irritated when her son was in the leadership role. At times, the clinician would ask for the family to "freeze" the motions and check in on how everyone was feeling. Sometimes the mother seemed suspicious or skeptical of Brad's behaviors, even at times that Brad was simply explaining the rules of the game. The therapist coached Brad to soften his approach, and Mom was thanked for trying so many times. "Both of you are very persistent," the therapist announced, "but this activity is supposed to be fun, not frustrating. . . . Let's figure out how you can all have some fun together."

Brad also chose to do emotional charades with his parents and encouraged them to write down a broad range of positive emotions as well as challenging ones. Everyone became comfortable acting out emotions, and Mother and Brad truly enjoyed watching Dad act out emotions. It turned out that Dad was rather comical and generated a lot of laughter when he was the actor.

After several family therapy sessions that used drama therapy activities to identify challenges, frustrations, and moments of positive connection, the clinician brought out a Family Band to give a concrete notion of family togetherness and cohesion. (The Family Band is available by phoning Marjorie Falk, in Towson, Maryland, at 410-449-0983.)

The family, as expected by now, approached this task with quizzical looks and general stiltedness. They were asked to rest into the band, to imagine it's been a long day and finally they can rest. The therapist modeled resting and breathing, and Brad followed easily. His parents seemed awkward and uncomfortable. After a while the therapist noted that she would be moving side to side and she wanted them to follow. Each person took a turn doing this, and it went well.

Finally, the therapist said,

> This is what a family is—everyone is in the same boat together, everyone has everyone else's back. What one person does affects the others. A family works together to make harmony. I know Brad has learned a lot about calming down, about feeling calm, about how his mind affects his body. I think he's working hard on making good choices. I also think that he is ready to receive what you have to offer, and I'm ready to help you all feel calmer and better about being with each other.

The therapist allowed those words to sink in, and then she asked everyone to put the band fabric over their heads, as if saluting the sun, then to bring it down to the ground crouching, and then to open their arms to salute the sun. With this the session ended, and the therapist invited the family to come in for more family sessions that would include drama, play, and family art activities designed to enhance their attachment to one another.

Brad's presenting problems were addressed through a series of play and drama therapy strategies provided individually, in dyads, and with full family cooperation. Play and drama therapies were chosen because Brad had a habit of presenting himself in superficial ways to others and yet was struggling with feelings of inadequacy and insecurity that he clearly demonstrated to his parents in ways that distressed and frustrated them. Drama therapy activities allowed him to become more engaged in therapy, push through some of his initial defenses, and learn ways to connect with the therapist and eventually his parents. Parents became more aware of their ambivalence toward this child, understood why he would act out the way he did, and began to respond to him by providing as much nurturance and acceptance as they could muster up. What started as a child therapy case eventually grew to be a family therapy case that included marital and dyadic parent– child therapy sessions.

EMPIRICAL SUPPORT

There have been a handful of studies on drama therapy with small sample sizes yet consistent results. Drama therapy has been shown to be particularly helpful for increasing social and emotional development (Amatruda, 2006; N. Feldman, 2008), building conflict resolution skills (Karatas, 2011), community interventions after traumatic events (Landy, 2010), building resilience (Folostina et al., 2015), clarifying narratives of foster and adoptive children (Moore, 2010), and children with histories of child abuse (James et al., 2005). Drama therapy has proven consistently most effective with adolescents and has been researched most with this population. These authors believe that younger children are natural candidates for dramatic play, particularly young boys who are less expressive, or those who find themselves conflicted about being factual about their experiences and subsequent feelings, such as victims of domestic violence, abuse, contentious divorces, or a host of other challenging family situations, and these children would be excellent candidates for future research.

SUMMARY AND CONCLUSION

Play therapists naturally use dramatic play in their work with children. This chapter talks a little about using specific drama therapy approaches to promote therapy goals and to deliver those activities in a purposeful way. Drama therapy by definition includes several dimensions that may or may not appear organically in play therapy. In particular, drama therapy prioritizes the use of movement, theater arts, embodiment, role-play, and mind–body connection to raise the client's awareness of the here and now and interconnectedness between thoughts, feelings, and actions. Drama therapy intersects with play in enlivening, dynamic, and exciting ways that can most definitely promote therapy goals in very specific ways.

REFERENCES

Amatruda, M. J. (2006). Conflict resolution and social skill development with children. *Journal of Group Psychotherapy, Psychodrama & Sociometry, 58*(4), 168–181.

Booth, P. B., & Jernberg, A. M. (2010). *Theraplay: Helping parents and children build better relationships through attachment-based play* (3rd ed.). Jossey-Bass.

Cassidy, S., Gumley, A., & Turnbull, S. (2017). Safety, play, enablement, and active involvement: Themes from a Grounded Theory study of practitioner and client experiences of change processes in Dramatherapy. *The Arts in Psychotherapy, 55*, 174–185. https://doi.org/10.1016/j.aip.2017.05.007

Cassidy, S., Turnbull, S., & Gumley, A. (2014). Exploring core processes facilitating change in Dramatherapy: A grounded theory analysis of published case studies. *The Arts in Psychotherapy, 41*(4), 353–365. https://doi.org/10.1016/j.aip.2014.07.003

Drewes, A., & Schaefer, C. E. (2014). Introduction: How play therapy causes therapeutic change. In C. E. Schaefer & A. A. Drewes (Eds.), *The therapeutic powers of play: 20 core agents of change* (2nd ed., pp. 1–7). John Wiley & Sons.

Emunah, R. (1994). *Acting for real*. Psychology Press.

Feldman, D., Ward, E., Handley, S., & Goldstein, T. R. (2015). Evaluating drama therapy in school settings: 4 case studies of the ENACT programme. *Drama Therapy Review, 1*(2), 127–145.

Feldman, N. (2008). Assisting children in the creation of new life performances: Expanding possibilities for social and emotional development. *Journal of Child & Adolescent Social Work, 25*, 85–97.

Folostina, R., Tudorache, L., Michel, T., Erzsebet, B., Agheana, V., & Hocaoglu, H. (2015). Using play and drama in developing resilience in children at risk. *Procedia: Social and Behavioral Sciences, 197*, 2362–2368. https://doi.org/10.1016/j.sbspro.2015.07.283

Fong, J. (2007). Psychodrama as a preventive measure: Teenage girls confronting violence. *Journal of Group Psychotherapy, Psychodrama, & Sociometry, 59*(3), 99–108.

Godsal, J. (2017). Neurodevelopmental approaches. In R. Houghman & B. Jones (Eds.), *Dramatherapy: Reflections and praxis* (pp. 99–122). Palgrave Macmillan Publishers.

Haen, C. (Ed.). (2011). *Engaging boys in treatment*. Routledge.

James, M., Forrester, A., & Kyongok, C. K. (2005). Developmental transformations in the treatment of sexually abused children. In A. M. Weber & C. Haen (Eds.), *Clinical applications of drama therapy in child and adolescent treatment* (pp. 67–86). Brunner-Routledge.

Johnson, D. R. (2009). Developmental transformations: Toward the body as presence. In R. Emunah & D. R. Johnson (Eds.), *Current approaches in drama therapy* (pp. 89–116). Charles C Thomas.

Jones, P. (1996). *Drama as therapy*. Routledge.

Karatas, Z. (2011). Investigating the effects of group practice performed using psychodrama techniques on adolescents' conflict resolution skills. *Educational Sciences: Theory and Practice, 11*(2), 609–616.

Landy, R. J. (2010). Drama as a means of preventing post-traumatic stress following trauma within a community. *Journal of Applied Arts & Health, 1*(1), 7–18. https://doi.org/10.1386/jaah.1.1.7/1

McNiff, S. (1981). *The arts and psychotherapy*. Charles C Thomas.

Moore, J. (2010). A story to tell: Use of story and drama in work with substitute families. *Dramatherapy, 31*(3), 3–9. https://doi.org/10.1080/02630672.2010.9689781

Nash, E., & Haen, C. (2005). Healing through strength: A group approach to therapeutic enhancement. In A. M. Weber & C. Haen (Eds.), *Clinical applications of drama therapy in child and adolescent treatment* (pp. 121–135). Routledge.

Orkibi, H., Azoulay, B., Snir, S., & Regev, D. (2017). In session behaviours and adolescents' self-concept and loneliness: A psychodrama process-outcome study. *Clinical Psychology & Psychotherapy, 24*(6), O1455–O1463. https://doi.org/10.1002/cpp.2103

Perry, B., & Szalavitz, M. (2006). *The boy who was raised as a dog.* Basic Books.

Reynolds, A. (2011). Developmental transformations: Improvisational drama therapy with children in acute inpatient psychiatry. *Social Work with Groups, 34*(3–4), 296–309. https://doi.org/10.1080/01609513.2011.558820

Schwartz, R. C. (2011). *An introduction to the internal family systems model.* Trailheads Publishing.

Weber, A. M. (2005). "Don't hurt my mommy": Drama therapy for children who have experienced domestic violence. In A. M. Weber & C. Haen (Eds.), *Clinical applications of drama therapy in child and adolescent treatment* (pp. 25–43). Routledge. https://doi.org/10.4324/9780203997666

10

SENSORY PLAY THERAPY

SIOBHÁN PRENDIVILLE

This chapter considers definitions and historical roots for sensory play therapy. It illustrates the critical role of sensory play in establishing safety and facilitating the establishment of a strong therapeutic alliance. Key sensory play techniques and strategies are outlined, and the multiple therapeutic powers of sensory play are highlighted. The case of Alex, a composite sketch that protects confidentiality by changes to names and identifying details, is used to exemplify the therapeutic powers of sensory play therapy.

DEFINING SENSORY PLAY

Essentially, sensory play involves using the body to experience the world through touch, smell, taste, sight, hearing, and movement. It is play that engages one, many, or all of the senses: tactile, olfactory, gustatory, auditory, visual, kinesthetic, vestibular, or visceral (S. Prendiville & Fearn, 2017, pp. 121–122). Usher (2010) defined *sensory play* as "play that provides opportunities for children and young people to use all their senses, or opportunities

https://doi.org/10.1037/0000217-011
Play Therapy With Children: Modalities for Change, H. G. Kaduson and C. E. Schaefer (Editors)

to focus play to encourage the use of one particular sense" (p. 2). Gascoyne (2011) shared a similar definition: "Sensory play differs [from] other types of play in that the sensory focus adds a significant and integral extra dimension to the play" (p. 2).

HISTORICAL ROOTS FOR SENSORY PLAY THERAPY

A definition for *sensory play therapy* does not yet exist; however, as explained next, it is a therapy that makes full use of the therapeutic powers of play by means of activating the child's senses. Other established therapies with a comparable emphasis on the therapeutic value of sensory play are presented next.

Developmental Play Therapy

Brody's (1978, 1993) developmental play therapy is built and based on the curative power of touch. Developmental play therapy is firmly grounded in attachment theory and the bonding process. It is a directive play therapy intervention in which the therapist leads the sessions and focuses on four main areas: "noticing the child, touching the child, responding to the child's cue, and bringing to the attention of the child, in undeniable fashion, the presence of an adult who meets her needs" (Brody, 1993, p. 9). Through creating and delivering these core conditions, Brody proposed that children will begin to "move, feel, think, talk, and above all, to relate to the [developmental play] therapist" (Brody, 1993, p. 23). Hair brushing, applying lotion, feeding, touching, cradling and rocking children, playing simple playful body contact games, hugging, kissing, speaking, and singing are all central sensory play techniques used in this model.

Theraplay

Theraplay (Booth & Jernberg, 2010) is an animated, playful, engaging treatment based on attachment theory that has been validated from a neurodevelopmental perspective. Sensory play and nurturing touch are used consistently in this model to enhance parent–child attachment. Theraplay focuses on modulating sensory input and recognizes the critical need to pay deep attention to the individual child's sensory reactivity level and provide appropriate soothing and/or stimulating sensory input (Munns, 2008, p. 163). Sensory play techniques, including rhythmic movement, song, touch, massage, and feeding, are used in the four Theraplay dimensions: structure, challenge, engagement, and nurture.

Dynamic Play Therapy

Dynamic play therapy (Harvey, 1994) also emphasizes the importance of sensory play when working with children and families. Parents are encouraged to develop more collaborative play with their children. Physical play involving touch is used to increase spontaneous play interactions and attunement. Full body physical activities, music, rhythmic rocking and movement, and play with visually appealing tactile materials are used, particularly when working with young children and their caregivers (Harvey, 2008).

Neuro-Dramatic-Play and Developmental Playtherapy

Jennings (1999) proposed that the body is the primary means of learning; sensory play is critical in both her Neuro-Dramatic-Play (NDP) and developmental playtherapy models. NDP and developmental playtherapy are two interweaving developmental paradigms that uniquely chart the progression of dramatic play from 6 months before birth to 7 years. Jennings (2011) coined *Neuro-Dramatic-Play* to describe the sensory, rhythmic, and dramatic play that takes place between a mother and her unborn or newborn baby. She proposed that NDP principles and techniques can be used in play therapy with children of all ages to enhance and repair attachments. She suggested three components of play: sensory play and messiness, rhythmic play and ritual, and dramatic play and mimicry—work to enhance the primary attachment (Jennings, 2011, p. 78). Each component is firmly grounded in sensory play techniques. The embodiment stage, essential in the development of the "body self," focuses on early physicalized experiences, which are mainly expressed through body movement and the senses. Gross and fine body movement, rhythmic chanting and dancing, sensory movement, and play are paramount.

Sensory Play in Play Therapy or Sensory Play Therapy?

Play therapy relies on the therapeutic powers of play to act as agents of change. Play therapists place significant emphasis on the establishment of a safe, warm, playful, and accepting relationship. The use of sensory play within play therapy is grounded in developmental research on play, attachment theory, and neurobiology, all of which propose that sensory input is necessary to establish safety and regulation, develop play skills, and create and foster secure attachments and meaningful relationships. I propose that the previously undefined term, *sensory play therapy*, makes intentional use of sensory play within the play therapy process to address therapeutic and developmental needs through the application of the therapeutic powers of play. The use of *sensory play therapy* applies only to the portion of the play therapy process in which this intervention is clinically appropriate. The intentional introduction and use of sensory play put the play therapist into the lead, planning appropriate sensory play interventions, interacting with and engaging the child, and possibly their carers, in therapist-led sensory play activities. However, the therapist allows the clients to take the lead and direct the sensory play experiences as they become engaged and engrossed in the process. It is a gentle balancing act, much like we see in healthy parent–child relationships when the parent takes charge of the safety and regulation needs of a child but then can take a step back and allow the child to explore the environment, make discoveries, and create their own learning.

THERAPEUTIC BENEFITS

Without regulation, play capacity is compromised; if children cannot play, they cannot access its wonderful therapeutic powers. Sensory play can be a gateway to children's imaginative play. If age-appropriate regulation is not yet established, sensory play can facilitate the ability to calm or ignite a child's arousal system, allow them to make contact with the play materials and therapist and become fully engrossed and engaged in the play process.

Therapeutic Relationship

Safety is critical in therapy; it is "vital in facilitating the client's engagement and healing" (E. Prendiville, 2017, p. 8). E. Prendiville (2017) identified that feeling safe or unsafe is physiological in nature and is responsive to the environment. She proposed that therapists not only must focus on creating safety through structuring and predictability but also must provide safety cues and introduce interventions that communicate and establish safety through rhythmic sensory-based play interventions (Perry, 2006).

Positive Emotions

"Positive emotions cannot and will not happen unless clients feel safe" (Kottman, 2014, p. 113). Engaging in sensory play can bring not only safety but also a rapid increase in play, playfulness, and mirth. Sensory play is fun and engaging (Beckerleg, 2009), it absorbs the player (Fearn, 2014, p. 116), brings delight (S. Prendiville & Fearn, 2017), and provides for joyful, shared interactions (Sherborne, 2001). Panksepp (1998) told us that play is the major source of joy for our brains. Sensory play engenders positive emotions, a key therapeutic power of play (Kottman, 2014).

Attachment

Providing healthy and productive touch is a critical element in the attachment process (Harlow & Zimmermann, 1959). Sensory play facilitates active engagement of both parties in the parent–child relationship. It brings joy, smiles, and laughter into this crucial relationship; ignites playful connection and fun; and facilitates bonding and attachment (Nelson, 2008). It facilitates right brain to right brain connection, which is a critical component in the development of regulation and attachment (Cozolino, 2010; A. N. Schore, 2005; J. Schore & Schore, 2008). Additionally, the therapist's use of modeling, direct feedback, positive reinforcement, and scaffolding of appropriate responses is critical.

Stress Management and Self-Regulation

Sensory play, including rhythmic and repetitive movement and play with sensory materials, effectively engages the lower brain areas to calm and stimulate the nervous system (Perry, 2006) and positively impact stress modulation. It engages both brain hemispheres and supports regulation, organization, and integration (S. Prendiville & Fearn, 2017, p. 121). Children often will use sensory play for stress reduction without prompting (Bemis, 2014). However, it is also important that the therapist be attuned to each client's arousal levels as well as being on hand to offer prompts, suggestions, and support for soothing or alerting sensory play as clinically appropriate. Through consistent experiences and adult support, the play of clients can enhance the capacity for self-regulation.

Self-Esteem

Sensory play provides rich opportunities for children to experience a sense of control and freedom. The free nature of this play affords opportunities to experiment and explore, create and destroy, make discoveries, and play without any expectation of an end goal. Children learn about their preferences and their competencies through feelings of mastery, power, and control. Physical sensory play also allows children to use their bodies to figure out what they can and cannot do. The therapist can support exploration, delight in the child's discoveries, and acknowledge efforts and achievements. Feelings of self-worth and competence emerge and grow.

Self-Expression

Bennett and Eberts (2014) stated, "No matter what the play therapist's approach might be, an overarching goal of play therapy is to give children the opportunity to express themselves" (p. 16). Axline (1947) believed that play is the most developmentally appropriate means of expression for children. Ginott (1960) asserted that toys are the words of children and play is their language. Pretend play offers children an ideal means of safely expressing thoughts, feelings, and behaviors. The distance provided by play with puppets, props, and make-believe characters helps to create safety, which fosters self-expression (Schaefer, 2012). As a somatic form of play, sensory play can benefit children who have not yet developed imaginative play skills. It offers a safe means of expression and making meaning of experiences.

Access to the Unconscious

Explicit memory is associated with the left hemisphere of the brain. It is both conscious and rational and is accompanied by language that can be used to describe feelings and thoughts and to assign narrative to past events. Implicit memory, on the other hand, is associated with the right hemisphere and is linked to early life experiences, sensory and somatic learning, and trauma memories. Explicit memory activates at around 3 years of age and is associated with the hippocampus. Implicit memory is active from birth and is rooted in the limbic region. Trauma memories are stored as implicit memories (E. Prendiville, 2017, p. 13). Memories are often sensory, somatic, and non-verbal in nature. Sensory-based play interventions can express "the language of the right hemisphere made up of sensory-motor-sensations, kinesthetic and visceral sensations, and visual images" (Crenshaw & Tillman, 2014, p. 27).

Accelerated Psychological Development

Play is a causal agent in children's development (S. Prendiville, 2014), and success in play is critical in a child's holistic development (Stagnitti, 1998). Sensory play is regularly used in interactive play therapy sessions to extend and enrich the client's play. It provides for joint attention and mutual joy and is a wonderful vehicle for two-way interaction (Greenspan & Wieder, 1998, 2006). Sensory play fosters development across all domains, improves play skills, and enables clients to move into projective and role-play (Jennings, 1999).

Creative Problem Solving

Pretend play is often associated with various types of creative problem solving (Russ & Wallace, 2014). Sensory play can also facilitate the development of problem-solving skills. When children make and create sensory play products such as slime, play dough, or imaginary creations, they practice divergent thinking. They generate and explore many possible solutions to problems like sticky dough or activating slime.

Social Competence

Blundon Nash (2014) stated that "developmentally, one of the earliest forms of play in which children engage that promotes acquisition of social skills is rough and tumble play" (p. 187). The therapist can take on the role of the regulated other in rough-and-tumble play and can model and teach parents to do the same. This supports children to remain cheerful, playful, and non-aggressive while engaged in rough-and-tumble play, and thus ensure it has a positive impact on social competence. Joint interactive sensory play can also improve social competence. Through relationships, shared experiences, and participation, children can develop the capacity to take turns, to wait, to pay attention to another, to plan, and to work together.

Empathy

Gaskill (2014) stated, "Empathy is a complex neurobiological process with both affective (low-brain) and cognitive (high-brain) components" (p. 197). Empathy cannot develop in isolation; it is an elaborate neurobiological process that involves many components, including observation, memory, reasoning, and knowledge (Decety & Lamm, 2006). Gaskill (2014) explored how repetitive relational experiences with caregivers and sensory-motor play contribute to the development of empathy. Repetitive sensory motor-play, physical play, and physical nurturing interactions between therapist and child—and parent and child—can provide both cognitive and affective empathic learning. "Sensory-motor play has been shown to have multiple positive outcomes with deeply troubled children including gains in empathic abilities" (Gaskill, 2014, p. 201).

Catharsis

Catharsis allows for the release and completion of previously restrained or interrupted affective release via emotional expression or activity. Sensory play offers ample opportunities for the indirect expression of feelings such as anger, sadness, frustration, and anxiety. The physical nature of much sensory play allows "the release of both muscle tension and negative affect" (Drewes & Schaefer, 2014, p. 74). The fun, joy, and laughter that so often accompany sensory play balance the purging of negative affect and can act as a release for both psychological and physical tension.

Abreaction

In abreactive play, children reenact and relive stressful and traumatic experiences, often in symbolic form, and gain a sense of empowerment over the emotional content that was previously experienced as overwhelming (E. Prendiville, 2014). The unresolved, troublesome, sensory, and somatic elements of implicit memories can safely and gradually emerge in a playful context. Activation of the PLAY system (Panksepp, 1998) allows for engagement with, rather than retreat from, the difficult emotions associated with such memories and allows the child to experience a sense of mastery.

CORE TECHNIQUES

The core techniques associated with sensory play therapy and described next can be used in individual, group, parent and child, and family play therapy sessions.

Physical Play

Body-focused physical play activities, incorporating touch and movement, are central in any sensory play therapy intervention. This type of play does not rely on many play materials or toys; the body is the primary means of learning, and the aim is to get the body moving in many different playful ways. When children engage in self-initiated physical play, the therapist can follow the child's lead and make use of nonintrusive tracking and reflective responses. At other times the therapist can take on a more directive role, structure physical play activities, initiate play ideas, and interactively and playfully engage the child in play.

The following are examples of useful physical play techniques:

- gross body movement: running, climbing, jumping on a trampoline, crawling

- fine body movement: wriggling fingers and toes, pinching and picking things up

- full-body physical activities: incorporate these into moving in and out of small and large spaces—for example, climbing in and out of a large cardboard box

- playful interaction involving basic body movements: for example, action rhymes, dances, crawling alongside a child

- cooperation and resistance play: working with (e.g., both working together to carry objects across the room with each having only one finger touching the item) and working against (e.g., one partner pretends to be superglued to the floor while the other tries to move them) physical play

- games such as Simon Says incorporating gross and fine body movements
- obstacle courses
- crawling and moving through tunnels and tents
- rhythmic rocking and movement
- action songs that include moving, dancing, and naming body parts
- clapping games and songs
- popping bubbles with various body parts
- games encouraging children to move as different creatures (e.g., a lion, a frog, a monster)
- walk, crawl, roll on different textures (e.g., carpet, tiles, grass, sand, mud)
- ball and balloon games: catching, throwing, kicking
- physical play with scarves, dancing to music with scarves or ribbons
- physical play with foam swords
- roll a gym/yoga ball over and back on a child's body

Parent-Child Relational Play

Sensory play, touch, movement, and rhythm are paramount when working on parent–child relational play (S. Prendiville & Fearn, 2017, p. 128). Such play involves sensory play experiences involving touch and massage, gentle blowing, textures and smells, visual movement and colors, sucking and taste, soothing sounds and music, and loving gestures and words provide playful opportunities for human contact, which is a critical element in the attachment process (Harlow & Zimmermann, 1959). Rhythmic play experiences involving movement and rocking, cradling, clapping, humming, chanting, drumming, songs and music with clear rhythms, and finger rhymes provide playful opportunities for parents to develop and strengthen their contingent responsiveness toward the child while helping the child internalize a sense of repetition and predictability (Jennings, 2011). Both qualities have been identified as critical in the development of a secure attachment (Isabella, 1995). Dramatic play experiences incorporating consonant play, echo play, mimicry, mirroring, and singing games and stories incorporating sounds and gestures facilitate the development of synchrony between parent and child, another essential element in the attachment process. Such play also promotes the child's formation of a sense of self-identity and self-esteem and helps to develop the potential for empathy (Jennings, 2011). Consonant play refers to playful experiences in which parent and child are engaged in the same activity. These range from simple movements such as rocking while holding a child, dancing together, having a parent bounce a child on their lap while moving, and humming to mutual kisses and tickles. Echo play, mimicry, and mirroring occur in healthy early parent–baby interactions. The parents can initiate playful ways that encourage a child to echo sounds and movements of the parent, and for the child and parent to imitate each other. This dramatic play enables the child to perform actions and observe their parent performing the same action, an activity that is known to activate mirror neurons (Gallese, 2009). It is now believed that these mirror neurons contribute to a child's ability to understand the behaviors of others and can play an important role in how children learn about the world, how to act, and how to play (Stagnitti, 2009).

When facilitating parent–child relational play in sensory play therapy, therapists will initially adopt a directive role. They will initiate play ideas, model and lead the play, and in time support the parent/caregivers to lead and facilitate the play. Therapists' commentary will give direct feedback to what is happening in the moment. They will notice and comment on the special and unique qualities of the children, the relational moments between child and parent, and work to reframe any cognitive distortions that become apparent during the play. As the play develops and the parent's play facilitation skills strengthen, therapists will shift back into more nonintrusive responses, using tracking and reflective commentary and also esteem-building responses for both child and parent.

The following list provides examples of useful parent–child relational play techniques:

- Theraplay activities (if the therapist is Theraplay trained; Booth & Jernberg, 2010)
- safe massage (upper back, hand, arm, shoulders)
- creating simple story massages, such as the weather massage (Jennings, 2005)
- rhythmic movement games, such as Row Your Boat
- peek-a-boo and hide-and-find games
- swinging the child in a blanket or pulling them around in a blanket
- singing to a child while holding him/rocking him/swinging him in a blanket
- clapping, humming, chanting, drumming together

- joint rhythmic movements, including rocking and cradling
- using songs and rhymes, incorporate actions and movements to, for example, head shoulders knees and toes
- finger rhymes and finger plays (e.g., Round and round the garden like a teddy bear)
- make up personalized songs and stories about the child, tell/sing the songs to the child using sounds and gestures
- mirroring and copying games (can include movement and/or sounds)
- parent and child engagement in physical play (e.g., horsey, piggyback rides, wheelbarrow walks; also see the ideas listed in the previous section)
- parent and child engagement in interactive sensory play (details next)

Interactive Sensory Play

Interactive play is used to help foster and develop reciprocal communication, socioaffective relationship, and play skills in children (Seach, 2007). It focuses on shared attention and mutual joy and is particularly useful for children who have not yet developed imaginative play skills (S. Prendiville, 2014, p. 260). Sensory play strategies are critical in enabling the therapist to connect with these clients, to share communication, and to develop play skills (Seach, 2007) by making use of opportunities to extend and enrich the child's play. The play therapist takes an active role, bringing the therapist's own playfulness and creativity to make the sessions fun, engaging, and stimulating and to motivate the child to play. The use of sensory-based play materials helps to facilitate this and enables the therapist to respond appropriately to the child's reactivity level. The play therapist may demonstrate how materials can be used, model play skills, bring the child to the play space, and act in a playful way. Play starts from where the child is at, using whatever interests them.

The following are useful interactive sensory play techniques:

- peek-a-boo games

- making silly faces and/or blowing raspberries

- play with balloons, bubbles, feathers

- physical contact games

- play with a simple attention grabber kit, which includes a range of sensory play materials (e.g., bubbles, a spinning top, a feather, a glove puppet, a party blower, a yo-yo, a colorful ball, cotton wool balls)

- interactive play with a treasure basket or heuristic play materials

Regulatory Play With Fidgets and Sensory Materials

Sensory play with fidget toys and other sensory materials enables clients to regulate, stimulate their senses, and promote sensory integration (S. Prendiville & Fearn, 2017). Fidget baskets, which include a range of tactile toys that can be moved, stretched, and squeezed, can be included in the play therapy room at each stage of the therapy process. Likewise, regulatory sensory play materials such as colored rice, lentils, pasta, dough, sand, water, and scent bottles/bags are useful at various stages in a child's play therapy process to help establish core state regulation, if necessary. They can also be used as grounding and stress reduction tools to support and facilitate regulation when dysregulation occurs. The therapist may direct a client to some of these regulatory sensory materials, modeling ways in which they can be used and verbalizing their soothing effects. At other times children will simply go to and use the materials themselves. It is critical that the therapist can act as a coregulator and move in to redirect and support soothing/stimulating sensory input when necessary.

The following list presents useful sensory regulatory play materials:

- tactile toys and sensory balls that can be moved, stretched, and squeezed; include a variety of textures and colors to inspire and stimulate children
- colored rice, rice, lentils, spaghetti, split peas, shells, beans, colored sand for tactile play
- scent bags (add scented oils to cotton wool and place in small organza bags)
- lollipops, hard sweets, chewing gum

Messy Play

Expanding sensory play materials to include a wider variety of messy play material and stimuli is also beneficial to children with a wide range of referral issues and can be particularly effective in helping children resolve traumatic experiences and help manage anxiety. Play with gooey, sticky substances such as custard, jelly, cooked spaghetti, shaving cream, whipped cream, gloop, slimes, and homemade dough can be extremely powerful in the play therapy process. In facilitating messy play, the therapist must first have played with and explored all of the materials themselves. It is, as always with sensory play, vital to pay deep attention to the child's responses and reactions and take great care not to bombard the client with too many sensations at one time, and not to force a client to play with or explore any particular media. It is important to start with dry messy play and gradually introduce wetter stimuli. If a client does become overwhelmed or dysregulated, the therapist will move to support regulation through coregulation and appropriate sensory input.

The following are useful messy play materials:

- dry messy play materials: cereals, flour, shredded paper, fake snow, moon-sand, sawdust, sand, crushed biscuits, talcum powder, dried leaves, cous-cous, cocoa powder, cotton wool, popped popcorn

- wet messy play materials: water, jelly, custard, rice pudding, baked beans, cooked spaghetti, mashed potato, whipped cream

- shaving cream, slime, gloop/oobleck, homemade dough (Beckerleg, 2009)

Initially, when children play with sensory and messy play materials, they will explore them on a purely sensorial level, experiencing their unique physical properties and the emotions and sensations they evoke on a physiological level. As the children's play develops, they can begin to play with the materials in a different way, shifting from purely sensory and embodiment play into more "ordered and controlled projective activity" (Jennings, 2014, p. 85). When this occurs naturally in play, the therapist can follow the child's lead, join in when invited and use the therapist's typical responses. At times the play therapist can decide to introduce a sensory-based projective play idea, where the therapist and the client (including family groups) will work together to create something from sensory materials. Useful projective play with sensory material activities include making slime, various play doughs, textured finger paints, glitter cool-down bottles, edible treats, and salt dough creations (e.g., handprints and footprints).

Outdoor Play

The outdoors offers great potential for sensory-rich play experiences. From jumping in muddy puddles to rolling down grassy banks, smelling flowers, kicking autumn leaves, and climbing trees, the possibilities for sensory exploration are endless. Fearn (2014) explored the use of the outdoors as a therapeutic space, presenting key concepts regarding safety and containment and a range of therapeutic play ideas to use with children in the outdoors.

CLINICAL APPLICATIONS

In general, children who have difficulty with regulation and have problems engaging in mutually satisfying relationships would benefit from the use of sensory play in their play therapy process (Jennings, 2011). Diagnostically this would include children with a history of trauma; attachment disruptions (Jennings, 2011); anxiety disorders; sensory-processing disorders (Beckerleg, 2009; Zimmer et al., 2012); autism spectrum disorder (Stagnitti, 1998), attention-deficit/hyperactivity disorder (Ray, 2010), disruptive, impulse control, and conduct disorders (Bemis, 2014; Gaskill, 2014); children with intellectual disabilities or delay (Stagnitti, 1998); and any children with poorly developed play skills (S. Prendiville, 2014; Stagnitti, 2009). Children with coordination disorders (Beckerleg, 2009), elimination disorders (Bemis, 2014), and eating disorders may also find sensory play helpful.

CASE ILLUSTRATION

This case illustration is a composite sketch. At 10 years of age, Alex was referred for play therapy by his parents. They had just received a particularly negative report from Alex's school. At the time of referral, Alex's parents reported major concerns about his impulsive tendencies, anxious disposition, and challenging behaviors. Alex was extremely active, and his parents described him as "being in motion all of the time." He was very impulsive and tended to act out a lot, kicking, hitting, spitting, and shouting at others. His parents noted that he was particularly aggressive toward his younger sister, classmates in school, and his mother. Alex's mother admitted that Alex scared her, as he had physically hurt her on numerous occasions. Alex's teacher reported that he had poor play skills; he found it difficult to join in play with his peers and often ruined their play scenes. His teacher described him as being "argumentative" and "aggressive." Alex's mother noted that he had a very high pain threshold; she said he rarely felt pain and discussed how difficult it was to know when he was sick, as he would not tell her that he felt unwell. Alex also presented as being extremely anxious. He worried about many things such as death, monsters, crime, and also simple things such as what to bring for school lunch, what clothes to wear, and where his dog went when he left the house. Alex's mother described her pregnancy with Alex as being stressful, as her mother was terminally ill at the time. Her mother died when Alex was 3 months old. Alex's mother described how unavailable she was to Alex at this time. She cried at intake as she told the therapist that she often feels guilty about this.

The play therapist worked with Alex and his family over an 8-month period, with a mixture of parent sessions, parent–child sessions, and individual psychotherapy using play therapy sessions for Alex. She also liaised with personnel in Alex's school. Initially, the therapist adopted a client-centered approach. In these sessions, Alex's anxiety was extremely high; he was unable to engage in any play in the room. The therapist decided to shift into using more interactive sensory play techniques with Alex, aiming to facilitate therapeutic alliance and connection, enrich and develop Alex's play skills, and establish the types of sensory input that were soothing and stimulating for Alex. The therapist became more directive in her interactions, introducing physical games, dancing, singing, and rhythmic movement. She would make silly faces and introduce and play with simple attention grabber toys such as a glove puppet, bubbles, balloons, and party blowers. This began to hold Alex's attention; he started to laugh and join in the play. As time passed, he began to take the lead in the games, initiating play ideas in the playroom. He loved exploring the sensory play materials and engaging in physical movement-based play. Throughout these sessions, Alex also spent a great deal of time engaging in self-directed regulatory play with fidget toys and other sensory materials. Bubble blowing; playing with play dough, dry sand, and squidgy toys; bouncing on a gym ball; jumping; and listening to music all proved extremely regulating for him. The therapist and Alex also engaged in lots of joint sensory-play–based projective activities such as making slime, various sensory doughs, glitter bottles, and stress balls and fidgets.

As Alex's play skills developed further, the therapist no longer needed to make use of interactive play strategies. She now shifted into more nonintrusive responding and cofacilitation (Yasenik & Gardner, 2012) when appropriate. The increase in Alex's capacity for self-directed play ensured that he could continue to access the therapeutic powers of play. Alex began to feel empowered, less confused, and more self-assured. Through his play he developed a more positive self-concept and became more self-directing, self-accepting, and self-reliant. He developed coping skills and the ability to use his defenses adaptively.

The therapist used parent–child relational play activities at the start and end of each play therapy session. She introduced interactive games that were based on sensory interaction. Alex was hesitant initially, but he quickly realized these games were fun and soon began to join in easily, really enjoying the special time with his parents. Physical and rhythmic games such as Row Your Boat, piggyback rides, horsey games, and wheelbarrow walks brought laughter, touch, and connection. Cradling, cuddling, and rocking soon followed. Bubble and ball games, simple feather touching games, making up special handshakes, and mirroring and copying games soon became firm favorites too. Simon Says, traffic light games, and Mother May I? came next. Alex particularly loved being pulled around the room in a blanket. After time this moved into his being swung in a blanket while his mother sang him a very special song about how loved and safe he is. The therapist worked with his parents and school to support them in incorporating daily sensory play rituals into both environments. She used information gleaned from Alex's therapy sessions to support them in selecting appropriate regulating play activities.

As the lower brain learns by repetition, it was crucial that Alex experience sensory play daily, not just during his play therapy sessions.

When therapy ended, significant improvements were evident in each of the areas in which Alex had previously struggled. He had many positive relationships in his life, with family and friends, and he was managing comfortably in school and at home.

EMPIRICAL SUPPORT

Compelling findings from the field of neuroscience support and validate the use of sensory play interventions in therapy. The use of repetitive rhythmic activities, such as those incorporating movement, music, touch, and sensory activities, is now known to appropriately activate lower regions of the brain (Gaskill & Perry, 2014; Jennings, 2011; Malchiodi, 2014; Perry, 2006). The brain develops in a hierarchical fashion, and regulation in the lower region of the brain supports the development and integration of the interconnected functions of the brain. When working with children and teenagers who have experienced trauma and/or developmental difficulties, it is vital that we work on regulating the lower regions of the bran through sensory-based, repetitive, rhythmical activities before engaging in more cognitive-play-based approaches.

Human contact is recognized as a critical element in the attachment process (Booth & Jernberg, 2010; Harlow & Zimmermann, 1959; Jennings, 2011; Sori & Schnur, 2013; Whelan & Stewart, 2014). Encouragingly sensory play techniques provide ample opportunities to engage parents and their children in touch in playful, engaging, and fun ways.

In addition to the neuroscience evidence, therapeutic interventions that incorporate sensory play techniques have been found to be beneficial. In particular, Theraplay has achieved evidence-based status. It has been accepted by the U.S. Substance Abuse and Mental Health Services Administrator for inclusion on the National Registry for Evidence-based Programs and Practices (The Theraplay Institute, n.d.).

A study investigating sensory integration therapies for children with developmental and behavioral difficulties (Zimmer et al., 2012) examined occupational therapists' use of sensory-based therapies and concluded that such therapy may be acceptable as one of the components of a comprehensive treatment plan. Roberts et al. (2018) investigated the relationship between sensory processing and pretend play in typically developing children. They found that sensory-processing factors of body awareness, balance, touch and social participation were predictive of the quality of children's pretend play.

Ryan et al. (2017) explored the successful use of trauma-informed play therapy, incorporating a range of sensory play techniques in conjunction with filial therapy and a therapeutic classroom when working with children who have experienced trauma. They concluded that each of these "are essential to reverse the behavior patterns established by these early experiences [trauma] and should include multiple somatosensory relationally safe experiences" (p. 120).

SUMMARY AND CONCLUSION

This chapter has highlighted the main sensory play approaches that can be applied by play therapists. The critical role of sensory play in establishing safety and facilitating the establishment of a strong therapeutic alliance was explored, as were the multiple therapeutic powers of sensory play. Key sensory play techniques and strategies were outlined, and a working definition of sensory play therapy was presented.

REFERENCES

Axline, V. A. (1947). *Play therapy*. Ballantine Books.

Beckerleg, T. (2009). *Fun with messy play: Ideas and activities for children with special needs*. Jessica Kingsley Publishers.

Bemis, K. (2014). Stress management. In C. E. Schaefer & A. A. Drewes (Eds.), *The therapeutic powers of play: 20 core agents of change* (2nd ed., pp. 143–152). John Wiley & Sons.

Bennett, M. M., & Eberts, S. (2014). Self-expression. In C. E. Schaefer & A. A. Drewes (Eds.), *The therapeutic powers of play: 20 core agents of change* (2nd ed., pp. 11–24). John Wiley & Sons.

Blundon Nash, J. (2014). Social competence. In C. E. Schaefer & A. A. Drewes (Eds.), *The therapeutic powers of play: 20 core agents of change* (2nd ed., pp. 185–195). John Wiley & Sons.

Booth, P. B., & Jernberg, A. M. (2010). *Theraplay: Helping parents and children build better relationships through attachment-based play* (3rd ed.). John Wiley & Sons.

Brody, V. A. (1978, November). Developmental play: A relationship-focused program for children. *Child Welfare, 57*(9), 591–599.

Brody, V. A. (1993). *The dialogue of touch: Developmental play therapy*. Developmental Play Training Associates.

Cozolino, L. (2010). *The neuroscience of psychotherapy: Healing the social brain*. W. W. Norton.

Crenshaw, D., & Tillman, K. (2014). Access to the unconscious. In C. E. Schaefer & A. A. Drewes (Eds.), *The therapeutic powers of play: 20 core agents of change* (2nd ed., pp. 25–38). John Wiley & Sons.

Decety, J., & Lamm, C. (2006). Human empathy through the lens of social neuroscience. *The Scientific World Journal, 6*, 1146–1163. https://doi.org/10.1100/tsw.2006.221

Drewes, A., & Schaefer, C. E. (2014). Catharsis. In C. E. Schaefer & A. A. Drewes (Eds.), *The therapeutic powers of play: 20 core agents of change* (2nd ed., pp. 71–81). John Wiley & Sons.

Fearn, M. (2014). Working therapeutically with groups in the outdoors: A natural space for healing. In E. Prendiville & J. Howard (Eds.), *Play therapy today: Contemporary practice for individuals, groups and carers* (pp. 113–129). Routledge. https://doi.org/10.4324/9780203740286-8

Gallese, V. (2009). Mirror neurons, embodied simulation, and neural basis of social identification. *Psychoanalytic Dialogues, 19*(5), 519–536. https://doi.org/10.1080/10481880903231910

Gascoyne, S. (2011). *Sensory play: Play in the EYFS*. MA Education.

Gaskill, R. (2014). Empathy. In C. E. Schaefer & A. A. Drewes (Eds.), *The therapeutic powers of play: 20 core agents of change* (2nd ed., pp. 195–207). John Wiley & Sons.

Gaskill, R., & Perry, B. D. (2014). The neurobiological power of play: Using the neurosequential model of therapeutics to guide play in the healing process. In C. Malchiodi & D. A. Crenshaw (Eds.), *Play and creative arts therapy for attachment trauma* (pp. 178–194). Guilford Press.

Ginott, H. G. (1960). A rationale for selecting toys in play therapy. *Journal of Consulting Psychology, 24*(3), 243–246. https://doi.org/10.1037/h0043980

Greenspan, S. I., & Wieder, S. (1998). *The child with special needs: Encouraging intellectual and emotional growth*. DaCapo Press.

Greenspan, S. I., & Wieder, S. (2006). *Engaging autism: Using the floortime approach to help children relate, communicate, and think*. DaCapo Press.

Harlow, H. F., & Zimmermann, R. R. (1959). Affectional responses in the infant monkey; orphaned baby monkeys develop a strong and persistent attachment to inanimate surrogate mothers. *Science, 130*(3373), 421–432. https://doi.org/10.1126/science.130.3373.421

Harvey, S. A. (1994). Dynamic play therapy: Expressive play interventions with families. In K. O'Connor & C. E. Schaefer (Eds.), *Handbook of play therapy, advances and innovations* (Vol. 2, pp. 85–110). John Wiley & Sons.

Harvey, S. A. (2008). Dynamic play with very young children. In C. E. Schaefer, S. Kelly-Zion, J. McCormick, & A. Ohnogi (Eds.), *Play therapy for very young children* (pp. 3–23). Jason Aronson.

Isabella, R. A. (1995). The origins of infant–mother attachment: Maternal behaviour and infant development. *Annals of Child Development, 10*, 57–81.

Jennings, S. (1999). *Introduction to developmental play therapy*. Jessica Kingsley Publishers.

Jennings, S. (2005). *Creative play with children at risk*. Speechmark.

Jennings, S. (2011). *Healthy attachments and neuro-dramatic-play*. Jessica Kingsley Publishers.

Jennings, S. (2014). Applying an Embodiment-Projection-Role framework in group-work with children. In E. Prendiville & J. Howard (Eds.), *Play therapy today: Contemporary practice for individuals, groups, and carers* (pp. 81–96). Routledge.

Kottman, T. (2014). Positive emotions. In C. E. Schaefer & A. A. Drewes (Eds.), *The therapeutic powers of play: 20 core agents of change* (2nd ed., pp. 103–120). John Wiley & Sons.

Malchiodi, C. A. (2014). Neurobiology, creative interventions and childhood trauma. In C. Malchiodi (Ed.), *Creative interventions with traumatized children* (2nd ed., pp. 3–23). Guilford Press.

Munns, E. (2008). Theraplay with zero- to three-year-olds. In C. E. Schaefer, S. Kelly-Zion, J. McCormick, & A. Ohnogi (Eds.), *Play therapy for very young children* (pp. 157–170). Jason Aronson.

Nelson, J. (2008). Laugh and the world laughs with you: An attachment perspective on the meaning of laughter in psychotherapy. *Clinical Social Work Journal, 36*(1), 41–49. https://doi.org/10.1007/s10615-007-0133-1

Panksepp, J. (1998). *Affective neuroscience: The foundations of human and animal emotions*. Oxford University Press.

Perry, B. D. (2006). Applying principles of neurodevelopment to clinical work with maltreated and traumatized children. In N. B. Webb (Ed.), *Working with traumatized youth in child welfare* (pp. 27–52). Guilford Press.

Prendiville, E. (2014). Abreaction. In C. E. Schaefer & A. A. Drewes (Eds.), *The therapeutic powers of play: 20 core agents of change* (2nd ed., pp. 83–103). John Wiley & Sons.

Prendiville, E. (2017). Neurobiology for psychotherapists. In E. Prendiville & J. Howard (Eds.), *Creative psychotherapy: Applying the principles of neurobiology to play and expressive arts-based practice* (pp. 7–20). Routledge.

Prendiville, S. (2014). Accelerated psychological development. In C. E. Schaefer & A. A. Drewes (Eds.), *The therapeutic powers of play: 20 core agents of change* (2nd ed., pp. 255–268). John Wiley & Sons.

Prendiville, S., & Fearn, M. (2017). Coming alive: Finding joy through sensory play. In E. Prendiville & J. Howard (Eds.), *Creative psychotherapy: Applying the principles of neurobiology to play and expressive arts-based practice* (pp. 121–137). Routledge.

Ray, D. (2010). Play therapy for children exhibiting ADHD. In J. N. Baggerly, D. C. Ray, & S. C. Bratton (Eds.), *Child-centered play therapy research: The evidence base for effective practice* (pp. 145–162). John Wiley & Sons.

Roberts, T., Stagnitti, K., Brown, T., & Bhopti, A. (2018). Relationship between sensory processing and pretend play in typically developing children. *The American Journal of Occupational Therapy, 72*(1), 1, 8.

Russ, S. W., & Wallace, C. E. (2014). Creative problem solving. In C. E. Schaefer & A. A. Drewes (Eds.), *The therapeutic powers of play: 20 core agents of change* (2nd ed., pp. 213–225). John Wiley & Sons.

Ryan, K., Lane, S. J., & Powers, D. (2017). A multidisciplinary model for treating complex trauma in early childhood. *International Journal of Play Therapy, 26*(2), 111–123. https://doi.org/10.1037/pla0000044

Schaefer, C. E. (2012). *The therapeutic powers of play* [Unpublished manuscript].

Schore, A. N. (2005). Back to basics: Attachment, affect regulation, and the developing right brain: Linking developmental neuroscience to pediatrics. *Pediatrics in Review, 26*(6), 204–217. https://doi.org/10.1542/pir.26-6-204

Schore, J., & Schore, A. (2008). Modern attachment theory: The central role of affect regulation in development and treatment. *Clinical Social Work Journal, 36*(1), 9–20. https://doi.org/10.1007/s10615-007-0111-7

Seach, D. (2007). *Interactive play for children with autism*. Routledge.

Sherborne, V. (2001). *Developmental movement for children: Mainstream, special needs and pre-school* (2nd ed.). Worth Publishing.

Sori, C. F., & Schnur, S. (2013). Integrating a neurosequential approach to the treatment of traumatized children: An interview with Eliana Gil, Part II. *The Family Journal, 22*(2), 251–257.

Stagnitti, K. (1998). *Learn to play. A program to develop a child's imaginative play skills*. Co-ordinates Publications.

Stagnitti, K. (2009). Play intervention: The learn to play program. In K. Stagnitti & R. Cooper (Eds.), *Play as therapy* (pp. 87–101). Jessica Kingsley Publishers.

The Theraplay Institute. (n.d.). *Research.* https://theraplay.org/what-is-theraplay/research/

Usher, W. (2010). *Sensory play resource book.* Kids.

Whelan, W. F., & Stewart, A. L. (2014). Attachment. In C. E. Schaefer & A. A. Drewes (Eds.), *The therapeutic powers of play: 20 core agents of change* (2nd ed., pp. 171–183). John Wiley & Sons.

Yasenik, L., & Gardner, K. (2012). *Play therapy dimensions model: A decision making guide for integrative play therapists.* Jessica Kingsley Publishers.

Zimmer, M., Desch, L., Section on Complementary and Integrative Medicine, Council on Children with Disabilities, & the American Academy of Pediatrics. (2012). Sensory integration therapies for children with developmental and behavioral disorders. *Pediatrics, 129*(6), 1186–1189. https://doi.org/10.1542/peds.2012-0876

11
CLAY PLAY THERAPY

JULIE MEIGHAN

Since the establishment of play therapy, clay has always been an important tool for therapists (Landreth, 2012; White, 2006). Clay is engaging and invites sensory interaction. It allows children to express their creativity as well as enabling them to articulate their thoughts and feelings in a nonverbal way. Children are naturally attracted to clay and are drawn to its visual appeal. It is a strong expressive medium and is ideal for enhancing children's development and holistic learning (Henley, 2002; Landreth, 2012; White, 2006). Sherwood (2004) propounded that clay therapy has significant potential to influence the therapeutic process; however, Goryl's survey (as cited in Sherwood, 2004) indicates that only 25% of therapists used clay in their practice, whereas 99% of therapists stated that clay was therapeutic. Although many therapists acknowledge the therapeutic benefits of clay, it is not present in many play therapy rooms, as it is perceived to be a messy material by both the client and the therapist (Bratton & Ferebee, 1999). Oaklander (1978) posited that individuals who do not connect with their senses struggle to recognize and express their emotions. The anxiety of touching the clay or making a mess using clay should be investigated further by therapists, as it could be intrinsically linked to an individual's emotional well-being. Moreover,

https://doi.org/10.1037/0000217-012
Play Therapy With Children: Modalities for Change, H. G. Kaduson and C. E. Schaefer (Editors)

Souter-Anderson (2010) claimed that clay is not widely available in play therapy practices because therapists lack confidence in handling and manipulating the material. Clay is a resource that holds great promise. The discourse on clay in play therapy needs to be explored fully for practitioners to understand and demarcate clay within the field of play therapy.

This chapter identifies the therapeutic benefits of clay and discusses its clinical application in a play therapy context. A variety of practical clay therapy techniques are suggested in conjunction with a case study that helps illustrate the therapeutic powers of clay. There is a paucity of research, articles, and books on the use of clay in play therapy (Sherwood, 2004; Sholt & Gavron, 2006; Souter-Anderson, 2010); however, relevant empirical evidence related to clay therapy is identified and examined in this chapter.

THERAPEUTIC BENEFITS

Drewes and Schaefer (2014) identified 20 core therapeutic powers of play across all play therapy models. "The therapeutic powers of play refers to the specific changes in which play initiates, facilitates their therapeutic effect. These play powers act as mediators that positively influence the desired change in clients" (Drewes & Schaefer, 2014, p. 2). Clay can activate therapeutic powers that can encourage self-expression, connect the conscious to the unconscious, foster catharsis, and improve attachment bonds.

Self-Expression

Young children have difficulty expressing their conscious thoughts and feelings because of a lack of vocabulary and limited abstract thinking. The malleability and physical qualities of clay facilitate self-expression, as clay can embody a symbolic or a concrete shape (Kimport & Robbins, 2012). Once the form has emerged from the clay, it may become fixed and permanent, crushed or rolled. It is clay's physical qualities that enable children to shape the substance into tangible, defined representations. These representations may have significant emotional importance attached to them (Sholt & Gavron, 2006; Woltmann, 1993). The three-dimensionality of the clay allows children to express their thoughts and ideas. It affords children the opportunity to observe different sculptures from more than one angle or perspective, which may in turn alter, influence, clarify, or modify their views (Jørstad, 1965; Sholt & Gavron, 2006). It is through self-expression that children resolve and explore their internal conflicts and experiences (Erickson, 1977).

The transformative nature of clay enables it to represent metaphorical symbols, which can evoke inner emotions and memories (Anderson, 1995).

By using the clay to create metaphors, which are symbolic representations of thoughts and feelings, children can connect their conscious with their unconscious. Through symbols and metaphors, children can convey dynamics and capture meaning that is beyond the capacity to conceptualize and articulate through language (Sunderland, 2003). Working with clay during therapy is an effective way of confronting serious emotional issues, as it enables children to express their feelings in a way they can control, transform, or destroy. Acceptance of metaphors during play therapy deepens the therapeutic relationship between a child and therapist and facilitates the therapeutic process.

Access to the Unconscious

Touch is the most fundamental of human experiences, and tactile contact is the first mode of communication that babies learn (Winnicott, 1971). Clay is an intense sensory experience of touching and haptic involvement that can link clients to a preverbal stage in their life where their core attachment is formed (Elbrecht, 2013). Nez (1991) used clay to facilitate healing with adults who had experienced traumatic and abusive childhoods. He found that clay encouraged a more spontaneous and less control expression and response than other art mediums and that it connected his clients with primitive sensations and emotions. According to Damasio (2010), preverbal trauma memories are primarily stored and processed in the amygdala part of the brain. These memories of traumatic events are often not conscious and cannot be recalled automatically. Body movement and touch are interlinked when molding clay as feelings move through the hands into the clay, making the invisible visible. According to Oaklander (1978), real memories and the path to the unconscious can be unlocked through touch and movement. The physical and sensual experience that the clay facilitates may be helpful for children who are defensive or lack the ability or confidence to verbally express themselves (Sholt & Gavron, 2006).

Catharsis

Clay is an earthy substance that is cathartic in nature. Catharsis allows for the discharge of previously restrained and interrupted affective release via emotional expression such as pounding, kneading, or squashing the clay (Drewes & Schaefer, 2014). Clay play therapy provides the child with a medium to work through issues such as anger, grief, and fear and facilitate the therapeutic process. When children feel frozen, angry, or overwhelmed by life challenges, the therapeutic qualities of clay provide a safe place for releasing repressed feelings and emotions and discarding old, destructive, or unproductive habits. Some children find clay soothing, and it can be useful for releasing tension; others use it as a safe outlet to express frustration and aggression (Sholt & Gavron, 2006). When using clay to promote an emotional release, play therapists should ensure that it is "preceded and followed with emotional and cognitive support designed for insight, integration, reframing, and re-education" (Drewes & Schaefer, 2014, p. 77).

Attachment

Traumatic childhood experiences can have a serious impact on a child's brain function. The connection between the two cerebral hemispheres can be severely affected (Gerhardt, 2015; Siegel & Bryson, 2012). Emotional and cognitive regulation is interrupted and often does not develop because of very early childhood traumatic events (Elbrecht, 2013). According to Elbrecht (2015), secure attachment manifests as balance in a child, whereas insecure attachment such as divorce, death, or abandonment causes imbalance. In her work in the Clay Field, Elbrecht (2015) stated that imbalance occurs when children use only one hand when manipulating the clay. The use of clay in therapy can have a positive influence on a child's brain by assisting them to address imbalances. By using both hands simultaneously in the creative therapeutic process, clay can help to stimulate and connect the left and right brain hemispheres (Malchiodi, 2015; Meijer-Degen & Lansen, 2006).

Clay's constructive and deconstructive qualities allow children to understand object constancy (Winnicott, 1971). Object constancy is the emotional equivalent of object permanence and is considered a cognitive skill that children develop between 2 and 3 years of age. It occurs when children start to realize that an emotional bond is maintained with an absent person even when that person cannot be seen, touched, or sensed (Piaget, 1962). Clay play therapy enables children to represent and prepare "for the real world as a continuum of constant change of encounter and separation, of comings and goings of loved ones and event, of endings and beginnings" (Elbrecht, 2013, p. 15). Clay is a primal ancient material that originates from the earth. The earth is the root of all, hence working with clay offers a powerful and therapeutic experience (Sherwood, 2004; White, 2006).

CORE TECHNIQUES

Clay can be an effective therapeutic intervention in both nondirective and directive play therapy. The most appropriate types of natural clay used for play therapy are terra-cotta (red) clay and buff (gray) clay. However, man-made substitutes such as Play-Doh, Plasticine, Silly Putty, or Model Magic may be used instead. Edible clays are also an option, particularly for younger children. The various substances have different qualities. For example, Silly Putty is beneficial for stress relief and relaxation, but it is difficult to shape, whereas natural clays are easy to manipulate into different forms; however, they tend to harden quickly. Some children may be drawn to the stickiness of natural clay, whereas others may prefer not to touch the clay directly but instead elect to use it with the carving tools, cutters, or other materials. Offering many types of clay or clay substitutes in the play therapy room is helpful to children who have different sensory preferences. The following materials/resources may be included in the play therapy room:

- natural clay/man-made alternatives: Play-Doh, Silly Putty, Model Magic, Plasticine, edible clay
- rolling pin
- clay board/smooth surface
- water—put in a spray bottle; water can be used to moisten the clay to soften it or just to give it a wetter consistency
- carving tools: plastic knives, spoons, popsicle sticks
- an assortment of shape cutters—shapes that represent real and imaginary worlds and convey symbolic meaning
- garlic press
- potato masher
- pounding tools: hammer, mallet
- art materials: pencils, markers, pipe cleaners, google eyes, pompoms, feathers, gems, craft sticks, toothpicks
- cloth/sponge—to clean hands
- clay wire cutters
- plastic bucket—a place to put discarded clay
- access to a sink, if possible, as some children may become anxious because of the clay's messy nature

The following sections present core nondirective/directive clay therapy techniques that can be used in play therapy practice.

Free Clay Play Technique

The play therapist invites the child to choose a piece of clay and then offers him a basket of suitable tools. The child's imagination is stimulated by handling the clay. He can freely touch, feel, pat, and manipulate the lump of clay. This can lead to sensory play, which can relieve the child's stress levels, help him to relax, and increase his sense of well-being. If he wishes, he can assign meaning to the lump of clay. The important aspect of this approach is that the child leads the way and the play therapist follows. The child can mold the clay in silence, or he can reflect on its appearance, texture, size. This technique helps establish a positive and safe therapeutic relationship between the child and the therapist.

Mirroring Technique

The child chooses to take some clay. The therapist copies the child's actions with the clay. For example, if the child forcefully throws the clay on the table, the therapist does the same with similar force. The mirroring technique promotes empathy and is very effective for deepening the therapeutic relationship between the child and the therapist.

Make Friends With the Clay Technique

The therapist invites the child to choose a piece of clay and make friends with it (Geldard, Geldard, & Foo, 2018; Oaklander, 1978). She explores and examines the texture, size, and appearance carefully. The therapist can give the child a series of instructions, such as the following:

- Flatten the clay.
- Fold the clay.
- Break it up into little pieces.
- Roll into a ball.
- Turn it into a snake.

The child is given the opportunity to tell the therapist what it was like to make friends with her clay and discuss her favorite part of the task. When the session is finished, it is important that the therapist gives the child a choice about what she wants to do with the clay. She might want to deconstruct it, or she might leave it where it is or keep it safe so she can use it in her next play therapy session. All options should be available to the child. Oaklander (1978) suggested playing music during this technique.

Family Sculpture Technique

The child uses the clay to shape abstract versions of his family members. The therapist suggests that he situate the members in a manner that signifies the family dynamics. The child could discuss the reasons for his sculpting choices and location. If the child feels comfortable, he could perform a role-play where the different sculptures interact with one another (Malchiodi, 2015). This technique is useful in determining family dynamics, including "the exclusions, alliances, coalitions, conflict, boundaries, and strengths in the family system" (Banker, 2008, p. 296).

Self-Sculpting Technique

This technique is effective with older children or teenagers when they are at a developmental stage where self-confidence and self-esteem are being established. The therapist invites the child or adolescent to create a mold of herself from the clay. The mold can be abstract or concrete. Once the mold is completed, the therapist invites the child or adolescent to talk about her creation. This technique allows the child or adolescent to verbally identify and express her inner thoughts and feelings as well, giving the therapist insight into her self-awareness, self-image, and self-concept.

Personification Technique

The therapist encourages the child to make a clay mold of her choosing. The mold can be a human, an animal, or an inanimate object. Once the clay sculpture is completed, the therapist invites the child to talk to her sculpt. For example, if she created a dragon, she could speak to it about why it feels the need to breathe fire. If the child feels comfortable, the therapist can invite the child to answer as the dragon (Souter-Anderson, 2015). By creating a dialogue with the clay, the child reveals information about the sculpture and herself, which can result in the child reflecting on positive aspects of herself as well as recognizing and expressing blocked emotions and feelings. When facilitating this technique, it is very important that the therapist is fully present, as unexpected answers are often given.

Smash Technique

The child makes from the clay an object, person, or symbol that makes him angry. The therapist instructs the child to smash the clay sculpture with his fists or with one of the pounding tools previously listed. This technique is useful for the therapist to understand the source of the child's anger, and it shows him how to release his emotions in an appropriate way.

CLINICAL APPLICATIONS

Clay is used therapeutically with children who experience grief and loss (Sherwood, 2004; Souter-Anderson, 2015). Henley (2002) explored the subject of clay and loss in his book *Clayworks in Art Therapy: Plying the Sacred Circle*. Children who experience loss by being separated or abandoned by a parent or family member through divorce or death can use clay to express or project the agony, anger, sadness, and frustration that is associated with their mourning and grief. Due to its three-dimensional nature, clay can be used more effectively than other two-dimensional art materials, such as painting or drawing, to represent a concrete image or symbol of whom or what was lost. This provides children with the opportunity to recount and explore their loss in a safe and supportive manner. Physical activities such as punching, dismantling, or throwing clay pieces can lead to a release of repressed emotions associated with the grief; this can facilitate an increase in a child's psychological well-being.

All children experience some level of anxiety during childhood, but generally these anxieties are natural and transient. If a child experiences excessive worry, distress, or fear that is disproportionate to the situation and inappropriate for the child's age and level of development, it is a cause for concern. Anxiety in children manifests itself in a variety of disorders such as panic disorders, general anxiety disorder, social phobia, obsessive-compulsive disorder, or selective mutism. Clay manipulation in therapeutic practice is soothing and can provide a relaxing and cathartic experience. It can reduce tension and stress by facilitating emotional expression while promoting well-being and decreasing emotional responses (Kimport & Robbins, 2012; Sholt & Gavron, 2006).

Clay involves touching, which is a primal mode of expression and communication. (Bowlby, 1969, 1980). The sense of touch is closely linked to early attachments, as it is the primary nonverbal way a baby relates to its mother. *Attachment* is the bond that develops between a baby and its primary caregiver, and it is characterized by the interaction patterns, which develop to fulfill the infants' needs and emotional development. An insecure attachment in early life can have a variety of detrimental effects on a child, such as depression, anxiety, aggression, low self-esteem, or other emotional issues. These difficulties can filter through to adulthood (Bowlby, 1969, 1980). Souter-Anderson (2010) stated that many therapists see their clients' relationship with clay as a metaphor for their attachments with different people in their lives. The medium of clay has its own specific qualities, and "it responds and reacts and has to be grappled with, in the same way as a human relationship does if it is to progress" (Ward, 1999, p. 112). Using clay in play therapy can not only help children to explore their early attachment bonds but also allow them to examine and explore their current relationships.

Working with clay can be rewarding for children who are hesitant about their creativity. Clay is the most malleable, flexible, and transformative of all art material, which affords children the opportunity to manage and manipulate it without fear of failure. This makes it a suitable material to use with children who need to increase their self-confidence and develop a stronger self-concept (Bratton & Ferebee, 1999; Henley, 2002). When using clay during play therapy, the play therapist does not enforce any expectations or boundaries on the child; he can express himself freely in a confident manner and without restraint. An important aspect of using clay within the therapeutic process is that it provides children with unlimited opportunities to create and enables them to produce lasting pieces. This permanency of creation promotes confidence and self-efficacy, which consequently enhances a child's self-esteem. When functional pieces are produced (e.g., cups, bowls), children see themselves as capable of engaging in a truly purposeful activity (Schaefer & Kaduson, 2006). Projective techniques such as clay sculpting or personification are effective in helping children explore their negative self-image in order to boost their self-esteem (Oaklander, 1978). Clay also arouses tactile and kinaesthetic senses; consequently, it can help children reconnect with repressed sensory and emotional experiences, which can result in their expressing their feelings and thoughts in a more confident manner (Geldard et al., 2018).

Clay provides a powerful intervention to work through many core issues and advance the therapeutic process in a group setting (Anderson, 1995; Nez, 1991). In a study carried out by Sweeney and Thomas (as cited in Souter-Anderson, 2010), clay was the second most popular medium after sandtray work used in group play therapy. Using clay in group play therapy with children helps them coprocess their own experience as well as others in the group. The tangible product makes interaction and feedback easier, as children will often exchange ideas and suggestions on how something can be made; being able to show another child how to make something can be particularly rewarding (White, 2006). Clay in group play therapy promotes and develops children's intrapersonal and interpersonal skills in a creatively mutual environment and should be included in all group play therapy practices.

CASE ILLUSTRATION

John was a 10-year-old boy.[1] He had suffered the loss of his grandmother the year before he started play therapy. He was her only grandchild, and they had a special bond. He was deeply saddened by her death. He was referred to play therapy because he was increasingly isolating himself from his classmates, friends, and parents. He was a bright student, but his schoolwork was deteriorating, as he was finding it difficult to concentrate. His parents were

---

[1]Permission to use the client's history and treatment was granted by his father, and confidentiality is protected in this chapter by changes to names and identifying details.

concerned about his lack of interaction, and he was becoming increasingly aggressive toward them. He refused to eat with them or engage with them beyond a superficial level. He was spending most of his time playing games on his Sony PlayStation. If they tried to take it from him, he would become very angry and hostile.

John was initially contracted to attend play therapy for 10 sessions. Of the initial 10 play therapy sessions, he used the clay six times. Although John had agreed to come to play therapy during the first session, there was a sense of reticence about the process. He entered the room and said very little except that most of the toys were too young for him. It was during this initial session that he first used the clay. He felt that it was one of the few age-appropriate materials. He sat at a table and broke off a lump of clay, then spent the session rolling it into a ball and then into a large snake. Throughout the session, the more he touched and manipulated the clay, the more he started to visibly relax, At the end of the session he smashed the lump and put it back with the rest of the clay. He said, "I'm not good at making stuff, but I liked this. It's smooth and cool and nice to touch."

During his third session, he used the clay again. He rolled it up into a ball. He stood up and fired it at the whiteboard. He did it again and then enthusiastically drew a shooting target bull's-eye on the board. His throws got more and more forceful as the session progressed. His anger and frustration were visibly being projected to the board. He turned around to the therapist, handed her a lump of clay, and said, "You try it. It's fun." At the end of the session, he said, "We enjoyed that, didn't we?" It was during this session that the therapist felt a therapeutic relationship was beginning to develop. He used the clay again in the following session. He had devised a game in which he would gain points if he hit certain targets on the board.

During the sixth play therapy session, John used the clay to make a face that showed no emotion. He studied it and began to change the shape of the mouth to display different emotions. While he was changing the different emotions on the mouth, he started to open up about his loss. He spoke freely about his grandmother and how much he loved her and how upset he was when she died. He spoke about his mother: "She got to say goodbye to her, but I didn't. She wouldn't let me." His grandmother had died of cancer, and his mother thought it would be too upsetting for him to see her in her last few days, as she was in a coma. He was very angry that he had not been able to say goodbye. He smashed and punched the face and said, "I told you, I can't make anything. I'm not good at it." He left the play therapy room without saying anything further.

During the ninth session, he used the clay again. He wanted to make a vase. He said his grandmother's favorite thing was flowers, and he would often pick them for her. He concentrated carefully while he was making it. He said very little throughout the process. At the end of the session, he asked if he could keep it in the playroom until the following week, as he wanted to decorate it. This was the first time during his therapy that he asked to keep anything that he had made. He had always thrown his artwork away. The following week, which was the final session, he decorated the vase and carved his grandmother's initials and his initials into the center of it. He was very proud of his creation and asked to take it home. At the end of the play therapy sessions, his class teacher noticed that he was interacting more with his classmates and his concentration and listening skills had improved. His parents reported that he had started to eat meals and was more engaged in family life.

EMPIRICAL SUPPORT

There is a lack of empirical studies for the therapeutic uses of clay. Much of the literature on clay therapy is based on case studies and anecdotal evidence. The empirical studies have gathered data that suggest clay therapy is effective in reducing anxiety, improving resilience, and alleviating depression.

A few relevant studies examine the link between clay therapy and the reduction of anxiety symptoms in children. Rahmani and Moheb (2010) examined the effectiveness of clay therapy and narrative therapy on the anxiety of 30 preschool children. Thirty 6-year-olds who were suffering from anxiety disorder were recruited. The children were divided and randomly assigned to one of three groups: a clay therapy group, a narrative therapy group, and a control group. Ten clay therapy and narrative therapy group sessions ran over a 5-week period. The results revealed there was a significant reduction in anxiety levels and symptoms in both the clay therapy and narrative groups compared with the control group, in which there was an increase in anxiety levels. There was no difference in the reduction of anxiety levels between the two experimental groups. Rahmani and Moheb's findings are supported by an Indonesian study that examined the anxiety levels of 20 preschool children who were hospitalized in October 2018. Prior to their play therapy sessions using Play-Doh, 85% of respondents experienced moderate to severe anxiety, but after the therapy sessions were completed a significant reduction in anxiety levels was recorded; 85% of the respondents experienced mild anxiety, and 15% (three) of the respondents experienced moderate anxiety.

Kimport and Robbins (2012) supported the preceding studies. They carried out the first randomized control trial, which examined the efficacy of clay work in improving mood. The 102 adult participants were randomly divided into four groups. One group created a pinch pot out of clay, the second group freely manipulated the clay, the third group tossed and caught a stress ball in the air, and the final group freely manipulated a stress ball. Results of the study showed that the clay groups were found to be significantly more effective in reducing anxiety and enhancing mood than either of the stress ball groups. The findings also revealed that creating a pinch pot—a structured activity—was more beneficial in reducing anxiety compared with free manipulation of clay, an unstructured activity. The study was limited by several factors: The intervention was not therapeutic or conducted by a qualified therapist, there was a lack of emotional disorders present among the participants, and the exposure period was brief.

Nan and Ho (2017) conducted the first randomized control trial that investigated the effectiveness of clay art therapy (CAT). The study included 106 adult participants, all of whom were diagnosed with major depressive disorder by a psychiatrist. The cohort was divided into two groups. The control group engaged in nondirective visual arts sessions with social care workers, and the experimental group engaged in CAT with trained art therapists. The results support that CAT was more effective than the visual arts sessions for improving the participants' daily functioning, mental health, and holistic well-being.

A Korean study by Jang and Choi (2012) examined effects that clay therapy had on the ego-resilience of 16 adolescents from a low socioeconomic background who were identified as needing emotional and psychological support. The participants' ego-resilience was measured before the first session and after the last session; the results demonstrated that clay therapy produced positive effects. These findings are attributed to the participants' successful experience of seeing clay becoming complete pottery through kiln firing and feeling the suppleness and plasticity of clay. The significance of this study lies in the finding that clay-based group art therapy produces positive effects on adolescents' ego-resilience, a personal trait that helps with mental and emotional adaptation in a changing and conflicting environment. There is a growing body of research in this discipline, but randomized control trials need to be conducted to support its efficacy. More studies and articles need to be published in peer-reviewed journals.

SUMMARY AND CONCLUSION

In the past, clay therapy has been viewed as the poor relation of other creative art therapies; however, it is an emergent discipline, and similar to sand play, music therapy, and therapeutic storytelling, it deserves recognition (Sherwood,

2004; Sholt & Gavron, 2006; Souter-Anderson, 2010). Clay makes the intangible touchable. Clay can represent both real-life objects and symbolic representations because of its three-dimensional qualities. Using it therapeutically allows the child to grab an emotion and look it in the face, touch it, shape it, and feel it. Clay is powerful and penetrating, and it enables an enormous release and transformation without the child having to verbalize their thoughts or feelings. Clay can tap into the unconscious mind and unlock hidden memories. It is an effective medium in group play therapy, as it encourages group interaction, builds social skills, and promotes empathy. Clay is a cathartic medium and an essential part of a play therapist's tool kit. However, it is important for play therapists to work with and get to know the medium in order to successfully implement it in their practice. Further research is needed to understand the specific therapeutic powers of clay and how it can be used effectively with children presenting with specific issues.

REFERENCES

Anderson, F. E. (1995). Catharsis and empowerment through group claywork with incest survivors. *The Arts in Psychotherapy, 22*(5), 413–427. https://doi.org/10.1016/0197-4556(94)00046-8

Banker, J. E. (2008). Family clay sculpting. *Journal of Family Psychotherapy, 19*(3), 291–297. https://doi.org/10.1080/08975350802269533

Bowlby, J. (1969). *Attachment and loss: Vol. 1. Attachment.* Basic Books.

Bowlby, J. (1980). *Attachment and loss: Vol. 3. Loss: Sadness and depression.* Basic Books.

Bratton, S., & Ferebee, K. (1999). The use of structured expressive art activities in group activity therapy with preadolescents. In D. Sweeney & L. Homeyer (Eds.), *The handbook of group play therapy: How to do it, how it works, whom it's best for* (pp. 192–214). Jossey-Bass Publishers.

Damasio, A. (2010). *Self comes to mind: Constructing the conscious brain.* Pantheon Press.

Drewes, A. A., & Schaefer, C. E. (2014). *The therapeutic powers of play: 20 core agents of change* (2nd ed.). John Wiley and Sons.

Elbrecht, C. (2013). *Trauma healing at the clay field: A sensorimotor art therapy approach.* Jessica Kingsley Publishers.

Elbrecht, C. (2015). The clay field and developmental trauma in children. In C. A. Malchiodi (Ed.), *Creative interventions with traumatized children—Creative arts and play therapy* (2nd ed., pp. 191–210). Guilford Press.

Erickson, E. H. (1977). *Toys and reason.* W. W. Norton and Company.

Geldard, K., Geldard, D., & Foo, R. Y. (2018). *Counselling children: A practical introduction.* SAGE Publications.

Gerhardt, S. (2015). *Why love matters: How affection shapes a baby's brain* (2nd ed.). Routledge.

Henley, D. (2002). *Clayworks in art therapy: Plying the sacred circle.* Jessica Kingsley Publishers.

Jang, H., & Choi, S. (2012). Increasing ego-resilience using clay with low SES adolescents in group art therapy. *The Arts in Psychotherapy, 39*(4), 245–250. https://doi.org/10.1016/j.aip.2012.04.001

Jørstad, J. (1965). Clay forming in psychotherapy: A possible remedy to communication and insight. *Acta Psychiatrica Scandinavica, 41*(4), 491–502. https://doi.org/10.1111/j.1600-0447.1965.tb06168.x

Kimport, E. R., & Robbins, S. J. (2012). Efficacy of creative clay work for reducing negative mood: A randomized control trial. *Art Therapy: Journal of the American Art Therapy Association, 29*(2), 74–79. https://doi.org/10.1080/07421656.2012.680048

Landreth, G. L. (2012). *Play therapy: The art of the relationship.* Routledge. https://doi.org/10.4324/9780203835159

Malchiodi, C. A. (2015). *Creative interventions with traumatized children—Creative arts and play therapy.* Guilford Press.

Meijer-Degen, F., & Lansen, J. (2006). Alexithymia—A challenge to art therapy. *The Arts in Psychotherapy, 33*(3), 167–179. https://doi.org/10.1016/j.aip.2005.10.002

Nan, J. K. M., & Ho, R. T. H. (2017). Effects of clay art therapy on adults outpatients with major depressive disorder: A randomized controlled trial. *Journal of Affective Disorders, 217,* 237–245. https://doi.org/10.1016/j.jad.2017.04.013

Nez, D. (1991). Persephone's return: Archetypal art therapy and the treatment of a survivor of abuse. *The Arts in Psychotherapy, 18*(2), 123–130. https://doi.org/10.1016/0197-4556(91)90019-7

Oaklander, V. (1978). *Windows to our children: A Gestalt therapy approach to children and adolescents.* Real People Press.

Piaget, J. (1962). *Play, dreams, and imitation in childhood.* W. W. Norton and Company.

Rahmani, P., & Moheb, N. (2010). The effectiveness of clay therapy and narrative therapy on anxiety of preschool children: A comparative study. *Procedia: Social and Behavioral Sciences, 5,* 23–27. https://doi.org/10.1016/j.sbspro.2010.07.044

Schaefer, C. E., & Kaduson, H. G. (2006). *Contemporary play therapy: Theory, research and practice.* Guilford Press.

Sherwood, P. (2004). *The healing art of clay therapy.* Acer Press.

Sholt, M., & Gavron, T. (2006). Therapeutic qualities of clay-work in art therapy and psychotherapy. *Art Therapy: Journal of the American Art Therapy Association, 23*(2), 66–72. https://doi.org/10.1080/07421656.2006.10129647

Siegel, D. J., & Bryson, T. P. (2012). *The whole-brain child: 12 revolutionary strategies to nurture your child's developing mind.* Bantam Books.

Souter-Anderson, L. (2010). *Touching clay, touching what?* Archive Publishing.

Souter-Anderson, L. (2015). *Making meaning: Clay therapy with children & adolescents.* Hinton House.

Sunderland, M. (2003). *Using storytelling as a therapeutic tool with children.* Speechmark Publishing.

Ward, C. (1999). Shaping connections: Hands-on art therapy. In A. Cattanach (Ed.), *Process in art therapy* (pp. 103–131). Jessica Kingsley Publishers.

White, P. (2006). CLAYtherapy: The clinical application of clay with children. In C. E. Schaefer & H. G. Kaduson (Eds.), *Contemporary play therapy: Theory, research and practice* (pp. 270–292). Guilford Press.

Winnicott, D. W. (1971). *Playing and reality.* Basic Books.

Woltmann, A. G. (1993). Mud and clay. In C. E. Schaefer & D. M. Cangelosi (Eds.), *Play therapy techniques* (2nd ed., pp. 185–202). Guilford Press.

12 THE USE OF MUSIC AND MOVEMENT IN PLAY THERAPY

SUSAN A. TAYLOR

Humans are embodied, moving beings. We move through space, and we move to be. Internal movement regulates living—breath, circulation of blood, digestion, physiological arousal. External movement, or behavior, creates our communication with others—we move toward another for connection, move away for survival, offering subtle and not-so-subtle body-based cues to our needs, wants, and emotions. Movement is, therefore, the essence of living, of being. Movement is gestural and postural, fully embodied and occurring on the cellular level, interacting with the outside world and to our internal sense of self. Simply stated, all human clinicians are using movement, intentionally or not, in our work with clients in every moment.

Humans are also tonal and rhythmic beings. Our footfalls, heartbeats, breath, and vocalizations embody rhythm. Even native speakers of nontonal languages, like English, express meaning through the sounds of inflection and emphasis, tempo, pitch, dynamics of volume, repetition and recapitulations of theme, consonance and dissonance in speech. Human sound making, or sounding, communicates, vibrates, and resonates body-to-body and brain-to-brain. The music we make in sounded communication, whether verbal or

https://doi.org/10.1037/0000217-013
Play Therapy With Children: Modalities for Change, H. G. Kaduson and C. E. Schaefer (Editors)

nonverbal, transmits our intentions to others and expresses our conscious and unconscious feelings. Again, clinicians are using the music of breath and prosody of speech in our work with clients in every moment, with intention or not.

This chapter focuses on the ways that play therapists can begin to recognize their existing use of movement and music in sessions with clients of all ages (infants to elders) and develop more conscious, intentional choices. Presenting some basic components of music and movement, the chapter offers play therapists a window into more fully embodied clinician presence and clinician–client attunement. Next the chapter explores the therapeutic benefits of a wide range of core techniques to build the play therapist's toolbox. Last, a case vignette opens a window into the impact of music and movement in the life on one child, and a community of children and adults.

INTENTION IN BODY, BREATH, AND SOUND

Clinicians are continually searching for effective interventions. For clinicians to directly employ their ever-present use of movement and music in their work with clients, awareness is required. Reflective practice requires us to dive fearlessly into exploring what and how we are doing and examining the impact of our gestures and postures, tones and rhythms of sounds, speech, and song on those around us. When we are the embodiment of an intervention, examination of how we "bring our bodies to the party" is crucial. Listening into our own body messaging (the sensory and regulatory signals our bodies offer us to communicate our unconscious feelings and motivations) and carefully observing our resonance with those around us are the first steps in honing the awareness needed to use music and movement with intention.

IN APPRECIATION OF DANCE MOVEMENT THERAPY AND MUSIC THERAPY

Two effective modern disciplines—dance movement therapy and music therapy—have rich histories that stretch into the ancient past, vigorous training programs, and a great variety of methodologies from which we can draw inspiration. Each of these fields contains a wealth of diversity in practitioners, practices, and treatment settings, from large hospitals to private practice. Music therapy is shown to have significant effects on children and adolescents with a wide range of psychopathology, particularly developmental and behavioral disorders (Gold et al., 2004). Some recent research in music therapy looks at the ways in which singing and sounding with others increases well-being and bonding through neurochemical connection (Hallam & Creech, 2016; Keeler et al., 2015).

Marian Chase, one of the foremothers of dance movement therapy, saw the observation of and interaction with a client's verbal expression as potentially hidden or restrained, and she viewed a client's self-expression through movement as a primary source of clinical investigation (Chaiklin & Chaiklin, 1982). Well before our recent explorations into neuroscience and the renewed understanding of mind–body unity, Chase believed that human feeling and experience were inextricably linked with sensation, pointing to the embedding of bodily experience in the very term *emotion* (Chaiklin & Chaiklin, 1982).

Play therapists can learn a great deal from each of these professions and their highly trained and skillful practitioners. This chapter, however, encourages play therapists to reflect upon their conscious and unconscious use of movement and sound and to intentionally add somatic and sounded awareness and expression into their toolbox as therapeutic modalities within their scope of current practice of playful clinical work.

SOME BASIC MOVEMENT AND MUSICAL COMPONENTS

Our body is what is moving. With dedicated observation, we can identify increasingly specific and subtle areas of sensation, tension, ease, and impulse to move. We can study the quality of our breath as body sensation. Space, both in the world around us and inside of our own body's architecture, is where we are moving. Our movement relates to the structure of our body and how we imagine it divided: upper and lower, left side and right side, front and back. But our body also bends, extends, and rotates through our spine and joints. The dynamics of movement allow a window into the why or motivation behind movements. We vary our speed, pressure, and control. Our motivation, and therefore our quality of movement, differs as we reach out to touch a butterfly or slam a car door, push a refrigerator into place or hold a balloon. Our bodies know how to make shapes and can mold softly around a newborn baby or grow large and wide when threatened.

All sound is vibration, so our bodies are involved in the resonance of making and hearing music. We use our breath to make voiced sounds, and we can use our body as percussion (clapping, playing our tummy drums, stomping our feet). Singing is elongated speech on a pitch, ranging from high to low. Music uses speed (tempo), pressure, and control like bodies do. We use volume to create intensity. Rhythms vary from a heartbeat to an alarm bell to complex interrelated polyrhythms. Repeated short, sharp, loud sounds tend to mean something different to us than long, slow whispers do. Different cultures use a series of notes to create scales of music, which can offer varied feeling senses of emotion. Many Western readers may be surprised to find that "Do-Re-Mi" (Rodgers & Hammerstein, 1964) is only one way to organize notes in a scale.

By examining the component parts of movement and music, clinicians will begin to piece together what their clinical body sees, hears, and senses in the quality of a client's movement or sounded expression.

ATTUNEMENT THROUGH BODY AND SOUND AND SYMBOL

Attachment theory has brought a careful observation of preverbal and non-verbal cues into our work (Ainsworth et al., 1978; Beebe et al., 2016; Bloom, 2006; Bowlby, 1982; Tortora, 2006). In therapy, clinicians are simultaneously holding the client's experience in safety and maintaining a container for the capacity of clinical growth (T. H. Ogden, 2004). Although clinicians have long recognized their use of self to create a therapeutic relationship of attunement that leads to effectiveness in therapy, recent advances in biobehavioral research help us understand physiological cocreation of the safety necessary for clinical change, body-to-body and brain-to-brain (Geller & Porges, 2014). Play therapists draw from the syntax of symbolism and metaphor in the play of children to unveil their inner concerns, to communicate their realities and fantasies, and to move toward resolution (Chazan, 2001; Gil, 1991). An embodied and aware use of self is critical in creating therapeutic relationships in which clients of all ages feel safe (Carey, 2006), and it is happening through conscious and unconscious, symbolic, somatic (body and sound), and neurological attunement. Clients may ask, "Will my therapist stay with me through major and minor keys, or as I push through the metaphorical gelatin of my experiences, or as my body melts into release like an ice cube?" Our therapeutic relationships are based upon mutual willingness, but the foundation must be an ethical competence of the clinician dependent on training, experience, practice, self-reflection, and supervision. Please be certain to experiment and grow comfortable with any of the following techniques before jumping into them with clients.

THERAPEUTIC BENEFITS

As outlined by Schaefer and Drewes (2014), music and movement access all four of the major therapeutic powers of play therapy: facilitating communication, fostering emotional wellness, enhancing social relationships, and increasing personal strengths. Clinical implementation of music and movement in the playroom can be tailored to address the needs of clients—cognitive, emotional, and/or interpersonal (Schaefer & Drewes, 2014). The techniques that follow can activate mechanisms of change within clients and, through embodied reflective practice, within the person of the therapist as well.

Direct and Indirect Teaching

Music and movement can be used, directly and indirectly, to teach new or reinforce emerging skills while strengthening therapeutic or familial attachment and peer relationships and creating access to metaphor (Fraser, 2014; Schaefer & Drewes, 2014; Taylor de Faoite, 2014). The Build a Song technique is a useful vehicle for direct teaching—creating simply repetitive lyrics to deliver content. Yoga, creative movement, and body stories offer opportunities for clients to embody and explore symbols and metaphors.

Self-Expression and Self-Regulation

Although valuable therapeutic goals themselves, connecting to breath, song/sound-making, and body messaging enhances intra- and interpersonal connection to facilitate self-expression and self-regulation, particularly in clients who, whether developmentally or in response to trauma, are unable to speak their experiences (Beer & Birnbaum, 2019; Bennett & Eberts, 2014; Crenshaw, 2006; van der Kolk, 2014). Clinician-driven modulations of tempo and volume in sounding, as well as size (e.g., posture vs. gesture, close vs. expansive reach) and tempo in movement, offer clients embodied exploration of a variety of states of excitement and, eventually, the intentional pathways between them. Mirror and Opposite techniques build a menu of embodied experiences within clients from which they can learn to regulate themselves. All of the core techniques allow clients to access and study their inner experience and communicate their truths through embodied expression.

CORE TECHNIQUES

Our embodied selves enter the playroom, bringing the tones and rhythm of our sounds and the postures, gestures, and inner sensations of our bodies. Intentional use of music and movement allows clients to access body-based self-discovery and self-regulation through sensation, imagery, and symbolic play. The techniques outlined here assume a level of personal exploration and comfort on the part of the clinician within an ethical, reflective practice, thus guaranteeing safety in client exploration. This therapist recognizes that in contemporary Western culture, there is an unconscious understanding that singing and dancing belong to a category of performance by professionals. The clinical use of music and movement outlined here is not performance but a joining together in playful expressive resonance. Clinically, we can choose to follow the lead of our clients into musical and embodied play. Or we can choose a more directive approach. Because our bodies and our sound are ever-present in our work together, play therapists using child-centered or directive approaches have access to music and movement techniques. We can improvise together with our clients, trading the lead in play. The techniques outlined here offer suggestions for increasing our clinical awareness of, then amplifying and guiding, the musicality and embodiment of spontaneous expression and exploration of our clients.

Begin With Cultural Humility and an Invitation to Play Together

Moving our bodies and making music is our human birthright, but our approach to body consciousness, manners of moving, and creation of and interaction with music are deeply influenced by culture and, therefore, rife with potential clinical blind spots. Reflective practice and attention to the importance of a client's cultural elements that may differ from your own allow a clinician to use cultural humility to enhance the clinical relationship (Hook et al., 2013). There are myriad ways to move or contact our own body's messaging, and to sing, hear, sense, and respond in the richness of human diversity in sound. This is an invitation for you and your clients to play in music and in movement, trading the lead and improvising in turn. Particularly when stretching your skills, it is fine to introduce new methods slowly.

Recorded music can be a useful tool, but it comes with pitfalls. Experiment with a wide variety of what you may or may not consider music, and open your ear to cross-cultural resources, if you choose to use recordings. Music that sounds new or different to a client eliminates some of the cultural prescriptions around how-this-must-be-moved-to. Close your eyes for a moment and picture bodies moving to polyrhythmic drumming, a Viennese waltz, a tune by Cardi B, or a Grateful Dead jam. Do those elicit specific images, rules for moving, and conjure emotional cues that are specific to your personal narrative? Whereas offering familiar-to-them recorded music may initiate moving for some clients, it can come at an expressive and explorative cost. In the same way, clinicians need to be aware of their personal and dominant cultural preferences or strictures, falsely construed as universal. Each person exists within their own relative dualities of exertion and recuperation, soothing and activating, for example (Studd & Cox, 2013). What feels harsh to you may be comforting to your client. What follows are examples of incorporating the intentional use of movement, sound, and music into your practice.

Opposites

One easy way to explore affect and body messaging is though exploring opposing sensations and expressions. A long body stretch can be contrasted with shortening and contracting into a small ball. Loud, high, and fast voicing can be contrasted with soft, low, and sustained sounding. We can usually identify what we do not like, even when we cannot quite put our finger on what we do. Offering a menu of opposite experiences can both assist clients in accessing a broader range of possibilities and clarify their needs and intentions by tuning in. Opposites can be useful in guided imagery, through song and movement, or simply slipped into an existing play therapy experience.

Using Opposites in guided imagery can begin with the client in a seated or reclining position or moving in the space with closed or downcast eyes. The client practices connecting to their body messaging, using that information to uncover concerns, identify affect, recognize and alter behavior, and so on. It is crucial that the therapist has a clear command of their own vocal prosody for this technique. To introduce Opposites, ask a client to find a color that feels relaxing or soothing or safe. While you talk through a scan of the body (using your clinical judgment to choose which body parts or areas to mention), they imagine filling their body with this color. Textures, sounds, and emotions can also be used once you are both familiar with this form of inner body sensory imagining. If a client is having difficulty accessing a particular emotion, start with a toned-down aspect of it. "Where do you feel irritation in your body? What color is it? Does it have a sound?" Once the client explores their body's message, change to the opposite. "What does the opposite feel like? Where is it? What does is look like? What does it sound like?" Do not name the opposite but allow the client to find what it feels like and sounds like. This may be a key to release. It is fine to be fairly loose about the idea of opposite. Any difference will be useful at first. Clients tend to develop a broader vocabulary during the course of treatment.

Another way to access Opposites is to create a song that you and the client sing forward and backward. You can use "Row, Row, Row Your Boat" or any other tune that is comfortable for you and your client. As you sing, "Row, row, row your boat, gently down the stream," move in one specific way, or target one specific emotion. Next, sing (to the "merrily" part of the song), "Stream the down gently, boat your row, row, row," while moving in a contrasting way. As your clients explore their body messaging, they will develop a more sophisticated understanding of body tension, breath, somatic markers of trauma triggers, or the ways their body feels when they are safe. Singing lyrics backward takes some practice and can add a lighthearted element. For clients who easily experience frustration, feel free to write the lyrics on a poster, or just say "Switch!" before singing the regular second part of the song.

Repeat a Phrase

Repeat a Phrase, like Opposites, uses iterations of the same pattern for discovering contrast and thereby contact and explore body-felt emotions. You and the client can decide if this is sounded, sung, or spoken. With verbal phrases, you can use a single word (a name, place, object of meaning) or a phrase ("Come here," "It's good to see you," "That hurt," "I love you"; anything appropriate to the client's work) or nonverbal sounded phrases. Repeat a Phrase needs to be embodied, so please offer your client the freedom to move about the space. Each time the phrase is repeated, explore a different emotion. Using your clinical judgment, you and your client may devise a menu of feelings that range from easier to access to more difficult for them to explore. With Repeat a Phrase, a client has access to the felt sense of their body messaging and can hear the change in tonal and rhythmic qualities of spoken or sung voice.

Repeat a Phrase can also be used as Repeat a Gesture. In this case the movement phrase (reaching a hand, putting a foot onto the floor, sitting down) is the basic template through which different emotions are experienced in the body.

Build a Song

Build a Song is the process of creating a song for, or with, your client. You do not have to compose your own music, unless you like to do so. Feel free to use a wide range of familiar songs for tunes, such as "Mary Had a Little Lamb," "Rock a My Soul in the Bosom of Abraham," "Reuben and Rachel," or popular songs that have meaning for your client. Add words for the theme or purpose needed. Keep songs simple in both tune and lyrics. Remember that repetition is good, repetition is good, repetition is good. Songs can be used for ritual purposes (walking together from the waiting room to the playroom, or cleaning up, or self-containment at the end of a session), to educate (from songs about sneezes for public health reasons to songs that describe what happens in our bodies when we feel a specific emotion, from learning to wait to singing about how our bodies are private), to contain some clinical material (e.g., a client may compose a calming nightmare song), or to celebrate! If you and your client compose a tune, be sure to record it so that you both can remember it.

Build a Dance

Build a Dance comes from Build-a-Phrase in the rich resource of the Liz Lerman (n.d.) Atlas of Creative Tools. Build a Dance can embody a story or idea and, thus, describe a narrative in movement. This entails matching humming, chanting, song, or recorded music to the client movements that tell the story. Often I use Build a Dance to offer a set of clinical tools for both identifying body messaging associated with particular emotions or scenarios and pairing the emotion with postural or gestural release. If a client has an upcoming test in school, for example, you can explore together what she is experiencing in her body when she imagines the test and when she is preparing. You can then use the concepts in Opposites to find what feels like a sense of release for this particular client (be sure to explore breath, body tension, where the feeling is located in the body, and qualities of sound).

In either case, the client offers a gesture or movement, which you then work together to heighten and highlight, magnifying any not fully formed movement. If a client is shy, the clinician can model growing and embodying the movement. However, let the client lead in determining how the movement is done. Create repeated movement phrases of shorter or longer duration (depending on the emphasis needed and the form of the music you are using), or match phrases to specific parts of the music. Next, combine a few phrases into a pattern and repeat them. This is now your dance. So, dance it. After you dance, feel free to allow the client to alter it for their needs. You may find that it will change over time as the client transforms clinically. Often clients want to revisit their dance weekly or with significant clinical milestones.

Body Mirrors, Sound Mirrors

The Mirror metaphor is a powerful tool for a client to share their embodied experience with a clinician, to expand a client's expressive movement vocabulary, and for teaching self-regulation skills. A Body Mirror requires the participants to stand face-to-face, slowly and carefully matching the postural and gestural directions and qualities of each other. Who leads is a clinical decision. After some practice, a Body Mirror can happen almost simultaneously. A Sound Mirror requires careful listening to the singing or humming or sounding of the other. With increasing attunement, Sound Mirrors can move from turn-taking experiences to becoming more synchronous. Drums and other rhythm instruments can be used in Sound Mirrors.

Scarves, Drums, Rhythm Instruments, and Props

Scarves, drums, rhythm instruments, and props are useful in the playroom for increasing the reach of the body or sound and for making rhythm visible.

Any costume element can represent the metaphor and symbolism of the clinical embodiment. Scarves can reinforce the idea of separation and return. Drums or instruments can be used, as in Sound Mirrors, to first follow and match a client's heightened emotional state, with the option of gradually slowing the tempo and softening the touch to illustrate downregulation or to upregulate a consistently hypoaroused child.

Yoga, Body Stories, and Creative Movement

Clinicians can use yoga postures and creative movement to imaginatively explore body shapes in stand-alone experiences or blended into other activities. A yoga-therapy protocol may be appropriate for some therapists (Beltran et al., 2014). For others, simply infusing yoga into your existing work can offer clients a body postural framework for identifying emotions or grounding, stabilization, and self-regulation. Sitting or standing in a mountain pose allows a client to access a feeling sense of their body and the ground beneath them (Emerson, 2008). Yoga or creative movement can bring symbolic play into an exploration of body-felt awareness for clients. Postures can be used one at a time for a client to embody a warrior or bear (Flynn, 2015; Mond, 2018) or in a sequence like the Sun Salutation (Dance for PD, 2013). Clinicians and clients can also build a narrative of body transformations to work through a specific concern. Examples of a simple body story include a seed growing into a mighty tree, a stomping angry dinosaur that finds a baby to care for, or a star that is spinning wildly across space and experiments with shining down on a planet. A clinical dyad may build a series of movements without music simply for the study of mindful awareness and release that can lead to increasing tools of self-regulation (Nhat Hanh & Vriezen, 2008). Any story or sequence can be paired with self-made or recorded music, as in Build a Dance, for further expressive texture.

Individuals and Groups

Although these interventions are described in use with a single client, any of these techniques may be implemented effectively in family and group settings with a modicum of modification. For some clients, the inhibitions to dive deep and explore unfamiliar territory will be lessened in a group setting. Working playfully with music and movement can feel lighter in a group. However, some client choices may be inhibited by the sway of a dynamic member, a need to "do it the right way," copying others without personal exploration, or the rigid dynamics of a family system.

Build a Dance, in particular, works well to create group cohesion and meaning. Consider creating "our own special dance" as a way to begin a series of group therapy. In a group, it is important to allow each member to dance their own version. The therapist might say, "Great. Keisha offered her movement. Check in with yourself and see what feelings that brings up in your body. Express that feeling in your own way."

Although we might return to our dance during the series, we will always dance it together again at the end of the series—a dance that can exist only with this group of people for this specific reason at this time—to contain and celebrate our work together. Families can take their dance into their home life to hold on to the work of connection and attunement they create through the therapy.

CLINICAL APPLICATIONS

Music and movement techniques are applicable to a wide range of clinical concerns in children (Carmichael & Atchinson, 1997). Clients benefit from any increase in their emotional literacy, sensory awareness, and relational literacy. Music and movement-based interventions target all three. Play therapists may find that this modality enhances their therapeutic relationships by honing attunement and increasing connection. Many clients who have developmental delays find rhythmic, repetitive movement with a simple accompanying song or chant (e.g., one about brushing teeth) to be soothing, organizing, and regulating (Cosgrove et al., 2020). Children with speech delays can access singing and begin to communicate effectively using a "Waiting Song," or songs that describe what is happening in their daily routine (Cosgrove et al., 2020). A form of sounded or nonverbal role-play is particularly effective in experimenting with social skills, including proximity and boundaries.

Using music and movement interventions in children with a trauma history can be particularly effective. Recent research acknowledges that the effects of trauma and trauma reactions may remain housed in the body long after traumatic events and that these reactions can be worked through and processed into health with the careful, specific, and intentional use of movement, breath, and sound (P. Ogden et al., 2006; Rothschild, 2000, 2017; van der Kolk, 2014). Additionally, Beebe and colleagues (2000, 2016) have filmed parent–infant pairs and examined each dyad's micromomentary expressions, reactions, body coordination, and rhythmic sounding that reveal the establishment of lifelong attachment and relational patterns. Drawing the connection between these two streams of research, we understand that the relational interaction of therapy engages the sensory and verbal, body and sound, movement and music for clients of all ages. Clinicians constantly communicate and dance, brain-to-brain and body-to-body, with our clients (Schore, 2003; Wallin, 2007). Change becomes possible when a client's inner life is connected to sound and body (Beer & Birnbaum, 2019). The use of body-based experiences with a trusted clinician opens the possibility of integrating formerly held traumatic reactions, as well as creating new relational patterns suffused with self-efficacy (Roediger et al., 2018; Wallin, 2007).

CASE ILLUSTRATION

This case illustrates a movement and music circle time intervention for families of preschool children using a composite client, and confidentiality is protected by changes to names and identifying details. Jasmine, a frantically interactive just-4-year-old, is bouncing around and through the circle of preschoolers. Like all of the other children present, Jasmine and her mother, Ms. Franklin, are living in a shelter for families traumatized by their experiences of homelessness and community violence. Her preschool is both a school and an early intervention clinical program designed to address the emotional distress and developmental delays common in young children facing homelessness. Many of the children, including Jasmine, have experienced the accumulation of attachment-related difficulties in families impacted by interpersonal violence and intergenerational trauma. The family music circle is a clinical intervention designed specifically to address trauma, attachment, and emotional safety and regulation.

On this morning, Jasmine and her mommy arrived at preschool mid-conflict. Depositing Jasmine at the door, Ms. Franklin fled abruptly in a cloud of stomping anger with no goodbye kisses. Without her mommy, Jasmine found herself plopped into the family music circle, already underway—alone, sad, fearful, and simply unable to organize and contain her feelings. Jasmine ran through the center of the circle, poking at other children, moving quickly from one seated adult to another. Other children in the circle responded to Jasmine's dysregulation, becoming distracted and antsy. Adults in the circle stopped singing and grabbed at Jasmine to "get her to stop." The clinician changed tack in the therapeutic movement and music circle after first checking in with herself and then observing the shifts away from a stable state of coregulation in the others around her. She began to lead a song about emotions, inviting all of what Jasmine, and everyone else, was feeling to have clinically contained vocal and physical expression. The group sang and stamped out anger, using "our words"; they hugged themselves while they sang about feeling scared;

they reached up in a gesture of supplication while singing about needing help; they peeked out from behind fingers hiding faces to reassure themselves that what we cannot see now will return, like our mommies; singing a description of what they were doing, they placed their hands on their bellies and breathed in and out. They sang about love and safety, separation and return, varying the volume of their voices, the tempo and quality of each body's movements. Slowly, all of the children and adults in the circle began to regulate together, both up and down, finding their individual and collective Windows of Tolerance—the optimal area of arousal between hyperarousal and hypoarousal (P. Ogden et al., 2006). By the time the therapist began singing a settling song, "All the Way Down" (Cosgrove et al., 2020), Jasmine was able to tolerate the slower tempo, softer volume, and gentler movement. She melted like an ice-cream cone and came to "sit like a mountain tall" next to her beloved teacher. Now contained, Jasmine sang out brightly, "I can take a breeeaaaaattthhhh, allll the way down!" (Cosgrove et al., 2020).

In the weeks that followed, teaching and clinical staff members continued to support Jasmine with movement and musical regulation cues when she became dysregulated throughout her school day. Incorporating clinical techniques from the weekly music circle, Jasmine and her mommy began to use songs and movement play to cue regulation in the preschool and in their shelter home. Over the year she remained in the clinical preschool, Jasmine could often be seen sitting in her classroom singing to a doll about her mommy coming back at the end of the day, or "sitting and waiting for my turn" (Cosgrove et al., 2020).

EMPIRICAL SUPPORT

As recent research in neuroscience teaches that we know ourselves through recognizing and eliciting meaning from the sensations of our body, one pressing task of psychotherapy is to cocreate experiences for clients to move from alexithymia (inability to understand what is going on inside, or numbing) to growing interoception (van der Kolk, 2014).

From premature infancy to old age, live music-making is shown to promote social–emotional (including communication and social skills), personal, and cognitive development and well-being (including vital signs and sleep; Gerry et al., 2012; Hallam, 2015; Hallam & Creech, 2016; Loewy et al., 2013). The color of sound, or timbre, expresses affect in vocal communication. Using singing with developmentally and neurologically diverse children promotes social responsiveness, increasing both receptive and expressive communication (Beer & Birnbaum, 2019; Finnigan & Starr, 2010; Weeks, 2015). Prosocial behavior (including cooperation, helping, joint problem solving) is shown to increase more in children who make music together in pairs and in groups rather than other joint activities (Kirschner & Tomasello, 2010; Rabinowitch & Meltzoff, 2017). Moving and sounding in rhythm is linked to social interaction and may provide important neurodevelopmental stimulation to connect auditory and motor mechanisms (Dalla Bella et al., 2015).

As the use of expressive modalities increases with children, and professionals collaborate across disciplines, more research needs to be done (Irwin, 2006; van Westrhenen & Fritz, 2014).

SUMMARY AND CONCLUSION

By becoming aware of and skillfully using music and movement in play therapy, clinicians employ creative multisensory modalities to both model and make room for clients to embody change. Crenshaw (2006) reminded us that effective trauma treatment must reach beyond the essential need to access a sense of safety, soothing, and stabilization (thereby reducing internal and external aggression to the self and others) toward self-study with the goal of de-linking our somatic experiences from the memory of trauma. Investigating and observing moving and music-making, brings the client and clinician into the present moment. Music and movement in play connects and can integrate clients with the whole of themselves—in sensing body, in emotional sound, in spirit (Beer & Birnbaum, 2019). By entering treatment through a nonverbal door, we can bypass the offline speech areas of the brain and arrive with our client at here-and-now relational expression of their inner world and experiences (Beer & Birnbaum, 2019; Crenshaw, 2006; van der Kolk, 2014).

REFERENCES

Ainsworth, M. D. S., Blehar, M. C., Waters, E., & Wall, S. (1978). *Patterns of attachment: A psychological study of the strange situation.* Lawrence Erlbaum Associates.

Beebe, B., Cohen, P., & Lachmann, F. (2016). *The mother–infant interaction picture book: Origins of attachment.* W. W. Norton & Company.

Beebe, B., Jaffe, J., Lachmann, F., Feldstien, S., Crown, C., & Jasnow, M. (2000). Systems models in development and psychoanalysis: The case of vocal rhythm coordination and attachment. *Infant Mental Health Journal, 21*(1–2), 99–122. https://doi.org/10.1002/(SICI)1097-0355(200001/04)21:1/2<99::AID-IMHJ11>3.0.CO;2-%23

Beer, L. E., & Birnbaum, J. C. (2019). *Using music in child and adolescent psychotherapy.* Guilford Press.

Beltran, M., Brown-Elhillali, A., Held, A., DeBerardinis, C., Muyu, J., Deal, S., & Haverson, D. (2014). *Yoga based psychotherapy: A group protocol for children.* The Family Center at Kennedy Krieger Institute.

Bennett, M. M., & Eberts, S. (2014). Self-expression. In C. E. Schaefer & A. A. Drewes (Eds.), *The therapeutic powers of play: 20 core agents of change* (2nd ed., pp. 11–24). John Wiley & Sons.

Bloom, K. (2006). *The embodied self: Movement and psychoanalysis.* Karnac Books.

Bowlby, J. (1982). *Attachment and loss: Attachment* (Vol. 1). Basic Books.

Carey, L. (2006). Introduction. In L. Carey (Ed.), *Expressive and creative arts methods for trauma survivors* (pp. 15–20). Jessica Kingsley Publishers.

Carmichael, K. D., & Atchinson, D. H. (1997). Music in play therapy: Playing my feelings. *International Journal of Play Therapy, 6*(1), 63–72. https://doi.org/10.1037/h0089414

Chaiklin, H., & Chaiklin, S. (1982). Body awareness and its expression: A technique for social casework. *Social Casework, 63*(4), 237–240. https://doi.org/10.1177/104438948206300408

Chazan, S. E. (2001). Toward a nonverbal syntax of play therapy. *Psychoanalytic Inquiry, 21*(3), 394–406. https://doi.org/10.1080/07351692109348943

Cosgrove, K., Norris-Shortle, C., & Taylor, S. (2020). *Wee cuddle and grow* [Manuscript in preparation]. The Kennedy Krieger Institute.

Crenshaw, D. (2006). Neuroscience and trauma treatment: Implications for creative arts therapists. In L. Carey (Ed.), *Expressive and creative arts methods for trauma survivors* (pp. 21–38). Jessica Kingsley Publishers.

Dalla Bella, S., Berkowska, M., & Sowiński, J. (2015). Moving to the beat and singing are linked in humans. *Frontiers in Human Neuroscience, 9,* Article 663. https://doi.org/10.3389/fnhum.2015.00663

Dance for PD. (2013). *Sun salutation sample* [Video file]. https://danceforparkinsons.org

Emerson, D. (2008). *Yoga: For peace of body and mind. A manual for clinicians from the Trauma Center at JRI.* Justice Resource Institute.

Finnigan, E., & Starr, E. (2010). Increasing social responsiveness in a child with autism. A comparison of music and non-music interventions. *Autism: An International Journal of Research and Practice, 14*(4), 321–348. https://doi.org/10.1177/1362361309357747

Flynn, L. (2015). *Yoga 4 classrooms: Tools for learning. Lessons for life.* Edison Press.

Fraser, T. (2014). Direct teaching. In C. E. Schaefer & A. A. Drewes (Eds.), *The therapeutic powers of play: 20 core agents of change* (2nd ed., pp. 39–50). John Wiley & Sons.

Geller, S. M., & Porges, S. W. (2014). Therapeutic presence: Neurophysiological mechanisms mediating feeling safe in therapeutic relationships. *Journal of Psychotherapy Integration, 24*(3), 178–192. https://doi.org/10.1037/a0037511

Gerry, D., Unrau, A., & Trainor, L. J. (2012). Active music classes in infancy enhance musical, communicative and social development. *Developmental Science, 15*(3), 398–407. https://doi.org/10.1111/j.1467-7687.2012.01142.x

Gil, E. (1991). *The healing power of play: Working with abused children.* Guilford Press.

Gold, C., Voracek, M., & Wigram, T. (2004). Effects of music therapy for children and adolescents with psychopathology: A meta-analysis. *Journal of Child Psychology and Psychiatry, and Allied Disciplines, 45*(6), 1054–1063. https://doi.org/10.1111/j.1469-7610.2004.t01-1-00298.x

Hallam, S. (2015). *The power of music: A research synthesis of the impact of actively making music on the intellectual, social and personal development of children and young people.* International Music Education Research Centre.

Hallam, S., & Creech, A. (2016). Can active music making promote health and well-being in older citizens? Findings of the music for life project. *London Journal of Primary Care, 8*(2), 21–25. https://doi.org/10.1080/17571472.2016.1152099

Hook, J. N., Davis, D. E., Owen, J., Worthington, E. L., & Utsey, S. O. (2013). Cultural humility: Measuring openness to culturally diverse clients. *Journal of Counseling Psychology, 60*(3), 353–366. https://doi.org/10.1037/a0032595

Irwin, E. C. (2006). Peter: A study of cumulative trauma: From "robot" to "regular guy." In L. Carey (Ed.), *Expressive and creative arts methods for trauma survivors* (pp. 93–1114). Jessica Kingsley Publishers.

Keeler, J. R., Roth, E. A., Neuser, B. L., Spitsbergen, J. M., Waters, D. J. M., & Vianney, J. M. (2015). The neurochemistry and social flow of singing: Bonding and oxytocin. *Frontiers in Human Neuroscience, 9*, Article 518. https://doi.org/10.3389/fnhum.2015.00518

Kirschner, S., & Tomasello, M. (2010). Joint music making promotes prosocial behavior in 4-year-old children. *Evolution and Human Behavior, 31*(5), 354–364. https://doi.org/10.1016/j.evolhumbehav.2010.04.004

Liz Lerman. (n.d.). *Build-a-phrase.* http://www.d-lab.org/toolbox/view/Build-a-Phrase

Loewy, J., Stewart, K., Dassler, A.-M., Telsey, A., & Homel, P. (2013). The effects of music therapy on vital signs, feeding, and sleep in premature infants. *Pediatrics, 131*(5), 902–918. https://doi.org/10.1542/peds.2012-1367

Mond, S. (2018). *Yoga stories for kids: A path to resilience and growth.* Mind Mend Publishing.

Nhat Hanh, T., & Vriezen, W. (2008). *Mindful movements: Ten exercises for well-being.* Parallax Press.

Ogden, P., Minton, K., & Pain, C. (2006). *Trauma and the body: A sensorimotor approach to psychotherapy.* W. W. Norton & Company.

Ogden, T. H. (2004). On holding and containing, being and dreaming. *The International Journal of Psycho-Analysis, 85*(6), 1349–1364. https://doi.org/10.1516/T41H-DGUX-9JY4-GQC7

Rabinowitch, T. C., & Meltzoff, A. N. (2017). Synchronized movement experience enhances peer cooperation in preschool children. *Journal of Experimental Child Psychology, 160*, 21–32. https://doi.org/10.1016/j.jecp.2017.03.001

Rodgers, R., & Hammerstein, O. (1964). Do-Re-Mi [Song]. On *The Sound of Music.* RCA.

Roediger, E., Stevens, B. A., & Brockman, R. (2018). *Contextual schema therapy: An integrative approach to personality disorders, emotional dysregulation & interpersonal functioning.* Context Press.

Rothschild, B. (2000). *The body remembers: The psychophysiology of trauma and trauma treatment.* W. W. Norton & Company.

Rothschild, B. (2017). *The body remembers: Volume two: Revolutionizing trauma treatment.* W. W. Norton & Company.

Schaefer, C. E., & Drewes, A. A. (Eds.). (2014). *The therapeutic powers of play: 20 core agents of change* (2nd ed.). John Wiley & Sons.

Schore, A. N. (2003). *Affect regulation & the repair of the self.* W. W. Norton & Company.

Studd, K., & Cox, L. (2013). *Everybody is a body.* Dog Ear Publishing.

Taylor de Faoite, A. (2014). Indirect teaching. In C. E. Schaefer & A. A. Drewes (Eds.), *The therapeutic powers of play: 20 core agents of change* (2nd ed., pp. 51–67). John Wiley & Sons.

Tortora, S. (2006). *The dancing dialogue: Using the communicative power of movement with young children*. Paul H. Brookes Publishing.

van der Kolk, B. (2014). *The body keeps the score: Brain, mind, and body in the healing of trauma*. Viking Press.

van Westrhenen, N., & Fritz, E. (2014). Creative arts therapy as a treatment for child trauma: An overview. *The Arts in Psychotherapy, 41*(5), 527–534. https://doi.org/10.1016/j.aip.2014.10.004

Wallin, D. J. (2007). *Attachment in psychotherapy*. Guilford Press.

Weeks, K. (2015). Vowels—sonic gems of emotion for social communication: Practical singing strategies for non-musician teachers with developmentally diverse young children. *Early Childhood Education Journal, 43*(6), 515–522. https://doi.org/10.1007/s10643-014-0681-2

13 THERAPEUTIC USE OF BOARD GAMES WITH CHILDREN

JACQUELINE M. SWANK AND JO L. WEAVER

Game play is defined as the use of games in the counseling process (Schaefer & Reid, 2001). There are five features of game play: (a) competition, (b) goal orientation, (c) increased cognition ability due to evoked ego processes, (d) interpersonal interactions, and (e) rules (Reid, 2001). Sutton-Smith and Roberts (1971) described three types of games: (a) physical games, which rely on gross and fine motor skills; (b) strategy games, which rely on problem solving; and (c) games of chance, in which the outcome of the game is not controlled by the players. Board games typically involve players moving to designated spots outlined on a game board, and although board games are most commonly grouped within strategy games or games of chance, they may also encompass some features of physical games through the inclusion of tasks in which players engage as they navigate their journey across the board.

Clinicians have used games in therapy for decades, as either an adjunct or central to the counseling process (Nickerson & O'Laughlin, 1983). Loomis (1957) discussed using checkers to address children's resistance to discussing problem areas. Then, in the 1970s, support grew for using games to foster communication in session, and two therapeutic games were created: the Talking, Feeling,

https://doi.org/10.1037/0000217-014
Play Therapy With Children: Modalities for Change, H. G. Kaduson and C. E. Schaefer (Editors)

and Doing Game (Creative Therapeutics, Bohemia, NY) and the Ungame (Talicor Inc., Plainwell, MI; Reid, 2001). Games have continued to evolve across time, which has resulted in the development of both new traditional games and games designed specifically for counseling that include technology features, including games available through apps and virtual board games. This chapter focuses on the use of board games in counseling children and addresses the therapeutic benefits, strategies and techniques, application for use with various childhood concerns, a case illustration, and empirical support.

THERAPEUTIC BENEFITS

Play positively influences the therapeutic effect of many change agents, which Drewes and Schaefer (2014) referred to as the "therapeutic powers" of play. The development of the therapeutic relationship is a crucial step in the counseling process, and the clinician may use board games as a play therapy intervention to help develop relationships with children. Games can be especially helpful with this process when a client is reluctant to engage with the counselor (Matorin & McNamara, 1996; Reid, 2001). Games are fun, and this may help open the door for interacting with the child (Swank, 2008). Scholars (e.g., Reid, 2001) have reported that games may also be effective in helping reduce clients' anxiety during the initial stage of counseling.

Counselors can use games to create a natural play environment in which to observe a child. Reid (2001) reported that creating this natural environment allows the child to relax, which may result in the child expressing more typical behaviors and feelings, including both desirable and undesirable ones. The counselor may observe how the child responds to rules, how they interact with others (if there are other players), their level of engagement and focus, how they react to doing well or not doing well on turns and, ultimately, how they respond to winning or losing the game. These observations can help facilitate the assessment and diagnosis processes (Swank, 2008).

Games facilitate communication (Bellinson, 2002; Reid, 2001; Swank, 2008). Children may be more willing to talk while playing a game because the focus is on the game. Conversation occurs naturally through the course of the game play, and children do not perceive the counselor as pressuring them to talk during this time. A child might be less focused on screening what they share with the counselor because they are focusing on the game. Therefore, the discussion of topics, even difficult ones, arises naturally instead of the child feeling forced to share.

In addition to facilitating communication, counselors may use games to help children develop social skills (Bay-Hinitz & Wilson, 2005; Reid, 2001;

Serok & Blum, 1983). This may involve interactions solely between the counselor and the child or those among members of a group of children. Through engagement in the board game during the counseling session, the counselor can help support children as they interact with each other and help them develop healthy ways to respond to various situations that occur during the games (e.g., cheating, winning or losing, a player doing something that affects their turn) while also helping them translate these responses to situations that occur outside of the counseling session.

Through engagement in board games during counseling sessions, children also have the opportunity to develop insight into situations that arise during game play and how such situations are related to their real lives (Reid, 2001). This provides opportunities for problem solving in the moment that may also translate to addressing situations that occur beyond the counseling session. Counselors have the opportunity to help children develop healthy coping skills and strategies to address conflict and a range of feelings (e.g., anger, sadness) that occur during the session that they may then continue to practice using outside of counseling sessions. Games also create opportunities for reality testing (Bellinson, 2002; Reid, 2001). Children will not always like the outcomes of the game and, as in real life, they cannot always control the outcome, without trying to alter the rules, which also has consequences.

CORE STRATEGIES AND TECHNIQUES: STEP BY STEP

In their work with children, counselors may use a variety of traditional board games (games not designed for counseling), as well as games designed specifically for counseling. They also may create new games, or modify traditional board games, to focus on a variety of therapeutic topics or concerns; specifically, they may seek to modify existing games because games designed for therapy are not always appealing to children. Children who are reluctant to attend counseling or who do not perceive themselves as having a problem with anxiety, for example, could be reluctant to play a board game with the word "anxiety" in the title; however, they may be willing to play a traditional game with which they are familiar that the counselor has modified to integrate some components of addressing or coping with anxiety. Although we refer mostly to games commonly known in the United States in this chapter, counselors can use the steps described here to modify nearly any game.

Swank (2008) discussed areas to consider when deciding whether to integrate a game into counseling and what specific game to use in sessions. One consideration is the purpose of using a game with a particular client. Counselors may integrate games into their therapeutic work to help facilitate relationship building or focus on various concerns that may be the focus of counseling. Deciding whether to use or modify an existing game, or create a new game, is an important step. The counselor should consider what the child's therapeutic goals are and how the game may help in addressing those goals.

Another variable the counselor will want to consider is the child's developmental level. Counselors should keep in mind that some children may want to explore games that are not typically used with their age group or developmental level. For example, adolescents may want to play board games that they enjoyed as a child, or a younger child may want to play a game that they have played with an older sibling. If the counselor allows the child to play a game that is outside of their developmental level, the counselor may need to make accommodations, especially if the child's developmental level is below the level of the game. For example, if a game requires reading, and the child does not have a strong reading ability yet, the counselor may offer to help read the text on the game cards.

Reading level is especially important to consider when playing a game during a group counseling session; counselors must avoid embarrassing a child who may struggle with reading (Kendall, 2003). In groups where some children struggle with reading, counselors can make a rule that the counselor will read all of the question cards in the game (Swank, 2008). Counselors may also offer children the opportunity to change the rules of a game to be more congruent with their developmental level. During group or family sessions it is especially important that the rules are clear for everyone before the game is begun.

The level of autonomy that the counselor gives the child in regard to the selection of the game and decisions about how the game is played may relate to the counseling goals and the counselor's personal therapeutic approach (e.g., direct vs. indirect; Swank, 2008). For example, in using a child-centered approach, the counselor may allow the child full autonomy in deciding how to play the game and in leading the game. In contrast, a counselor using a cognitive-behavioral approach may be more directive in establishing the rules and how the game is played as well as challenge the child's maladaptive thoughts and behaviors while playing the game (e.g., challenge the child's statement "I'm stupid" when they answer a question incorrectly, lose a turn, or get sent backward while playing the game). In Adlerian play, the counselor's goal of the game may be to engender the "Crucial Cs" (connect, capable, count, courage), or address a goal of misbehavior (attention, power, revenge, inadequacy). The participants involved in the session is also a consideration given that counselors may choose to integrate games with children during individual, family, and group counseling sessions.

Swank (2008) discussed some additional areas to consider when modifying an existing game or creating a new game, including the integration into the game of a variety of learning styles and senses, facilitation of engagement with and fun for children, and consideration of multicultural aspects and the ability to adapt the game to diverse populations. In regard to the integration of learning styles and senses, the counselor may integrate a variety of questions or tasks within the game, including knowledge-based questions, scenarios, and activities or tasks. Knowledge-based questions are factual and provide an opportunity for the counselor to educate the child about the topic as well as test their knowledge about the subject. Scenarios provide an opportunity for children to apply knowledge by considering how they would respond to real-life situations. Finally, the integration of activities or tasks provides an active component to the game. This can be especially important for children who have difficulty sitting still for a long time. This component provides an opportunity to try out what is learned. For example, children can actively demonstrate a coping strategy that goes beyond talking about what they would do in a given situation.

Lowenstein (1999) and Swank (2008) both have described examples of modifying existing games to use in counseling; specifically, Swank discussed modifying Candy Land (Hasbro, Pawtucket, RI) to focus on anger by adding questions and activities to the game cards. An example of a knowledge-based item is "It is okay to feel angry (True or False)." This is a crucial aspect to address because children who struggle with coping with their anger in healthy ways may associate feeling angry with getting in trouble and therefore think it is bad to feel angry. An example of a scenario-type question related to anger that was included in the game was "Jacob feels angry because his brother grabbed the toy that he was playing with; what should Jacob do?" This question could also be modified to be an activity or task by wording it as "Jacob feels angry because his brother grabbed the toy that he was playing with; show me what Jacob can do to calm down." The counselor can also tailor the situation and activity questions to apply to a specific child by using the child's name and offer situations that the child may experience or has experienced. In addition, the counselor can integrate activities, such as ones that focus on specific coping skills that the child is working on integrating into their life at home, school, or other settings. This makes the game real for the child and may help the child apply what they learned during the game to their lives beyond the counseling session.

The active component is especially engaging to children, and the counselor may also make the game more fun and engaging by adding some questions or activities to the game that are silly (i.e., make your favorite animal noise, stand up and wiggle like Jell-O; Swank, 2008). When integrating these activities within the modified Candy Land game that was focused on anger within a group setting, the first author found that, in addition to having fun, the children often said they forgot what they were doing for a moment because they were laughing. The author used this as a teaching moment to share with them that sometimes when someone is angry, taking a break for a few moments helps them feel less angry.

Counselors can address multicultural considerations in a variety of ways. For example, in using scenario-based questions they can change the names of the people to reflect names consistent with a particular racial or ethnic group. They also can create scenarios to which a child can personally relate (e.g., scenarios about a younger brother if they have a younger brother, scenarios about the rules at a parent's house compared with rules at the other parent's house if their parents are divorced). If there are figures used as game pieces, the counselor can also have a variety of figures available that represent diverse groups. Swank (2008) discussed the use of miniatures from her sandtray collection as game pieces. When identifying game pieces it is important to preselect pieces for children to choose from that are small enough to fit on the game spaces and that will stand up on their own. Selecting options in advance for children will help facilitate this process. Selecting the game piece also makes the game more personal for children, and the counselor may also learn something new about a child based on the reason they selected a particular game piece.

When modifying a game or developing a new game, counselors may also consider involving children in this process by integrating this into counseling sessions. Smith and Renter (1997) discussed the development of games within family counseling and reported that children may develop the game on their own with the counselor, or the process may also involve the family. Children and their families could develop games that focus on a variety of topics, and involvement of parents in the process may help avoid a sole focus on the child as the root of the family's problem as well as reduce parents' resistance to participating in counseling (Smith & Renter, 1997). Swank (2008) discussed involving children in this process by explaining modifications made to Chutes and Ladders (Hasbro, Pawtucket, RI), also known as Snakes and Ladders, a game that dates back to the second century BC. In modifying this game, Swank cut out squares of blank paper the size of the spaces on the board and allowed children to draw pictures in the squares that represented choices and consequences from their own lives and then add them to the board. Children were then able to play the game with the counselor. This game could also be modified within a family session. It is important to note that developing or modifying a game in session takes time, and the counselor may need to allow multiple sessions to modify or create the game and then play it. It is unlikely that a counselor would be able to accomplish both of these tasks in a single session.

CLINICAL APPLICATIONS FOR USE WITH VARIOUS CHILDHOOD CONCERNS

A number of therapeutic board games address the gamut of childhood problems. As discussed, a clinician can also modify existing, child-friendly board games to address the child's presenting problem. To this point, board games can build emotional vocabulary, reinforce coping skills, and create an outlet for discussion. Board games can catalyze the child's developmental skills in the cognitive, affective, behavioral, and social domains (Jordan, 2002). Before introducing any game, the clinician should be cognizant of, and intentional with, their selection and modification to best address the child's needs. Therefore, in the sections that follow, we examine specific childhood concerns to which board games are particularly germane and offer suggestions on how to modify existing board games to address these concerns.

Anxiety

Children can experience heightened anxiety when first entering counseling. Researchers have highlighted the reciprocal relationship between the therapeutic alliance, which influences the outcome of therapy, and anxiety reduction, which improves the therapeutic alliance (Marker et al., 2013). Games can lower children's anxiety about beginning therapy (Reid, 2001). Counselors can use existing board games to provide a sense of structure and familiarity for clients and to neutralize the power differential between clinician and client (Swank, 2008). In these beginning sessions, the counselor may allow the child to choose a common board game, such as Chutes and Ladders. To promote a sense of mastery, the child can explain to the counselor how to play the game. Playing board games adds a component of fun to counseling and reduces stress and anxiety within the session.

As the therapeutic alliance forms, the counselor can also modify a game to address the child's anxiety that occurs in various settings. This presents a new, fun way to play the existing game that explores the child's anxiety and supports the development of healthy coping skills. For example, the counselor can modify Chutes and Ladders by generating ladder and chute cards. The ladder cards will be drawn as the client goes up the ladder, and these will include coping skills for the child and counselor to practice (e.g., deep breathing) or a question for the child to answer (e.g., "Whom can you talk to when you feel afraid?"). The child will draw the chute cards as he or she goes down the chute that includes questions and prompts to further explore the child's anxiety (e.g., "Name something that scares you. Is it real or pretend?"). As the child becomes accustomed to the game, the cards can be removed and, when they "fall down" the chutes on the game board they can describe times they were anxious during the week and, when "climbing up" the ladders discuss coping skills they used. Designing the game so that cards are drawn only on the ladders and chutes spaces is a strategy counselors can use to make the game therapeutic without overwhelming the child by having them answer a question on each turn.

Emotion Regulation

In children, emotion dysregulation includes an inability to effectively express their emotional responses, which usually results in a behavioral outburst (Roy et al., 2013). Board games can be a regulating tool for counselors as players learn emotional control and tolerance (Swank, 2008). Numerous traditional board games (e.g., Candy Land, Chutes and Ladders, Operation, Sorry!, and Trouble [also known as Frustration in the United Kingdom and as Kimble in Finland]; Hasbro, Pawtucket, RI) address emotion regulation through the outcome of their turn. For example, in Candy Land a player may draw a card that sends them close to the end of the board or back toward the beginning. In Chutes and Ladders, the spinner may land on a number advancing the player to a space that has a ladder or a chute on it. In Operation, the child might successfully grab the piece, or the buzzer may sound as they hit the side of an "operating area." Finally, in Sorry! and Trouble, in addition to the space they advance to based on their role or card, other players' moves may affect a child's place on the board. Thus, counselors have the opportunity to reflect feelings (thereby helping children develop a feeling vocabulary), set limits as needed, and help children process their emotions and develop healthy ways to cope with the outcome of their turn in traditional games without any modifications.

Counselors can also embed coping skills within the game. For example, the second author modified Operation by stating a coping skill, and the child was then asked to guess which game piece goes with the strategy (i.e., deep breathing for butterflies in the tummy, telling a joke for funny bone, writing down your feelings for writer's cramp). The labels of the body parts may have to be altered depending on the edition of the game. The game can be developed into a type of code for the child to remember these coping skills. For example, the child can practice the deep breathing when the counselor points to their tummy, and write down their feelings when the counselor makes a specified gesture with their hands (writer's cramp). The child and counselor can introduce these codes to the parents or teachers to remind the child of specific coping skills without having to directly state it in the moment. Also while playing Operation, the child has the opportunity to work on frustration tolerance and impulse control when they are unable to successfully remove a body part and during real life situations can use the coping skill they identified during these moments.

Anger management is also a common issue with children who exhibit emotional dysregulation. Swank (2008) and Reycraft (2007) both have suggested modifying Candy Land to focus on anger management. Reycraft discussed telling the saga of Lord Licorice's anger management problem and his siege of Candy Land. Players name positive ways for Lord Licorice to cope with his anger when they land on his spaces in addition to other black dots on the board. Including a story, as Reycraft suggested, can also add a component of fun to the game and increase engagement. Stories and metaphors provide children with an opportunity to experience therapeutic concepts in a developmentally appropriate way and can highlight social–emotional themes in children (Friedberg & Wilt, 2010; Russo et al., 2006). In addition, mutual storytelling is an Adlerian play therapy technique that illustrates the child's goals (i.e., attention, power, revenge, inadequacy) and the current behavior used to reach said goals (Kottman & Stiles, 1990). The use of storytelling in board games can further explore these themes and goals.

Disciplinary Problems at School

Children who experience disciplinary problems may be resistant to discussing them, especially with an authority figure. However, board games can engage these children and help build trust and create a safe environment in which they can address conflict by discussing their perspective about their behavior at school. Lowenstein (1999) modified Trouble to include cards depicting scenarios in which the child felt they did something wrong or got in trouble. The players would then brainstorm positive ways to cope with the situation.

Similar to what she did with Trouble, the second author used the board game Sorry! for clients to identify times they were sorry for their choice of words or actions. As with the traditional rules, a player who landed on the same space as another player would shout "Sorry!" when the other player had to return home. In addition, the player who said "Sorry!" would describe a time they had felt sorry for something they did, or that they regretted. If they had not apologized in the discussed situation, the player would explore ways to make amends, or practice how they would have liked to apologize in the moment. If they had apologized, the players discussed the outcome of the apology (i.e., how they felt afterward, how others responded). The counselor can also introduce a forgiveness component by instructing the player who returned to the home space to describe a time they forgave someone else.

Social-Emotional Learning

Games create an environment in which social learning can occur (Serok & Blum, 1983). Children can practice socialized competition, cooperation, and socioflexibility through game playing in counseling (Swank, 2008), especially in a group setting. Board games highlight social rules and boundaries, such as learning to take turns and expectations of appropriate behavior. Playing board games one on one or in a group can help the players learn socially acceptable behaviors they can then implement in other parts of their lives.

Counselors can also promote social–emotional learning by presenting board games that focus on identifying and articulating emotions. Again, counselors can use the popular board game Candy Land to help young clients develop emotional intelligence by labeling each color spot with an emotion (e.g., red for angry). The players must answer a prompt that is in accordance with these specific colors. The counselor can write the various prompts on cards. Examples of prompts include "Describe a time when you felt this emotion," "How do you identify this emotion in others?," and "What other words can you use to describe these emotions?" The counselor may also have a feeling word chart available depending on the child's developmental level. Counselors can do something similar to this with older children by associating each row of a checkers (also known as "draughts" in the United Kingdom) or chess board with a "Feeling" category and asking the questions related to the feeling associated with the row they move to during their turn. For example, a child may move to a row labeled "sad," and a question or task for that row could be, "Describe a healthy way to cope with sadness." Counselors can also modify bingo cards by labeling each space with feelings and asking children to name a time when they felt an emotion associated with the space on the card (Swank, 2008). Thus, counselors can use a variety of board games to address a multitude of counseling topics and concerns.

CASE ILLUSTRATION

We illustrate the use of board games in therapy with a fictional case. Kevin is an 8-year-old White male who was referred to a counselor because of his angry outbursts in the classroom, which involved screaming, throwing things, and calling his teacher and classmates inappropriate names. The outbursts typically ended with Kevin storming out of the classroom in tears. The school counselor, Cameron, is a 36-year-old Hispanic woman who had been an elementary school counselor for 7 years. Cameron often used board games in her sessions with students as a therapeutic tool for coping skills development and rapport building. In her office, she had a designated game-play area with popular board games. She often used games with students who appeared apprehensive about counseling.

When Kevin entered the counseling room, he appeared hesitant and shy. Cameron introduced him to her board game collection and prompted Kevin to pick his favorite game. Kevin quickly grabbed Chutes and Ladders and began to set up the game. Cameron asked if he wanted to explain to her the rules, and Kevin enthusiastically replied, "Yes!" While Kevin provided the general rules to the game, he added his own twists as well. Throughout the game, Kevin was a steadfast rule-keeper and would quickly point out if Cameron had violated one of his rules. Cameron took this opportunity to ask Kevin about his family and friends and what had been going on in the classroom. Kevin explained that he gets frustrated with other kids because they won't follow his rules. The other kids ignore his instructions, which makes him upset and unable to control his anger. Kevin reported that he hated getting into trouble but that he was not sorry for his actions because the other kids should listen to him. Cameron asked if they could play one of her favorite games in their next session, and Kevin agreed.

Cameron prepared the game Sorry! for their next session. Through their first session, she had built rapport with Kevin by allowing him to pick and lead their game, during which time he exhibited the issues he experienced in class. This week, she wanted to see how he could follow someone else's rules and work on learning how and when to apologize. For her version of Sorry! the player must draw a card when they land on the same space as another player. These cards included prompts on apologizing and forgiveness in various instances (e.g., "Describe a time at home you said 'sorry' or regretted your actions").

Kevin entered the room excited to play another round of games. He remembered that Cameron had a special game picked out for them. Cameron explained the rules and Kevin looked perplexed at the addition of the cards. He asserted that this was not how he played the game and proceeded to provide an elaborate set of rules. Cameron waited for him to finish and then began to reflect some of Kevin's feelings (e.g., frustration) about the game not including his rules. He got quiet and nodded his head. Cameron thought this could be a good time for Kevin to learn about working together and compromising. She explained the concept of compromise, and Kevin appeared confused. Cameron decided this could be a good time to model it with this game. She began by asking Kevin which one of his rules for this game was most important. After he described his rule, she explained a compromise would be keeping both her rule and adding his rule. She asked if this would be okay with Kevin, and he agreed, appearing suspicious.

Consistent with the previous session, Kevin constantly reminded Cameron of his rule. She acknowledged Kevin's strength in remembering his rule but reminded him that compromise meant that everyone's rules counted, and everyone wins. She asked if he could remind them of all the rules for the rest of the game. Kevin proudly replied, "Of course!" and began enforcing all the rules. However, regarding the cards, Kevin provided silly answers (e.g., "I felt sorry when I didn't give my dog a treat"). Cameron modeled the type of answers she was looking for during her turn, using situations from her childhood (e.g., yelling at her parents and telling them she hated them). Then, after a few times, Kevin drew a card that asked him about a time he apologized in class. He was stumped. He had always refused to apologize, which got him in more trouble. This prompted Cameron to ask Kevin when people should apologize. He sat silently and then began crying. He acknowledged the things he had said during his outbursts as being hurtful and that he regretted them. However, he felt too embarrassed to apologize after he had already cried in front of his classmates. This led to a discussion of how apologizing is an act of courage. Cameron and Kevin role-played how to apologize to his teacher and classmates. Kevin told Cameron he was going to do his best to apologize to everyone, but it might take some time. Cameron reassured him that was okay, and he returned to class.

Cameron used games to address Kevin's need to be in charge and applied Kevin's strength in rule-following to enforce a new rule of compromising with others. Kevin also learned the importance of apologizing as well as how to do this with his classmates and teacher. Before their next session, Kevin's teacher reported to Cameron that he had been explaining to the other students how to compromise during group activities and at recess. Kevin had also made the teacher an apology card, and she had overheard him apologizing to a few students for calling them names in the past. The teacher wondered about asking Kevin to teach the class about compromise. Cameron thought this was an excellent idea.

At their next session, Kevin reported his new responsibility was to teach other students how to compromise. He shared how his classmates listened to him more now. Cameron asked if he thought that was because he also listened to them, and he replied, "You know, you're probably right! Everyone wins with compromise! So, can we compromise on a game to play today?"

EMPIRICAL SUPPORT

Although counselors often use board games for multiple purposes, the effi-cacy of board games in counseling remains greatly undertested (Matorin & McNamara, 1996). To date, only a limited amount of research has focused on the outcomes of using board games in therapy, and most of this research "stems from clinician reports and nonscientific sources" (Matorin & McNamara, 1996, p. 9). We found only two studies that have examined the effectiveness of board games with children (Bay-Hinitz et al., 1994; Kaduson & Finnerty, 1995)

Bay-Hinitz et al. (1994) introduced cooperative and competitive games to 70 preschool children (ages 4–5), assigning the children to four groups. The preschool setting included both indoor play areas, which contained large desks, and outdoor play areas with playground equipment. The teachers were informed of the general structure of the study and provided a list of coopera-tive and competitive games to introduce to the children. The teachers led both types of games on the list for 30 minutes each day. The competitive games included Candy Land, Chutes and Ladders, Aggravation, Double Trouble, and Children's Trivial Pursuit, and the cooperative games included Max, Harvest Time, Granny's House, and Sleeping Grump. The children played the board games during the designated 30 minutes, and then the games were made inaccessible during free play. Trained observers recorded the cooperative and aggressive behaviors of all groups. The participants' behavior positively corre-lated with the type of board game being played that day. During both game time and free play, aggressive behavior increased when playing competitive games, and cooperative behavior increased when playing coop-erative games. These findings reveal the type of game can affect children's behavior during subsequent free play, which underlines the influence of games.

Kaduson and Finnerty (1995) compared the effectiveness of two game interventions—a cognitive-behavioral game and a biofeedback game that included self-control training—with a control group who engaged in struc-tured game play with board games without self-control training for children ages 8–12 with attention-deficit/hyperactivity disorder. In regard to the chil-dren's perceptions of self-control, the biofeedback group and the control group both demonstrated significant improvements, with children in the bio-feedback group showing the greatest improvement. In contrast, parents of children in all three groups reported significant behavioral improvements in sociability and attention, with parents of children in the control group indi-cating the greatest improvement in behavior. The control group also was the only group to demonstrate improvements in hyperactive symptoms. Thus, the researchers found support for using board games with children with attention-deficit/hyperactivity disorder.

As demonstrated by the aforementioned studies, in-session board game use can influence future behaviors of children. Bay-Hinitz and Wilson (2005) recommended evaluating cooperative games through observation and self-report. Counselors can assign one or more people to observe the child's aggressive behaviors in various contexts and document increases, decreases, or observable differences. Parents or teachers may also tally the number of times aggressive behaviors occur during cooperative game play. These observations can inform the efficacy of cooperative game play, along with any environmental differences in which the aggressive behavior occurs. Counselors can also use observation to track desired and undesired behaviors to measure the outcome of playing board games during sessions. Thus, it is crucial to observe children's behaviors before, during, and after the use of board games.

SUMMARY AND CONCLUSIONS

This chapter has focused on board games as a therapeutic modality in counseling children and adolescents. Board games provide counselors with a mechanism for fostering the therapeutic relationship with children as well as a means of addressing a variety of mental health concerns. In addition to existing board games, including those designed specifically for therapy, counselors may also embrace their own creativity to modify existing games and create their own games. The extant literature describes numerous potential benefits of using board games in counseling; however, minimal research in this area exists. Thus, counseling professionals are encouraged to continue to creatively engage in board game play with children and adolescents as well as engage in research regarding the effectiveness of this approach.

REFERENCES

Bay-Hinitz, A. K., Peterson, R. F., & Quilitch, H. R. (1994). Cooperative games: A way to modify aggressive and cooperative behaviors in young children. *Journal of Applied Behavior Analysis, 27*(3), 435–446. https://doi.org/10.1901/jaba.1994.27-435

Bay-Hinitz, A. K., & Wilson, G. R. (2005). A cooperative games intervention for aggressive preschool children. In L. A. Reddy, T. M. Files-Hall, & C. E. Schaefer (Eds.), *Empirically based play interventions for children* (pp. 191–211). American Psychological Association. https://doi.org/10.1037/11086-011

Bellinson, J. (2002). *Children's use of board games in psychotherapy.* Jason Aronson.

Drewes, A. A., & Schaefer, C. E. (2014). How play therapy causes change. In A. A. Drewes & C. E. Schaefer (Eds.), *The therapeutic powers of change: 20 core agents of change* (2nd ed., pp. 1–7). Wiley.

Friedberg, R. D., & Wilt, L. H. (2010). Metaphors and stories in cognitive behavioral therapy with children. *Journal of Rational-Emotive & Cognitive-Behavior Therapy, 28*(2), 100–113. https://doi.org/10.1007/s10942-009-0103-3

Jordan, K. B. (2002). Create-a-game. In R. W. Watts (Ed.), *Techniques in marriage and family counseling* (Vol. 2, pp. 105–108). American Counseling Association.

Kaduson, H. G., & Finnerty, K. (1995). Self-control game interventions for attention-deficit hyperactivity disorder. *International Journal of Play Therapy, 4*(2), 15–29. https://doi.org/10.1037/h0089359

Kendall, J. (2003). Using games with adults in a play therapy group setting. In C. E. Schaefer (Ed.), *Play therapy with adults* (pp. 317–323). Wiley.

Kottman, T., & Stiles, K. (1990). The mutual storytelling technique: An Adlerian application in child therapy. *Individual Psychology, 46*(2), 148–156.

Loomis, E. A., Jr. (1957). The use of checkers in handling certain resistances in child therapy and child analysis. *Journal of the American Psychoanalytic Association, 5*(1), 130–135. https://doi.org/10.1177/000306515700500107

Lowenstein, L. (1999). *Creative interventions for troubled children and youth.* Hignell.

Marker, C. D., Comer, J. S., Abramova, V., & Kendall, P. C. (2013). The reciprocal relationship between alliance and symptom improvement across the treatment of childhood anxiety. *Journal of Clinical Child and Adolescent Psychology, 42*(1), 22–33. https://doi.org/10.1080/15374416.2012.723261

Matorin, A. I., & McNamara, J. R. (1996). Using board games in therapy with children. *International Journal of Play Therapy, 5*(2), 3–16. https://doi.org/10.1037/h0089022

Nickerson, E. T., & O'Laughlin, K. S. (1983). The therapeutic use of games. In C. E. Schaefer & K. J. O'Connor (Eds.), *Handbook of play therapy* (pp. 174–187). Wiley.

Reid, S. E. (2001). The psychology of play and games. In C. E. Schaefer & S. E. Reid (Eds.), *Game play: Therapeutic use of childhood games* (2nd ed., pp. 1–36). Wiley.

Reycraft, J. (2007, Spring). Candy Land or angry land? *The Playful Healer, 13*, 7.

Roy, A. K., Klein, R. G., Angelosante, A., Bar-Haim, Y., Leibenluft, E., Hulvershorn, L., Dixon, E., Dodds, A., & Spindel, C. (2013). Clinical features of young children referred for impairing temper outbursts. *Journal of Child and Adolescent Psychopharmacology, 23*(9), 588–596. https://doi.org/10.1089/cap.2013.0005

Russo, M. F., Vernam, J., & Wolbert, A. (2006). Sandplay and storytelling: Social constructivism and cognitive development in child counseling. *The Arts in Psychotherapy, 33*(3), 229–237. https://doi.org/10.1016/j.aip.2006.02.005

Schaefer, C. E., & Reid, S. E. (2001). *Game play: Therapeutic use of childhood games* (2nd ed.). Wiley.

Serok, S., & Blum, A. (1983). Therapeutic uses of games. *Residential Group Care & Treatment, 1*(3), 3–14. https://doi.org/10.1300/J297v01n03_02

Smith, C. W., & Renter, S. G. (1997). The play is the thing: Using self-constructed board games in family therapy. *Journal of Family Psychotherapy, 8*(3), 67–72. https://doi.org/10.1300/J085V08N03_07

Sutton-Smith, B., & Roberts, J. M. (1971). The cross cultural and psychological study of games. *International Review for the Sociology of Sport, 6*(1), 79–87. https://doi.org/10.1177/101269027100600105

Swank, J. M. (2008). The use of games: A therapeutic tool with children and families. *International Journal of Play Therapy, 17*(2), 154–167. https://doi.org/10.1037/1555-6824.17.2.154

14 ELECTRONIC GAME PLAY THERAPY

KEVIN B. HULL

Electronic game play therapy is the application of computer, video, and tablet games in helping people overcome psychological and emotional problems (Hull, 2016). Researchers have discovered the benefits of incorporating everyday electronic games into play therapy (Baker, 2019; Hull, 2019; LaFleur et al., 2018) in addition to apps and games designed for specific therapeutic use. This chapter examines the benefits and effectiveness of electronic game play as well as core techniques and clinical applications. A fictional case study is presented to demonstrate the techniques and applications; this is followed by a discussion of the empirical support for electronic game play.

THERAPEUTIC BENEFITS OF ELECTRONIC GAME PLAY

Some of the "therapeutic powers of play" (Schaefer & Drewes, 2014, p. xiv) found in the application of electronic game play, such as facilitating communication, enhancing social relationships, increasing personal strength through creative problem solving and resiliency, and developing self-representation, are discussed in the following subsections.

https://doi.org/10.1037/0000217-015
Play Therapy With Children: Modalities for Change, H. G. Kaduson and C. E. Schaefer (Editors)

Facilitating Communication

Hull (2016) discussed how electronic game play provides a familiar platform for the child and helps with "communicating thoughts and feelings" (p. 616). Electronic game play is particularly useful for children with neurodevelopmental challenges, who may struggle with language because of developmental delays. Communication through electronic game play occurs as the child expresses thoughts, feelings, and behaviors during solitary and dual game play with the counselor. Communication also occurs when a counselor, armed with the information elicited by the child interacting with the game, reflects back to the child by providing affirmation, feedback, and encouragement (e.g., when a child whose parents are going through a divorce repeatedly makes his game character jump off a cliff to his death and remarks, "Nobody cares; that's just how it is"). This and other behavior in game play communicates to the counselor the child's feelings of abandonment and hopelessness.

Enhancing Social Relationships

Electronic game play enhances social relationships by creating a foundation for the development of the therapeutic alliance between the counselor and the child, which is characterized by trust and a sense of safety (Hull, 2016), in addition to providing a representation to the child of an affirming, collaborative relationship. Many electronic games, such as Minecraft (Mojang Studios, 2015), can be played together with the counselor, placing an emphasis on collaboration and social dynamics such as awareness, perspective taking, and protecting one another from enemies. The use of electronic games also allows the child to take on a teaching role, by enabling them to, for example, show the counselor how to play and various strategies to improve game play. Hull (2014) discussed the use of electronic games in therapy groups with children diagnosed with autism spectrum disorder (ASD) to teach social skills and noted that electronic gaming is useful in promoting prosocial behavior, in particular in games played together whereby the player interacts with others to accomplish goals and objectives (Jackson & Games, 2015).

Increasing Personal Strength Through Creative Problem Solving and Resiliency

Electronic game play also is beneficial for increasing personal strength and resiliency through the development of coping skills by means of creative problem solving. For example, overcoming challenges, making decisions, and conquering fear are common themes found in nearly every electronic game. Many electronic games contain situations that require players to craft creative solutions so they can reach goals and acquire abilities; this involves the skills of patience and dedication. Aspects of resilience, such as not giving up, learning from mistakes, and analyzing a problem in order to solve it also pop up in electronic game play and, through the affirmation of the counselor, the child can experience an increase in personal strength and resilience.

Developing Self-Representation

Self-representation encompasses emotional and cognitive factors, specifically, the sense of self that the child carries consisting of thoughts and feelings about oneself and the world around them (Harter, 2016). Specific elements of self-representation include a sense of self-worth and self-awareness, which leads to confidence in representing oneself to the world and the development of competency in relationships and achievements. Self-representation—being aware of the thoughts and feelings of the self and others and learning to take other's perspectives—is the foundation for forming and maintaining relationships. Perspective taking is something that develops in middle to later childhood and is lacking in children who have ASD and other psychological issues, such as trauma from abuse and neglect (Harter, 2016; Hull, 2016). Many children who come to therapy lack a sense of self, and they often suffer from a sense of low self-worth and struggle with perspective taking.

Electronic game play is helpful in developing self-representation. First, many games allow the player to create and use a unique character known as an "avatar." The avatar is a representation of the player within the context of the game as the player interacts with the elements of the game. Players can customize their avatar, and children love doing this. In fact, this can be a powerful part of the initial work of building self-representation and creating a sense of self-awareness for children with neurodevelopmental challenges (Hull, 2016). An avatar "helps individuals create a specific narrative for the character which may represent internal manifestations" (Bean, 2019, p. 98), thus providing the child a representation of self that they can generalize to the real world.

A second way electronic game play is helpful in developing self-representation is that electronic games are useful tools to create a self-narrative that leads to increased self-knowledge and self-worth. Apps such as Sock Puppets Complete (Smith Micro Software Inc., 2014) and Toontastic 3D (Google LLC, 2017) allow a player to create characters and customize their creation through the addition of music and a variety of voices. Customization of characters, in addition to creating a story, is a metaphor for establishing a sense of self and presenting that self to the external world. The LEGO Movie 2 Movie Maker (LEGO System A/S, 2019) app provides an opportunity to create stop-motion movies and bring a story to life. These games and apps provide a counselor with tools to reflect back to the child an awareness of self and to create an autobiographical memory experience. Using electronic games also gives the child the opportunity to take on the persona of a heroic persona, such as the characters in The Avengers, and to play out scenarios of escaping danger, rescuing people in distress, and feeling powerful and in control. For children with neurodevelopmental challenges, these games and apps are important because their working memory and autobiographical memory process are often delayed or offline during key periods of development.

A third application of using electronic game play in developing self-representation is by increasing perspective taking. A common theme in electronic games is how the player's character interacts with other characters during the game play experience. The other characters have several different qualities: Some are enemies, some are helpful, and some are neutral in that they are neither harmful nor helpful but simply just there. As children play games, bringing these other characters to their awareness can be useful in helping them process thoughts and feelings as they interact with these characters.

CORE TECHNIQUES

The following techniques demonstrate the application of key components in using electronic game play in therapy. These techniques are useful in forming a therapeutic alliance, providing a broader understanding of the client's world, and helping the client broaden perspective in understanding the world around them.

Adapting Game Themes and Metaphors to the Child

One of the most beneficial elements of electronic game play is that the themes found therein directly reflect the challenges that life presents on a daily basis. Overcoming problems, making decisions, forming and achieving goals, controlling impulses, gathering and managing resources, relying on others for help, developing attributes, dealing with loss and failure, and experiencing the joy of achievement through balancing risk and reward are all challenges children will face and ideally master in electronic game play (Hull, 2016). A child struggling with change due to loss or a transition can play out pertinent themes when, for example, the stage suddenly shifts in a "stage morph" in Super Smash Bros. (Nintendo, 2018). A child with impulse control problems must learn to wait for a special ability to become available during game play, or a child battling anxiety must face a "boss" at the end of a stage and defeat it.

Metaphors found in electronic games are the foundation of the process of providing "life applications" (Hull, 2016, p. 616), in which the counselor helps create awareness in the child's mind of the relationship between what is happening in electronic game play and the situation being faced in the real world. A child broken by fear and anger over losing his family and living in foster care can fight through immense odds in a survival game, dodging enemies, building and hiding in shelters, and making key decisions while relying on others to finish a series of missions. The counselor can reflect to a child who is ecstatic over his accomplishment as follows:

> You fought through many challenges, and you didn't give up! You used your brain to think and your ability to rely on others. This is just like what you are doing each day to make good choices and adapt to life's challenges!

Through the identification of themes and metaphors, electronic game play can be adapted to the various theoretical orientations of therapy. For example, the thinking process behind player's decisions can be examined (cognitive), electronic games can create trust and relationship between therapist and client (person centered), and the stories found in electronic games can be applied to the child's current challenges or experiences (narrative).

Electronic game play, whether used strategically to work on a specific problem, such as impulse control or anxiety, or done in a child-centered manner and simply allowing a child to freely express and discover important parts of the self, offers many tools to enhance clinical work. Noticing themes in the child's play, such as levels of frustration and perseverance, as well as striving for emotional control, allows the counselor to draw from metaphors in the game to assist the child in broadening perspective, gaining self-knowledge, and implementing tools and strategies to overcome emotional disturbances. Reflection of these themes is important to develop the child's awareness: "It seems that when you think you aren't going to make it to the end, you just give up. I wonder what you could try next time to keep going?" In addition, reflections that provide encouragement by pointing out new coping skills are important: "Hey, even though you got frustrated, you were able to reach your goal. That's just like what you are doing in school now."

Working Together: Joining in Play and Healing

Can electronic game play really be genuine play and therapeutic at the same time? Many factors provide a resounding "Yes!" to this question. Play is universal and necessary for the child to develop a sense of self and to learn about the exterior world and others. Play continues through the life span (Winnicott, 1989) and takes on many forms. Play is both a foundation and a conduit; it establishes a structure for acquiring knowledge about how to navigate novel situations while providing a practice ground for the application of skills necessary to ensure survival. Electronic game play incorporates these aspects in general, whether a single- or two-player game and regardless of the type of game. In a therapeutic sense, many dynamics of electronic game play allow counselors to join their youthful clients and apply elements of the game play to real-life situations, in addition to learning about a child from observing how the child plays and interacts with the game. Playing electronic games with children and integrating the games into therapy can be a powerful tool in helping reduce emotional disturbances and broadening perspective (Hull, 2016), as well as improving cognitive, emotional, and social functioning (Jackson & Games, 2015).

Electronic game play provides the counselor with the opportunity to assess the child's challenges and provide feedback to the child. The counselor can assess the level of the child's emotional disturbance in real time during game play, bring it to the child's awareness, implement techniques to reduce the emotional arousal, make new choices without autonomic nervous system arousal, and process the experience with the child. This process of increasing meta-awareness increases the child's sense of self-knowledge and self-awareness and strengthens neuroprotection through strategies to reduce emotional disturbances.

Playing two-player games with the counselor can be helpful for character interaction between counselor and child because it provides a reference point for the child to see and hear another's perspective through interacting in game play. This dimension of electronic game play generalizes to the child's experiences in the external world. Many children who come to therapy are dealing with varying levels of bullying and rejection. For example, a child playing Minecraft might make a connection during game play between the enemies in the game and the bullies in school. This can help creates a dialogue about finding solutions and metaphors in the game and reveal to the child that although ignoring and avoiding unpleasant others is an option, sometimes there is a place for direct confrontation. The child and counselor can process the child's thoughts and feelings during game play and brainstorm solutions. Two-player games played with the counselor send the message to the child that they are not alone in their struggles and that they can ask for help.

CLINICAL APPLICATIONS

Electronic game play is useful for addressing a range of clinical issues, such as understanding and tolerating negative emotions, and helping to put feelings into words. There are also many positive implications from the field of neuroscience as to the effectiveness of using electronic games in therapy.

Addressing Emotional Problems

Electronic game play is well suited for dealing with emotional issues because, during game play, emotions such as fear, frustration, and excitement may arise. Themes found in electronic games, such as overcoming challenges to reach goals, facing "mobs" or "bosses," and navigating risk and reward situations create emotional reactions in the player. Electronic games provide the chance for children who struggle with tolerating negative emotions to learn emotional control. Emotional control results in a sense of autonomy and self-control, which provides neuroprotection by warding off depression and anxiety and gives the child a sense of mastery. Described as "flow" (Jackson & Games, 2015, p. 22), this state of being involves an enjoyable experience of being in control with a reduced sense of self-consciousness and creates repeated positive emotional experiences. This state connects the child to a sense of safety that fosters neurodevelopmental growth and healing.

An effective example of a game designed specifically for therapeutic use with children who experience emotional disturbances is MindLight (GainPlay Studio, 2014), a cognitive behavior therapy–based video game designed to treat anxiety. MindLight teaches relaxation through biofeedback, exposure training, and "attention-bias modification" (Wols et al., 2018, p. 656). Play-Mancer (Fernández-Aranda et al., 2012) is another example of an effective "serious" game to increase impulse control by teaching relaxation skills and developing "emotional regulation strategies" (p. 364). Serious games are examples of an increasing genre that incorporates strategies of therapeutic interventions in a fun, relatable way. Since the invention of the iPad, several apps have been developed specifically for therapeutic use with people who experience emotional disturbances (Grant, 2019). The Virtual Sandtray app (Stone, 2016), a digital form of a sand tray, offers myriad backgrounds and materials for sand play on a portable platform. Effective with children experiencing emotional disturbances, the Virtual Sandtray is especially useful for counselors in rural areas and schools that are limited by a lack of play materials.

General electronic games and apps are effective in increasing frustration tolerance and emotional awareness, and two-player games are effective in building rapport between counselor and child (Hull, 2016). Two-player games increase social connection, communication skills, and incorporate the themes of trust building and working together to solve a problem. Children who have experienced emotional disturbances often feel isolated, and developmentally they have a hard time advocating for themselves and asking for help. Gaming with the therapist helps the child feel empowered and builds self-knowledge and self-worth while instilling a reference point that affirms the child is not alone in their struggles.

Developing Cognitive and Communication Strategies

Because of developmental delays and challenges of daily living, children who come to therapy often struggle with putting thoughts and feelings into words. Play is a vehicle for expression, and electronic game play provides a valuable tool for a child to enhance communication with others. As previously mentioned, children in therapy often have experienced trauma, and others struggle with ASD, attention-deficit/hyperactivity disorder (ADHD), and other neurodevelopmental challenges, which leave them with a fragmented sense of self. Using electronic games in therapy helps create autobiographical memories by creating a narrative of the gaming experience, thereby contributing to the child's self-narrative and instilling in them a sense of self through the gaming experience. This develops the child's self-knowledge and self-awareness and provides a practice ground for shifting attention in goal-oriented tasks. For example, having a child who battles ADHD play a game in which they must focus solely on the goal and block out other stimuli provides valuable practice for success in their daily life at school. In addition, electronic games can help a child verbalize thoughts and feelings as the counselor helps the child create a narrative of the process used to formulate a goal and work toward reaching that goal.

Electronic game play creates possibilities for a child to make meaning of experiences to further a sense of self-knowledge. Children who have experienced trauma, with neurodevelopmental challenges such as ASD, struggle with forming autobiographical memories, which results in "fragmented self-concepts" (Lind, 2010, p. 440). The complications of ASD bring to a halt the parts of the brain needed for interpretation of events, mainly the parts that create meaning from experiences and connect these memories with self-awareness. Electronic gaming and the gaming experience provide the opportunity for counselors to help children expand their cognitive awareness, in addition to helping them put thoughts and feelings into words.

Enhancing Healthy Brain Development

Neuroscience research has provided evidence that the previously discussed elements of electronic game play offer significant benefits in the treatment of neurodevelopmental challenges and enhancement of healthy brain development (Chan & Siegel, 2018). Part of this evidence involves two networks in the brain: (a) the default mode network (DMN)—a group of neural processes that are active in states of being in awareness of both the self and others, as well as remembering the past and planning for future events—and (b) the task positive network (TPN). Chan and Siegel (2018) discussed the role of the DMN and the relationship between it and play. The DMN seems to be most active during times of mind-wandering, that is, when the brain is not focused on a specific task but still active in a relaxed manner, such as in an attitude of play. According to Chan and Siegel, "this attitude is of play, in that play occurs in the context of focused and relaxed attention while being in a state of acceptance and receptivity" (p. 50). Research on the DMN is scarce, but there is supportive evidence that too much DMN activation can lead to anxiety or depression, and malfunctions of parts of the brain associated with this network contribute to memory problems as well as to neurodevelopmental delays and challenges (Raichle, 2015).

The TPN, a collection of parts of the brain that are activated when one is focused on a specific task, is an alternative network and opposite from the DMN. The DMN is an introspective process, whereas the TPN focuses on "extrospective activities, such as task performance" (Downar et al., 2016, p. 111). Activation of the TPN shuts off the DMN, and vice versa. Both have separate independent tasks and may seem to function in opposition to each other, but this is not the case (Beaty et al., 2018). In fact, these two networks complement each other and, although opposite in function, engage in a wonderful dance: The DMN allows for introspection and the creation of forward-focused thinking and ideas, and the TPN is the mechanism that generates a focus of energy that puts those thoughts and ideas into action. Therefore, a balance of the DMN and the TPN is vital for self-awareness, planning, and shifting energy to focus on tasks necessary to ensure survival and success (Ramírez-Barrantes et al., 2019).

The extant neuroscience research has many implications in regard to electronic game play as a therapeutic intervention. First, children in therapy struggle emotionally and psychologically because of trauma, loss, or neurodevelopmental problems, and most are having difficulty adjusting to changes and meeting the demands of daily living. In addition, the brains of children are still developing, and the DMN, in particular, is underdeveloped (Daniels et al., 2011) because parts of the brain in the DMN network are still "sparsely connected" (Daniels et al., 2011, p. 57). The DMN and TPN systems contribute to "theory of mind, prospection, and autobiographical memory" (Daniels et al., 2011, p. 57), all of which are still being developed in children ages 5 to 10. The formation of the elements of the brain that make up the DMN and the TPN are severely affected by trauma, neglect, and neurodevelopmental challenges such as ASD. Strategies from electronic game play enhance the engagement and development of the DMN and TPN networks and result in self-knowledge and self-awareness and provide "neuroprotection" (Ramírez-Barrantes et al., 2019, p. 1) from the devastating effects of anxiety, depression, and self-rejection.

A second implication from the field of neuroscience regarding the effectiveness of electronic game play is that gaming involves activation of both the

DMN and the TPN. As previously mentioned, achieving a balance between these two networks is key to successful living, in the form of self-awareness, planning, and carrying out important tasks. Although neither network can be engaged simultaneously (Buckner et al., 2008), it appears that electronic gaming engages parts of both the DMN and TPN. Parts of electronic gaming involving the DMN include map wandering, planning, introspection, and gathering resources, and those that utilize the TPN involve intense focus that results in intentional decision making and taking action.

Healthy children can disengage the DMN when focus is necessary for a new task, but this is hard for children with ADHD and those who have experienced trauma or are struggling with neurodevelopmental delays (Sassi, 2010). Games that are useful for these problems include both elements of the DMN and TPN; that is, they have "free play" options after the completion of missions or games that are set in large, expansive worlds, like The Legend of Zelda: Breath of the Wild (Nintendo, 2017), Minecraft, and LEGO Movie 2 Movie Maker.

A third implication from neuroscience as applied to electronic game play is the idea of "Openness to Experience," which has been described as a "personality trait epitomized by imagination and creativity" (Beaty et al., 2018, p. 812). Openness to Experience is a factor in creative and imaginative thinking and is found in people who shift between the introspective, planful nature of the DMN and the action-oriented TPN. Children who grapple with emotional, psychological, and neurodevelopmental challenges struggle to engage in imaginative thinking, thus finding it hard to take the perspective of others and situations or engage in future planning. As mentioned earlier, electronic game play engages characteristics of both the DMN and the TPN and provides a practice ground for young people to be aware of the process of engaging in imaginative, introspective thinking as well as noticing the shift to goal-directed thinking and, ultimately, behavior that results in goal achievement. This process of noticing of one's internal state along with awareness of the external world, or meta-awareness, "could be used to intentionally initiate, direct, and/or sustain attentional processes" (Ramírez-Barrantes et al., 2019, p. 4). Electronic game play creates an opportunity to heal from symptoms of posttraumatic stress disorder and opens up space for creativity to blossom, offering myriad opportunities to foster Openness to Experience.

CASE ILLUSTRATION

The following case illustration is a fictional account of treatment using electronic game therapy.

Sam is a 10-year-old boy who was referred for therapy because of anxiety and anger problems. Sam currently lives with his grandmother because of ongoing domestic violence accusations between his parents against each other in the context of a vicious custody battle. Sam's grandmother reports he has not been sleeping and has been wetting the bed. Sam's school performance has suffered, and Sam is in danger of expulsion because of fighting with peers. Upon entering the therapy room, Sam was thrilled to see a Nintendo Switch game console. Sam told Mike, the therapist, that Minecraft was one of his favorite games. He said that he and his dad used to play together "before all the bad stuff happened" and asked Mike if he would join Sam in two-player mode. Mike agreed, and after creating their characters Sam set up a game in "survival mode," the hardest game mode complete, with a variety of enemies and the risk of "dying" if the player's health meter went too low. "Oh, yeah," Sam said to Mike with a look of dread, "If you die, you lose everything!" Sam took the lead in the play, and together he and Mike built a series of strongholds underground with connecting tunnels. They stockpiled resources and crafted weapons and armor. Sam played very cautiously, not leaving the stronghold at night and always posting a series of torches when in caves so that he could find his way out. He told Mike, "Survival mode is really scary, but I've figured out if you're smart and careful you can get through it. You just can't do anything dumb, and it is nice to have a buddy 'cuz it's safer."

In the initial stages of play, Sam did not talk about his anxiety or the divorce. As the play became more intense and collaborative, however, he started to share his feelings and experiences with Mike. He told Mike his feelings of terror at night when his parents would fight, and how he felt like his heart had been "stabbed" when his dad left. Sam said he felt "paralyzed" sometimes because the thought of choosing between his father and mother was like being stuck in "No Man's Land" and shared that he could not concentrate in school or finish his homework. Mike reflected to Sam the themes of the game play and connected them to Sam's experience in real life. For example, there was a time during play when Sam's character was lost and separated from Mike's character as night was approaching. Sam became frantic as he saw Creepers, Cave Spiders, and Zombies appearing in the approaching darkness.

At this point during play, Sam nearly threw down his controller in complete panic, yelling, "I'm in 'No Man's Land!'" Mike reminded Sam of breathing exercises he had taught Sam and told him to think of something he could do to make himself safe until morning came. Sam said he could dig into the side of the mountain to make a cave, and when he did so he was surprised to find some valuable resources such as coal, iron ore, and a cave. He quickly "crafted" some torches and explored the cave, excited to see a vast array of resources. Mike pointed out to Sam that, when he calmed down, he could think, and then he took action, and good things came from it. Sam eventually discovered that the cave he was in actually connected to their stronghold, and he let out a yell of triumph when he broke through the wall and into the room where Mike's character was making new weapons.

Mike helped Sam see the connection between this play experience and feeling paralyzed in "No Man's Land" in real life. Sam pushed through his fear by taking action and using resources available to him. This led to a discussion of what Sam could do when these feelings surface in real life, and Sam remembered the strategies he had learned, such as breathing exercises, asking his teacher for help, and doing push-ups at home during homework to shift over to physical action instead of letting anger and frustration build up. From the metaphors found in game play, Sam applied this strategy at school and at home, and he was thrilled to realize his control over his reactivity and overall improvement in these previously stressful environments.

Because of this collaborative play, Sam learned to put thoughts and feelings into words and realized that he could rely on others for help when he felt overwhelmed or sad. Sam's grandmother reported that his sleeping problems and anxiety lessened significantly, his bed-wetting ceased, and his school performance and behavior improved.

EMPIRICAL SUPPORT

The application of electronic game play has steadily evolved over the past few decades, along with research that demonstrates the benefits of electronic game play (Granic et al., 2014; Snow et al., 2012). Examples of where application of electronic game play can help include areas such as impulse control and social anxiety (Gardner, 1991), emotional expression (Kokish, 1994), and establishing therapeutic trust and bonding (Aymard, 2002; Clarke & Schoech, 1994; Hull, 2016). Electronic game play is a useful way for children to express thoughts and feelings (Bertolini & Nissim, 2002) in addition to reducing emotional disturbances, increasing self-worth, and helping with developmental problems (Baker, 2019; Hull, 2009; Tanaka et al., 2010).

Electronic game play therapy is beneficial for specific problems with targeted populations. For example, it has been shown to be effective with children going through various medical procedures by increasing pain tolerance (Dahlquist et al., 2007), in addition to helping those with neurodevelopmental challenges such as ASD learn social skills, improve concentration, and increase emotional regulation (Grant, 2019).

Children with ASD find electronic game play attractive because of the sense of being in control and the immediate feedback that results, in addition to the clear expectations and boundaries that electronic games provide. Kaduson

(2019) discussed the use of electronic games to increase self-control and enhance working memory in children struggling with ADHD, a common problem presented in therapy. The familiarity of the games, in addition to the themes found in everyday games such as Minecraft, Roblox (Google LLC, 2005), Pokemon (e.g., Pokemon GO; Google LLC, 2016), and The Legend of Zelda, provide tools to help children develop their focusing abilities and working memory skills, which they can then generalize to real life situations. Stone (2019) discussed the use of electronic games with gifted children, who often struggle with extreme anxiety because of perfectionistic thinking. Electronic games not only provide a foundation of therapeutic trust and relationship but also are useful for assessing "frustration tolerance, strategic skills, inter- and intra- personal skills, and many more" (Stone, 2019, p. 159). Electronic games "enhance a variety of cognitive skills, some of which generalize to real-world contexts" (Jackson & Games, 2015, p. 20); increase creativity; enhance social skills; increase emotional stability; and increase motivation to model goal-directed behavior.

SUMMARY AND CONCLUSIONS

Electronic game play in therapy is useful in reducing emotional disturbances and increasing self-representation as well as in fostering a child's sense of self-knowledge that results in increased perspective taking. It also is useful for reducing emotional disturbances by creating a balance in brain states by shifting from a DMN-dominant state to activation of the TPN and providing a path for action through intentional behavior. It increases prosocial behavior through the modeling and practice of reliance on others as well as by helping children communicate thoughts and feelings and increasing their perspective taking, which results in a better understanding of others and of various circumstances.

Electronic game play is useful for increasing creativity and problem solving in that it presents themes and metaphors such as overcoming challenges and gathering resources necessary for reaching objectives, which mimic real life situations. It increases neuroprotection by increasing coping skills as they relate to negative emotions and thereby reducing stress. Finally, electronic game play provides a fun and familiar way for children to explore dimensions of the self that were previously unknown because of activation of the autonomic nervous system, resulting in self-awareness and self-acceptance.

REFERENCES

Aymard, L. L. (2002). "Funny Face": Shareware for child counseling and play therapy. *Journal of Technology in Human Services, 20*(1–2), 11–29. https://doi.org/10.1300/J017v20n01_05

Baker, L. (2019). Therapy in the digital age. In J. Stone (Ed.), *Integrating technology into psychotherapy: A clinician's guide to developments and interventions* (pp. 37–47). Routledge/Taylor & Francis.

Bean, A. M. (2019). I am my avatar and my avatar is me. In J. Stone (Ed.), *Integrating technology into psychotherapy: A clinician's guide to developments and interventions* (pp. 94–106). Routledge/Taylor & Francis.

Beaty, R. E., Chen, Q., Christensen, A. P., Qiu, J., Silvia, P. J., & Schacter, D. L. (2018). Brain networks of the imaginative mind: Dynamic functional connectivity of default and cognitive control networks relates to openness to experience. *Human Brain Mapping, 39*(2), 811–821. https://doi.org/10.1002/hbm.23884

Bertolini, R., & Nissim, S. (2002). Video games and children's imagination. *Journal of Child Psychotherapy, 28*(3), 305–325. https://doi.org/10.1080/0075417021000022667

Buckner, R. L., Andrews-Hanna, J. R., & Schacter, D. L. (2008). The brain's default network: Anatomy, function, and relevance to disease. *Annals of the New York Academy of Sciences, 1124*(1), 1–38. https://doi.org/10.1196/annals.1440.011

Chan, A., & Siegel, D. J. (2018). Play and the default mode network: Interpersonal neurobiology, self, and creativity. In T. Marks-Tarlow, M. Solomon, & D. J. Siegel (Eds.), *Play and creativity in psychotherapy* (pp. 39–63). W. W. Norton.

Clarke, B., & Schoech, D. (1994). A computer-assisted game for adolescents: Initial development and comments. *Computers in Human Services, 11*(1–2), 121–140.

Dahlquist, L. M., McKenna, K. D., Jones, K. K., Dillinger, L., Weiss, K. E., & Ackerman, C. S. (2007). Active and passive distraction using a head-mounted display helmet: Effects on cold pressor pain in children. *Health Psychology, 26*(6), 794–801. https://doi.org/10.1037/0278-6133.26.6.794

Daniels, J. K., Frewen, P., McKinnon, M. C., & Lanius, R. A. (2011). Default mode alterations in posttraumatic stress disorder related to early-life trauma: A developmental perspective. *Journal of Psychiatry & Neuroscience, 36*(1), 56–59. https://doi.org/10.1503/jpn.100050

Downar, J., Blumberger, D. M., & Daskalakis, Z. J. (2016). The neural crossroads of psychiatric illness: An emerging target for brain stimulation. *Trends in Cognitive Sciences, 20*(2), 107–120. https://doi.org/10.1016/j.tics.2015.10.007

Fernández-Aranda, F., Jiménez-Murcia, S., Santamaría, J. J., Gunnard, K., Soto, A., Kalapanidas, E., Bults, R. G., Davarakis, C., Ganchev, T., Granero, R., Konstantas, D., Kostoulas, T. P., Lam, T., Lucas, M., Masuet-Aumatell, C., Moussa, M. H., Nielsen, J., & Penelo, E. (2012). Video games as a complementary therapy tool in mental disorders: PlayMancer, a European multicentre study. *Journal of Mental Health, 21*(4), 364–374. https://doi.org/10.3109/09638237.2012.664302

GainPlay Studio. (2014). MindLight [Computer game]. http://www.gainplaystudio.com/mindlight/

Gardner, J. E. (1991). Can the Mario Bros. help? Nintendo games as an adjunct in psychotherapy with children. *Psychotherapy: Theory, Research, & Practice, 28*(4), 667–670. https://doi.org/10.1037/0033-3204.28.4.667

Google LLC. (2005). *Roblox* [Mobile app]. Google Play Store. https://play.google.com/store/apps/details?id=com.roblox.client&hl=en_US

Google LLC. (2016). *Pokemon GO* [Mobile app]. Google Play Store. https://play.google.com/store/apps/details?id=com.nianticlabs.pokemongo&hl=en_US

Google LLC. (2017). *Toontastic 3D* (Version 1.0.5). [Mobile app]. Google Play Store. https://apps.apple.com/us/app/toontastic-3d/id1145104532

Granic, I., Lobel, A., & Engels, R. C. M. E. (2014). The benefits of playing video games. *American Psychologist, 69*(1), 66–78. https://doi.org/10.1037/a0034857

Grant, R. J. (2019). Utilizing technology interventions with children and adolescents with autism spectrum disorder (ASD). In J. Stone (Ed.), *Integrating technology into psychotherapy: A clinician's guide to developments and interventions* (pp. 124–136). Routledge/Taylor & Francis.

Harter, S. (2016). *The construction of the self: Developmental and sociocultural foundations.* Guilford Press.

Hull, K. (2009). *Computer/video games as a play therapy tool in reducing emotional disturbances in children* (Doctoral dissertation). UMI No. 3380362. Available at https://digitalcommons.liberty.edu/cgi/viewcontent.cgi?article=1282&context=doctoral

Hull, K. (2014). *Group therapy techniques with children, adolescents, and adults on the autism spectrum.* Jason Aronson.

Hull, K. (2016). Technology in the playroom. In K. J. O'Connor, C. Schaefer, & L. D. Braverman (Eds.), *Handbook of play therapy* (2nd ed., pp. 613–627). Wiley.

Hull, K. (2019). Replacing hesitancy and doubt with competence and skill: The technologically minded therapist. In J. Stone (Ed.), *Integrating technology into psychotherapy: A clinician's guide to developments and interventions* (pp. 24–36). Routledge/Taylor & Francis.

Jackson, L., & Games, A. (2015). *Video games and creativity.* Elsevier, Academic Press. https://doi.org/10.1016/B978-0-12-801462-2.00001-1

Kaduson, H. G. (2019). "See, I can focus": How video games can be used to enhance working memory and self-control for children with attention-deficit hyperactivity disorder (ADHD). In J. Stone (Ed.), *Integrating technology into psychotherapy: A clinician's guide to developments and interventions* (pp. 137–148). Routledge/Taylor & Francis.

Kokish, R. (1994). Experiences using a PC in play therapy with children. *Computers in Human Services, 11*(1–2), 141–150.

LaFleur, L. B., Hebert, Z. J., & Dupuy, A. S. (2018). Leveling up your game: The use of video games as a therapeutic modality. *Journal of Creativity in Mental Health, 13*(1), 58–67.

LEGO System A/S. (2019). *LEGO® Movie 2™ movie maker* (Version 1.3.0). [Mobile App]. App Store. https://apps.apple.com/us/app/the-lego-movie-2-movie-maker/id1436158065

Lind, S. E. (2010). Memory and the self in autism: A review and theoretical framework. *Autism, 14*(5), 430–456. https://doi.org/10.1177/1362361309358700

Mojang Studios. (2015). *Minecraft* [Video game series]. Stockholm, Sweden: Mojang Studios.

Nintendo. (2017). *The Legend of Zelda: Breath of the Wild* [Video game series]. Kyoto, Japan: Nintendo.

Nintendo. (2018). *Super Smash Bros.* [Video game series]. Kyoto, Japan: Nintendo.

Raichle, M. E. (2015). The brain's default mode network. *Annual Review of Neuroscience, 38*(1), 433–447. https://doi.org/10.1146/annurev-neuro-071013-014030

Ramírez-Barrantes, R., Arancibia, M., Stojanova, J., Aspé-Sánchez, M., Córdova, C., & Henríquez-Ch, R. A. (2019). Default mode network, meditation, and age-associated brain changes: What can we learn from the impact of mental training on well-being as a psychotherapeutic approach? *Neural Plasticity,* Article 7067592. https://doi.org/10.1155/2019/7067592

Sassi, R. B. (2010). Abstract thinking: The brain "at rest"—Default mode network in children. *Journal of the American Academy of Child & Adolescent Psychiatry, 49*(9), 861. https://doi.org/10.1016/j.jaac.2010.06.016

Schaefer, C., & Drewes, A. A. (2014). *The therapeutic powers of play: 20 core agents of change* (2nd ed.). Wiley.

Smith Micro Software Inc. (2014). *Sock puppets complete* (Version 2.0.4). [Mobile app]. App Store. https://itunes.apple.com/us/app/sock-puppets-complete/id547666894?mt=8

Snow, M. S., Winburn, A., Crumrine, L., Jackson, E., & Killian, T. (2012, September). The iPad playroom: A therapeutic technique. *Play Therapy, 7*(3), 16–19.

Stone, J. (2016). The virtual sandtray [Online app]. Google Play Store.

Stone, J. (2019). Connecting with gifted people. In J. Stone (Ed.), *Integrating technology into psychotherapy: A clinician's guide to developments and interventions* (pp. 149–165). Routledge/Taylor & Francis.

Tanaka, J. W., Wolf, J. M., Klaiman, C., Koenig, K., Cockburn, J., Herlihy, L., & Schultz, R. T. (2010). Using computerized games to teach face recognition skills to children with autism spectrum disorder: The Let's Face It! program. *Journal of Child Psychology and Psychiatry, and Allied Disciplines, 51*(8), 944–952.

Winnicott, D. W. (1989). *Playing reality*. Routledge.

Wols, A., Lichtwarck-Aschoff, A., Schoneveld, E. A., & Granic, I. (2018). In-game play behaviours during an applied video game for anxiety prevention predict successful intervention outcomes. *Journal of Psychopathology and Behavioral Assessment, 40*(4), 655–668. https://doi.org/10.1007/s10862-018-9684-4

15

THERAPEUTIC EXTENDED REALITY

RICHARD LAMB AND ELISABETH ETOPIO

Extended reality (XR) is an umbrella term that combines several types of constructed reality technologies—virtual reality, augmented reality, and mixed reality—that allow the user to control the level of immersion into virtual environments. *Virtual reality* (VR) is a completely computer-generated simulated environment in three dimensions with which a person can interacted in a seemingly real and physical way using a specialized set of goggles with a screen inside of it as well as other electronic equipment, such as gloves and sensors. In *augmented reality* (AR), computer-generated information (e.g., data about a building or a person) is superimposed on the user's view of the real world. *Mixed reality* (MR) is the merging and coexisting of real-world objects and computer-generated objects for the purposes of interacting in real time. Taken together, these multiple forms of generated realities form a continuum of immersion (see Figure 15.1). These forms of XR are potentially important tools counselors can use to engage both children and adults in therapeutic settings. This chapter addresses the potential therapeutic uses and clinical applications of XR. The chapter concludes with a short case study that illustrates the use of XR with a child.

https://doi.org/10.1037/0000217-016
Play Therapy With Children: Modalities for Change, H. G. Kaduson and C. E. Schaefer (Editors)

FIGURE 15.1. A Continuum of Immersive Environments

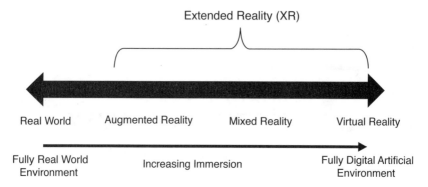

Extended Reality (XR)

Real World   Augmented Reality   Mixed Reality   Virtual Reality

Fully Real World   Increasing Immersion   Fully Digital Artificial
Environment   Environment

Note. Starting on the left with the real world, which has no immersion, and moving to the right, immersion increases until the client is completely immersed in a fully artificially constructed environment (i.e., virtual reality).

Practitioners across multiple disciplines, working in a variety of contexts, including those who work with children who need mental health intervention, often make use of multiple activities to advance their approaches and strengthen therapy sessions. However, despite the wide availability of AR, VR, and MR, there has been little adoption of these technologies in the augmentation of therapeutic approaches, such as play therapy (Ramsey et al., 2016). Despite this, there has been a near-ubiquitous adoption of these technologies in other fields, such as education, business, emergency response, entertainment, and military (Lamb & Etopio, 2019a; Lamb, Miller, et al., 2018).

Whereas VR can result in complete immersion in a virtual, constructed environment, AR allows a combination of a virtual and real-life environment in which the latter is augmented with information about the real world. MR is a hybrid reality in which the digital reality and the real world simultaneously exist and interact with one another. XR takes interactions among the user, real life, and virtual environments one step further and allows for the mixing of real and virtual combined environments by means of computers and wearables.

In a conceptual sense, the XR technologies illustrate the four essential components of play: (a) within XR the child has the capacity to make their own decisions and experience the consequences; (b) the activity in the XR environment is intrinsically motivating, thereby promoting problem solving; (c) the child experiences full immersion in the moment, allowing genuine expression of emotion and assuredness; and (d) play is enjoyable, spontaneous, and not scripted, thus increasing self-awareness and awareness of others (Bodrova & Leong, 2015). These characteristics are consistent with the desired outcomes of play therapy: (a) development of responsible behaviors and successful strategies to negotiate barriers that cause anxiety and depression (Shen, 2002); (b) creation of new solutions to problems, promoting greater self-esteem and locus of control (Post, 1999); (c) respect and acceptance of self and others (Fall et al., 1999); and (d) development of social and relational skills (Webster-Stratton & Reid, 2009).

Because the framework for development of therapeutic XR arose from play that can be therapeutic, it is important to distinguish that therapeutic play and play therapy are very different. *Therapeutic play* is defined as a framework of activities centered on play that take into account the cognitive and developmental state of the child to further develop the child's emotional and physical well-being (Koukourikos et al., 2015). This framework is often implemented in hospitals to promote recovery. In contrast, *play therapy* is a psychotherapeutic approach used with children to freely explore and express aspects of their lives and emotions through play. Play therapy has been proven helpful in work with children to alleviate anxiety, depression, grief, and anger, among other emotions. Although there may be some overlap between play therapy and therapeutic play, their distinctions become important when one is considering implementation of the techniques associated with each.

Cost-effective XR technologies for therapeutic purposes have only recently become available; historically, therapeutic (t), XR technologies (i.e., tVR, tAR, tMR) conceptually have arisen from the modification of frameworks associated with serious games and serious educational games (SEGs; Lamb, Etopio, & Lamb, 2018) and have only recently begun to be redeveloped as a tool for play therapy.

Therapeutic XR has its roots in predecessor technologies such as serious games, SEGs, and simulations. Serious games are electronic or computer-based games that were designed not for commercial purposes but for training users in a specific skill set. For example, the U.S. military has been the leader in serious games, using them to train soldiers on combat missions that could not be replicated completely in training in the physical world. SEGs are juxtaposed with serious games in that they target the development of disciplinary content knowledge using specific pedagogical approaches as opposed to specific skills. SEGs allow teachers and students to connect real-world scenarios with common school content. A simulation, by our definition, has duel characteristics of a serious game and a SEG but does not keep a score or have an economy, so in essence there is no endpoint and determination of completion that is easily identified. Therapeutic XR environments allow the development of skills, strategy, and content understanding through specific therapeutic approaches (Lamb & Etopio, 2019a, 2019c). As technology integration in therapeutic settings increases, more attention has been and will continue to be placed on the components of therapeutic XR that can supply greater realism, fluidity, and immersion with extensive environmental control. The increased realism and functionality associated with therapeutic XR situate it as an up-and-coming tool for use in therapeutic sessions.

The four overarching elements of therapeutic XR that allow its wide application in play therapy approaches have been outlined by Lamb (2015) and Tabak et al. (2017). These elements are (a) familiarity with the environment and activities (i.e., immersion), (b) distracting elements and graded exposure to stressors (i.e., interactivity), (c) graduated activity (i.e., visualization), and (d) provision of feedback and/or requested input from user (fluidity). Visualization, fluidity, interactivity, and immersion form the basis of treatment enhancements in therapeutic XR and are the foundations for its environments.

THERAPEUTIC BENEFITS

Many components of therapeutic XR inherently lend themselves to aspects of therapeutic factors related to play (Schaefer & Drewes, 2011). Integration of the therapeutic factors is inherent in the nature of constructed environments (e.g., therapeutic XR). One of the critical factors that links therapeutic XR play to effective therapeutic approaches is the increased level of engagement and the opportunity for children to practice and facilitate communication, foster emotional well-being, improve personal strengths, and develop social relationship skills. In many XR environments it is possible to have interactive characters in the same environment, which can promote greater self-expression and empathy. Therapeutic XR further links to play therapy approaches in the sense that the child will engage with therapeutic XR in therapeutic settings because, for some children, this may be a more enjoyable option than others offered by the therapist. Children at all age levels already interact with technologies and electronic games for both educational and noneducational purposes. Therapeutic XR environments allow direct and indirect learning by means of play narratives and interactive fantasy play. For many children, play using a board game or nonvirtual materials is unfamiliar and does not allow the levels of interaction and fantasy available in therapeutic XR environments (Plowman & McPake, 2013).

In addition to the potential positive aspects of therapeutic XR for children, therapeutic XR provides the opportunity for a therapist to tactfully observe, record, measure, and assess the child's abilities to engage in multiple processes through "stealth assessment," an approach in which the assessment of progress is embedded within the activities in the digital environment (DiCerbo et al., 2017). For example, a child in a therapeutic XR environment may have to use strategies that help promote self-regulation, empathy, or stress management as they were discussed and practiced in prior therapeutic sessions. The use of these strategies in therapeutic XR may occur as a part of the normal functioning of the therapeutic XR environment when a child is interacting with a digital character. Therapeutic XR allows the child to use these strategies in a simulated authentic environment that approximates real life. Stealth assessment is thought to provide a more reliable and valid measurement of a child's actions so the therapist can make therapeutic decisions about the actions the child takes. Some abilities that can be readily examined using therapeutic XR are creative problem solving, social competence, empathy, stress management and inoculation, and self-expression (Didehbani et al., 2016).

In addition to cognitive and emotional skills practice, therapeutic XR can be used to promote prosocial practices that will benefit the child. Therapeutic XR provides the therapist with a view of the child's ability to cooperate and coordinate activities within themselves and others, thereby promoting moral and psychological development through play. This is advantageous because play is regarded as the most effective setting in which to assess cognitive, social, and behavioral characteristics for children in a controlled environment (Knell & Dasari, 2016).

As this form of technology continues to develop, therapeutic XR will provide greater opportunities to work with children through play because of the immersive nature, interactivity, and customizability of the environments (i.e., the broad interactivity and the realism of action). Computer-based therapeutic XR environments will allow children and clinicians to examine phenomena at multiple levels, with transitions occurring as needed by the clinician and child to promote therapy (Lamb & Etopio, 2019c). An important feature of therapeutic XR that separates it from other therapeutic technologies is real-time interactivity in three-dimensional environments. Put more specifically, a therapeutic XR system is responsive to gestures and user inputs with relatively little lag in environmental changes, which helps augment activities such as block play, balloon play, and sensory play during play therapy sessions. Interactivity, control, and therapeutic XR's ability to respond to gesture promotes the sensation of immersion by responding to user actions on a screen, allowing for greater self-expression than with other technologies, which may rely only on a flat monitor. This allows users not only to visually interact with objects but also to manipulate graphic objects; that is, the client is able to touch and feel the objects using auditory, haptic, and tactile inputs (Jafari et al., 2016). Accordingly, clients using therapeutic XR feel and interact with objects while more of their senses are fully engaged in the experiences. To a degree, users often "forget" they are in a virtual world and in a therapeutic setting; this increases the therapist's ability to understand the child's world and how they behave. As confidence and mastery are gained, skills practiced in therapeutic XR may be transferred into real-life settings.

Therapeutic XR technologies have intrinsic properties that activate thoughts and emotions that help engage direct and indirect teaching, meaningful learning, discussion, and problem solving (Lamb & Firestone, 2017). Through repetitive play and reenactment children can relieve stress and gain mastery over and resolve traumas. Increases in environmental control can promote changes in thinking and behavior and increase positive emotion and associations. In follow-up discussions, participants in therapeutic XR research have cited realism and its resultant empathy as a key factor in their feeling of immersion and engagement in the sessions (van Loon et al., 2018). Neuroimaging and psychophysiological studies also have confirmed that the perceived realism and interactivity found in therapeutic XR environments triggers responses from people in therapeutic XR environments that are similar to those experienced n the real world (Lamb & Firestone, 2017).

Most recent therapeutic XR work has used three-dimensional video from the real world in ultra high resolution, creating ultrarealistic content. Infusion of digital content and information into virtual environments enhances the experience, making it nearly indistinguishable from reality and more likely that users will transfer skills learned in therapeutic XR to the real world. For example, a fully scaled environment in therapeutic XR, such as a forest with trees or rocks that are of photo quality, allows the user to walk around, see the size of the trees, touch animals and plants, and experience the responses. Such experiences allow them to engage in activities such as social scripting, environmental control, and exploration in safe, low-risk environments. Thus, therapeutic XR technology engages children and adults in an immersive context through authentic experiences while still providing a large degree of environmental control by the practitioner and user.

CORE TECHNIQUES

In developing play therapy–based approaches using therapeutic XR it is important to remember that traditional aspects of play therapy, such as relationship building between the therapist and child, home contingencies, drawing, and other forms of creative ventilation (i.e., the free and full expression of feelings and emotions using creative outlets), are important and are not replaced by therapeutic XR. In many ways, therapeutic XR in play therapy is a tool to enhance and augment these and other play-based approaches. When considering how to integrate therapeutic XR into therapeutic approaches, some specific recommendations related to activities are warranted. Activities and experiences with which therapists can engage include social scripting; environmental control; and exploration in safe, low-risk environments. For example, a child with severe anxiety may use the therapeutic XR headset to role-play interactions and activities or to become familiar with environments before experiencing them in the real world. A child may have the opportunity to interact with virtual playmates or practice specific social skills. While the child is immersed in the environment, the therapist can see what the child sees, and hear what the child hears, and either the child or therapist can control the level of immersion through computer controls (see Figure 15.2).

It is important to note that actions taken in the therapeutic XR environments occur in a soft-failure environment to allow a gradual release of control from therapist-directed to child-directed activities and expressions as skills and strategies are learned and applied. A *soft-failure* environment is one in which not being successful is not catastrophic in nature and additional opportunities are available without consequence. For example, if a child is playing a video game and is unsuccessful in completing a task, the game does not end; instead, the child is given multiple opportunities to complete the task from the point at which they were unsuccessful. This approach allows children to attempt multiple strategies and to directly and indirectly learn from their state of impasse.

FIGURE 15.2. Diagram of Therapeutic Extended Reality (XR) Setup for a Therapy Session

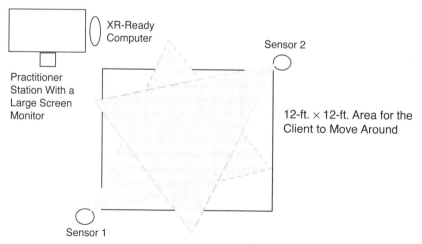

Note. Although the 12-ft. × 12-ft. area is optimal, other room sizes are acceptable, including a seated, nonmobile version.

A therapist may initially consider using a less realistic environment, meaning one that is less complex and less real-world like. The intent is to use an environment with fewer interactions and less realism to promote comfort, attachment to characters, and increase the opportunities to apply specific strategies and approaches. As the child gains understanding and practice, the therapist may slowly use more and more realistic environments. The use of less realistic environments promotes play and greater fantasy. Many environments are available at no cost with the caveat that they are often just settings, not specific to therapy, with objects for interaction. For example, an extremely realistic forest setting is available in one XR program, A Walk in the Woods (Brightdawn Entertainment, 2020), with some areas that allow a person to virtually climb a tree, pick flowers, or choose a specific walking path. The number of people who may simultaneously engage in the same therapeutic XR environment currently is limited to two to three people. Simultaneous immersion by multiple people (i.e., the therapist and child in the same environment) can be leveraged, allowing the therapist to see how the child is behaving without the therapist being seen in the environment. The therapist and child can both wear separate therapeutic XR goggles, with the child being able to interact with the environment and the therapist just being able to see the activities in which the child is engaging. This can more directly allow the therapist to experience the child's world while the child is in the therapeutic XR environment.

Use of therapeutic XR has occurred in educational and counseling contexts with children as young as age 4 years, at a maximum of 10 minutes per session, with rest periods of 30 minutes and a maximum of two sessions per day. In both contexts, the young child is exposed to experiences that may not be available in the real world. For example, in one educational context children were placed in an undersea environment and allowed to interact with jellyfish and sea turtles (Lamb et al., 2019; Lamb & Etopio, 2019b). In a counseling context, a child who was refusing to attend school because of anxiety was able to virtually walk through the actual school before the first day of school (Adjorlu et al., 2018). This points to the potential of therapeutic XR to be used with younger children. However, given the time limitations it is important to ensure that multiple activities in and outside of the therapeutic XR environment are planned for each session. The amount of time for each session and rest between sessions increases and decreases, respectively, up to a maximum of 1 hour for adults per session. At present there is little research on the topic of the number of hours of therapeutic XR with which a child can engage, but research is currently ongoing.

Therapeutic XR is thought to have considerable potential for therapeutic approaches, especially its effectiveness regarding cognitive retraining (Bashiri et al., 2017), feedback (Laver et al., 2015), interest (Tussyadiah et al., 2018), emotion regulation (Rodríguez et al., 2015), self-regulation, and mindfulness.

Therapeutic XR should not be thought of as a separate technique unto itself but as a tool to augment existing therapies; one example of this is therapeutic XR–enhanced dialectical behavior therapy. Although there are many benefits associated with therapeutic XR, some potential aspects of it, such as XR-based motion sickness or simulation sickness, may affect clients. It is important that potential side effects be explained clearly to the child's guardian and that he or she sign an informed-consent form before treatment proceeds. For more information about side effects, please contact the authors of this chapter. Therapeutic XR simulation sickness occurs when there is a disconnect between a person's movement in the virtual environment and the person's perceived motion in real life (i.e., a mismatch between the visual and the vestibular systems; Ng et al., 2019). A person experiencing simulation sickness may show symptoms of general discomfort, headache, disorientation, or dysphoric events that reduce immersion and enjoyment. Simulation sickness is not a serious condition or concern and occurs in only a small percentage of the population. The discomfort and symptoms generally resolve with the removal of the VR headset. Reduction or prevention of simulation sickness may be achieved by the following means:

- Clear a sufficiently large area and set up the therapeutic XR system in accordance with manufacturer recommendations.
- Demonstrate the boundaries to the client.
- Familiarize the client with the therapeutic XR equipment prior to use.
- Stop use of the headset when there are performance problems (i.e., frame rate reductions or skipping).
- Use the headset sitting if possible.
- Use gradual acclimation and increase headset usage slowly.
- Rest between sessions or whenever a client feels the need to do so.

Always provide supervision when a person is in a therapeutic XR environment. If comfortable, the operator (the person outside of the headset) should be within about 1.5 arms' lengths of the client.

The East Carolina University Neurocognition Science Laboratory can provide a sample protocol for therapeutic XR use.[1] The protocol provides an overview of suggested rest and usage times for therapeutic XR along with daily maximum usage time recommendations. If maximum usage times are reached, participants should not use therapeutic XR headsets or similar devices for 24 hours. For example, the maximum time a 9-year-old is recommended

---

[1]To obtain a copy of the protocols, please use the contact email lambr19@ecu.edu.

to use the headset is 25 minutes, with a 45-minute rest and then no use of therapeutic XR or other such devices for 24 hours. "Rest" in this context means complete removal of the headset from the person's head and face and a change to a nontherapeutic XR–based activity. Upon session completion, the therapist should remove the headset and debrief the client to ensure they are well. If the person does not indicate any problems, rest can consist of low-demand activities as tolerated without the therapeutic XR headset (e.g., mindfulness-based cognitive therapy, games, or guided imagery).

CLINICAL APPLICATIONS

Therapeutic XR has been found to be an important tool for play therapy and in other therapeutic activities when used with specific approaches for development of self-expression, social competency, and moral development (Barajas et al., 2017; García-Vergara et al., 2014; Riva, 2005). In addition, it allows therapists to experience firsthand the strategies and approaches a child may use to self-regulate or manage stress. For example, if a child was referred for aggression, then the therapist may have an opportunity to experience the aggression as the child bangs or breaks items in the therapeutic XR environment without harm to themselves or the child. The therapist can also help the child learn self-regulation by responding with appropriate strategies. Furthermore, therapeutic XR–enhanced distraction therapy has been found to outperform standard pharmacotherapy in the treatment of anxiety and hyperactivity (Pourmand et al., 2017). Distraction therapy is the process of developing specific strategies to divert or shift attention from a current negative thought process to a neutral or positive thought process. This approach is the underpinning of multiple play therapy–based techniques and promotes the child's ability child to engage in creative problem solving and stress inoculation from anxiety, trauma, or depression (Millett & Gooding, 2017; Parsons, 2015). This occurs through completion of activities in the therapeutic XR environment in which the child practices and is assessed in their ability to show multiple emotional and unconscious behaviors (e.g., resiliency, self-esteem, and more general psychological development) through play (Tabak et al., 2017). For example, Tabak et al. (2017) found that in these environments, children had to pick fruits and vegetables or clean up their room, all in a specific sequence, helping them build self-control. Their results indicated a relatively wide acceptance of the therapeutic XR environment by the child. Children can also engage in role play, free drawing and building in three dimensions, moving and dancing, and even bubble play.

CASE ILLUSTRATION

This case illustration shows how therapeutic XR–based technology was a key component in the success of K,[2] a 10-year-old boy referred for hyperactivity and distractibility in the classroom. Reviews of diagnostic visits by K provided evidence of intact perceptual systems and an understanding of conceptual ideas but also the presence of a parent who has provided rigid prescribed scheduling and significant control of K's real-world environments as long as K could recall. K did not demonstrate other clinically significant symptoms. Many of K's sessions, when the mother brought him, were spent immersed in a simulation of tropical forest with wide-open areas to explore. The simulation included animals, rivers, trees, caves, and cliffs. It is important to understand that this environment has multiple components that lend themselves to play therapy techniques. These include toy and object play, storytelling, role playing, and other creative techniques. Throughout this process it was necessary for the therapist to coordinate the play therapy techniques with available therapeutic XR content. The open and interactive nature of these environments allowed K to interact and maneuver through the available activities at his planning. These aspects of the technology allowed K to explore his surroundings in low-risk environments with large amounts of environmental control.

K was initially trained in the use of the VR controls by means of a small virtual robot avatar contained inside of the VR environment. The robot taught K skills such as how to grasp objects, how to interact with the environment, how to walk and move around the environment, and how to cooperate with it to accomplish tasks such as building a structure or moving large objects. The robot also responded with emotional cues when it was struck or something fell on it. One aspect to note is that the therapeutic XR system allows full movement with cues demarcating boundaries, thereby promoting exploration and self-determination. During the initial immersive experiences in the environment, K exhibited aggressive exploratory behaviors and a lack of inhibition in exploring areas such as the cave and river components. Lack of self-regulation caused K to approach exploration with a lack of concern and understanding of consequences, resulting in repetition of mistakes and frustration.

During the therapeutic XR sessions K would often run through the XR environment and discuss how the number of interactive elements in the environment overwhelmed him. During this time he became frustrated and

---

[2] Identifying information has been changed to ensure the case study materials are anonymous.

was unclear regarding how to express his frustration. Over time, and with assistance from his therapist through storytelling and emotion identification, K was more able to apply learned strategies, such as mindfulness, along with more indirectly learned approaches, such as cooperation (in this case with the robot avatar, which was required to open new areas within the environment for exploration). The discussions before, during, and after the VR sessions often focused on how K felt, how he could use strategies to approach activities that overwhelmed him, and how to handle events when the environment contained several new items and disrupted his initial plans.

In each of the environments, K needed to continually reason, make use of learned strategies, cooperate with others in the execution of tasks, express plans, engage with unknowns, regulate his aggressive responses, and use socially acceptable responses and appropriate releases of aggression. After several sessions over a period of 6 months, K came to understand the virtual environment, learned to generalize the thoughts of how he felt to thoughts of how another person might feel, and became more aware of how others may respond to his actions. Ultimately, K was able to move from specific self-referencing of his actions and responses to assessing the impact of his activities in a multiperson interactive environment. Over time, K's impulsiveness and need to act in an effort for stimulus slowly diminished, and he began to function more easily in both the VR environment and the real world.

EMPIRICAL SUPPORT

Multiple studies have illustrated the effectiveness of therapeutic XR technologies for the treatment of social anxiety (Bouchard et al., 2017), impulse control difficulties (Smeijers & Koole, 2019), trauma (Beidel et al., 2019), and related conditions. We examined multiple studies ($N = 233$, $K = 6$) to assess the relative effectiveness of therapeutic XR as an augmentative therapeutic tool. An analysis of the effects illustrated a medium overall effect, indicating that therapeutic XR technologies are more effective as an augmentative tool than individual approaches alone. This result is limited by the lack of examination of moderators of the effect. An example from a study conducted by the authors and a colleague illustrates the effectiveness of therapeutic XR augmentation in therapy (Lamb, Etopio, & Lamb, 2018; see Figure 15.3).

In examining the multiple findings from the research, we noted that therapeutic XR–based therapies, compared with time-delayed groups, are superior to comparison conditions in regard to the reduction of symptoms. This finding is consistent with those of other studies (i.e., Kampmann et al., 2016; Opriş et al., 2012). Examinations of therapeutic XR–enhanced treatments and

FIGURE 15.3. Comparison of Dialectical Behavior Therapy (DBT) and Virtual Reality (VR)-Enhanced DBT

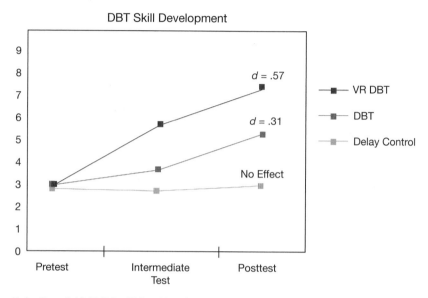

Note. Copyright 2019 by Richard Lamb. Reprinted with permission.

standard treatments revealed no significant difference in effect sizes. The results in general indicate that therapeutic XR–enhanced treatments tend to be efficacious, with no significant evidence that they lead to less benefit than traditional treatments, such as imaginal exposure, an approach in which the client is asked to imagine feared situations and confront them. Imaginal exposure is often used when it is not safe, or possible, to directly confront the fear or situation. It is important to note that therapeutic XR, compared with traditional approaches, engenders greater engagement and client compliance with therapeutic requests (e.g., Välimäki et al., 2014).

SUMMARY AND CONCLUSIONS

The potential benefits of therapeutic XR justify the need for additional high-quality trials and intervention developments. More research with increased methodological rigor would aid the existing body of literature and improve the generalizability of findings related to therapeutic XR as an augmentative play therapy tool. Therapeutic XR treatments have potential advantages over traditional therapies, including greater acceptability, increased engagement, and the ability to engage with strategies in a soft-failure environment. Potential future research should evaluate the effects of therapeutic XR exposure as a part of other play therapy techniques. Such interventions, possibly delivered through inexpensive mobile phone applications and using inexpensive therapeutic XR hardware, perhaps through teletherapy, will provide an option to people who may not have the ability to purchase this equipment.

REFERENCES

Adjorlu, A., Hussain, A., Mødekjær, C., & Austad, N. W. (2018). Head-mounted display-based virtual reality social story as a tool to teach social skills to children diagnosed with autism spectrum disorder. In *2017 IEEE Virtual Reality Workshop on K–12 Embodied Learning Through Virtual & Augmented Reality (KELVAR)*. IEEE.

Barajas, A. O., Al Osman, H., & Shirmohammadi, S. (2017, April). A serious game for children with autism spectrum disorder as a tool for play therapy. In N. Diaz (Ed.), *2017 IEEE 5th International Conference on Serious Games and Applications for Health* (pp. 1–7). IEEE. https://doi.org/10.1109/SeGAH.2017.7939266

Bashiri, A., Ghazisaeedi, M., Safdari, R., Shahmoradi, L., & Ehtesham, H. (2017). Improving the prediction of survival in cancer patients by using machine learning techniques: Experience of gene expression data. A narrative review. *Iranian Journal of Public Health, 46*(2), 165–172.

Beidel, D. C., Frueh, B. C., Neer, S. M., Bowers, C. A., Trachik, B., Uhde, T. W., & Grubaugh, A. (2019). Trauma management therapy with virtual-reality augmented exposure therapy for combat-related PTSD: A randomized controlled trial. *Journal of Anxiety Disorders, 61,* 64–74. https://doi.org/10.1016/j.janxdis.2017.08.005

Bodrova, E., & Leong, D. J. (2015). Vygotskian and post-Vygotskian views on children's play. *American Journal of Play, 7*(3), 371–388.

Bouchard, S., Dumoulin, S., Robillard, G., Guitard, T., Klinger, É., Forget, H., Loranger, C., & Roucaut, F. X. (2017). Virtual reality compared with *in vivo* exposure in the treatment of social anxiety disorder: A three-arm randomised controlled trial. *The British Journal of Psychiatry, 210*(4), 276–283. https://doi.org/10.1192/bjp.bp.116.184234

Brightdawn Entertainment. (2020). *A walk in the woods* [Video game]. Steam. https://store.steampowered.com/app/557900/A_Walk_in_the_Woods/

DiCerbo, K., Ferrara, S., & Lai, E. (2017). Principled design and development for embedding assessment for learning in games and simulations. In H. Jiao & R. Lissitz (Eds.), *Technology enhanced innovative assessment: Development, modeling, and scoring from an interdisciplinary perspective* (pp. 163–175). Information Age.

Didehbani, N., Allen, T., Kandalaft, M., Krawczyk, D., & Chapman, S. (2016). Virtual reality social cognition training for children with high functioning autism. *Computers in Human Behavior, 62,* 703–711. https://doi.org/10.1016/j.chb.2016.04.033

Fall, M., Balvanz, J., Johnson, L., & Nelson, L. (1999). A play therapy intervention and its relationship to self-efficacy and learning behaviors. *Professional School Counseling, 2*(3), 194.

García-Vergara, S., Brown, L., Park, H. W., & Howard, A. M. (2014). Engaging children in play therapy: The coupling of virtual reality games with social robotics. In A. Brooks, S. Brahnman, & L. Jain (Eds.), *Technologies of inclusive well-being* (pp. 139–163). Springer. https://doi.org/10.1007/978-3-642-45432-5_8

Jafari, N., Adams, K. D., & Tavakoli, M. (2016). Haptics to improve task performance in people with disabilities: A review of previous studies and a guide to future research with children with disabilities. *Journal of Rehabilitation and Assistive Technologies Engineering, 3.* https://doi.org/10.1177/2055668316668147

Kampmann, I. L., Emmelkamp, P. M., Hartanto, D., Brinkman, W. P., Zijlstra, B. J., & Morina, N. (2016). Exposure to virtual social interactions in the treatment of social anxiety disorder: A randomized controlled trial. *Behaviour Research and Therapy, 77,* 147–156. https://doi.org/10.1016/j.brat.2015.12.016

Knell, S. M., & Dasari, M. (2016). Cognitive-behavioral play therapy for anxiety and depression. In L. A. Reddy, T. M. Files-Hall, & C. E. Schaefer (Eds.), *Empirically based play interventions for children* (pp. 77–94). American Psychological Association. https://doi.org/10.1037/14730-005

Koukourikos, K., Tzeha, L., Pantelidou, P., & Tsaloglidou, A. (2015). The importance of play during hospitalization of children. *Materia Socio-Medica, 27*(6), 438–441. https://doi.org/10.5455/msm.2015.27.438-441

Lamb, R., & Etopio, E. (2019a). Preservice science teacher preparation using virtual reality. In K. Graziano (Ed.), *Proceedings of Society for Information Technology & Teacher Education International Conference* (pp. 162–167). Association for the Advancement of Computing in Education. https://www.learntechlib.org/primary/p/208478/

Lamb, R., & Etopio, E. (2019c). VR has it: A framework for virtual reality integration into therapy. In J. Stone (Ed.), *Integrating technology into modern therapies: A clinician's guide to developments and interventions* (pp. 80–93). Routledge.

Lamb, R., Etopio, E., & Lamb, R. E. (2018). Virtual reality play therapy. *Play Therapy Magazine, 7*(22), 22–25.

Lamb, R., Miller, D., Lamb, R., Akmal, T., & Hsiao, Y. J. (2018). Examination of the role of training and fidelity of implementation in the use of assistive communications for children with autism spectrum disorder: A meta-analysis of the Picture Exchange Communication System. *British Journal of Special Education, 45*(4), 454–472. https://doi.org/10.1111/1467-8578.12243

Lamb, R. L. (2015). Video games and student assessment. In M. Spector (Ed.), *Encyclopedia of educational technology* (pp. 808–810). Sage.

Lamb, R. L., & Etopio, E. (2019b). Virtual reality simulations and writing: A neuroimaging study in science education. *Journal of Science Education and Technology, 28*(5), 542–552. https://doi.org/10.1007/s10956-019-09785-9

Lamb, R. L., Etopio, E., Hand, B., & Yoon, S. Y. (2019). Virtual reality simulation: Effects on academic performance within two domains of writing in science. *Journal of Science Education and Technology, 28*(4), 371–381.

Lamb, R. L., & Firestone, J. B. (2017). The application of multi-objective evolutionary algorithms to an educational computational model of science information processing: A computational experiment in science education. *International Journal of Science and Mathematics Education, 15*(3), 473–486. https://doi.org/10.1007/s10763-015-9705-7

Laver, K., George, S., Thomas, S., Deutsch, J. E., & Crotty, M. (2015). Virtual reality for stroke rehabilitation: An abridged version of a Cochrane review. *European Journal of Physical and Rehabilitation Medicine, 51*(4), 497–506.

Millett, C. R., & Gooding, L. F. (2017). Comparing active and passive distraction-based music therapy interventions on preoperative anxiety in pediatric patients and their caregivers. *Journal of Music Therapy, 54*(4), 460–478. https://doi.org/10.1093/jmt/thx014

Ng, A. K., Chan, L. K., & Lau, H. Y. (2019, March 18–March 22). *A study of cybersickness and sensory conflict theory using a motion-coupled virtual reality system.* Paper presented at the 2018 IEEE Conference on Virtual Reality and 3D User Interfaces (VR), Reutlingen, Germany. https://doi.org/10.1109/VR.2018.8446269

Opriş, D., Pintea, S., García-Palacios, A., Botella, C., Szamosközi, Ş., & David, D. (2012). Virtual reality exposure therapy in anxiety disorders: A quantitative meta-analysis. *Depression and Anxiety, 29*(2), 85–93. https://doi.org/10.1002/da.20910

Parsons, J. A. (2015). Holistic mental health care and play therapy for hospitalized, chronically ill children. In E. Green & A. Myrick (Eds.), *Play therapy with vulnerable populations: No child forgotten* (pp. 125–138). Rowman & Littlefield.

Plowman, L., & McPake, J. (2013). Seven myths about young children and technology. *Childhood Education, 89*(1), 27–33. https://doi.org/10.1080/00094056.2013.757490

Post, P. (1999). Impact of child-centered play therapy on the self-esteem, locus of control, and anxiety of at-risk 4th, 5th, and 6th grade students. *International Journal of Play Therapy, 8*(2), 1–18. https://doi.org/10.1037/h0089428

Pourmand, A., Davis, S., Lee, D., Barber, S., & Sikka, N. (2017). Emerging utility of virtual reality as a multidisciplinary tool in clinical medicine. *Games for Health Journal, 6*(5), 263–270. https://doi.org/10.1089/g4h.2017.0046

Ramsey, A., Lord, S., Torrey, J., Marsch, L., & Lardiere, M. (2016). Paving the way to successful implementation: Identifying key barriers to use of technology-based therapeutic tools for behavioral health care. *The Journal of Behavioral Health Services & Research, 43*(1), 54–70. https://doi.org/10.1007/s11414-014-9436-5

Riva, G. (2005). Virtual reality in psychotherapy: Review. *Cyberpsychology & Behavior, 8*(3), 220–230. https://doi.org/10.1089/cpb.2005.8.220

Rodríguez, A., Rey, B., Clemente, M., Wrzesien, M., & Alcañiz, M. (2015). Assessing brain activations associated with emotional regulation during virtual reality mood induction procedures. *Expert Systems with Applications, 42*(3), 1699–1709. https://doi.org/10.1016/j.eswa.2014.10.006

Schaefer, C. E., & Drewes, A. A. (2011). The therapeutic powers of play and play therapy. In C. E. Schaefer (Ed.), *Foundations of play therapy* (pp. 15–35). Wiley.

Shen, Y. J. (2002). Short-term group play therapy with Chinese earthquake victims: Effects on anxiety, depression and adjustment. *International Journal of Play Therapy, 11*(1), 43–63. https://doi.org/10.1037/h0088856

Smeijers, D., & Koole, S. L. (2019). Testing the effects of a virtual reality game for aggressive impulse management (VR-GAIME): Study protocol. *Frontiers in Psychiatry, 10.* https://doi.org/10.3389/fpsyt.2019.00083

Tabak, M., Cabrita, M., Schüler, T., Hörst, D., Heuven, R., Kinast, B., & Thomas, A. (2017). Dinner is ready! Virtual reality assisted training for chronic pain rehabilitation. In *The ACM SIGCHI Annual Symposium on Computer–Human Interaction in Play* (pp. 283–289). Association for Computer Machinery. https://doi.org/10.1145/3130859.3131331

Tussyadiah, I. P., Wang, D., Jung, T. H., & tom Dieck, M. C. (2018). Virtual reality, presence, and attitude change: Empirical evidence from tourism. *Tourism Management, 66,* 140–154. https://doi.org/10.1016/j.tourman.2017.12.003

Välimäki, M., Hätönen, H. M., Lahti, M. E., Kurki, M., Hottinen, A., Metsäranta, K., Riihimäki, T., & Adams, C. E. (2014). Virtual reality for treatment compliance for people with serious mental illness. *Cochrane Database of Systematic Reviews.* https://doi.org/10.1002/14651858.CD009928.pub2

van Loon, A., Bailenson, J., Zaki, J., Bostick, J., & Willer, R. (2018). Virtual reality perspective-taking increases cognitive empathy for specific others. *PLOS One, 13*(8), e0202442. https://doi.org/10.1371/journal.pone.0202442

Webster-Stratton, C., & Reid, M. J. (2009). Parents, teachers, and therapists using child-directed play therapy and coaching skills to promote children's social and emotional competence and build positive relationships. In C. E. Schaefer (Ed.), *Play therapy for preschool children* (pp. 245–273). American Psychological Association. https://doi.org/10.1037/12060-012

Index

About the Editors

Heidi Gerard Kaduson, RPT-S, PhD, specializes in evaluation and intervention services for children with a variety of behavioral, emotional, and learning problems. She is past president of the Association for Play Therapy and Director of The Play Therapy Training Institute in Monroe Township, New Jersey. She has lectured internationally on play therapy, attention-deficit/ hyperactivity disorder, and learning disabilities. Dr. Kaduson has edited and authored many books on play therapy: *Prescriptive Play Therapy: Tailoring Interventions to Specific Childhood Problems*; *Contemporary Play Therapy*; *Short-Term Play Therapy for Children, Third Edition*; *101 Favorite Play Therapy Techniques*; as well as *101 More Favorite Play Therapy Techniques* and *101 Favorite Play Therapy Techniques, Volume III*. Dr. Kaduson has trained and supervised thousands of individuals across the world. She maintains a private practice in child psychotherapy in Monroe Township, New Jersey.

Charles E. Schaefer, RPT-S, PhD, is professor emeritus of clinical psychology at Fairleigh Dickinson University in Teaneck, New Jersey. He is cofounder and director emeritus of the Association for Play Therapy. Dr. Schaefer is the author/coauthor of more than 100 research articles and author/editor of more than 70 professional books, including *Handbook of Play Therapy, Second Edition*; *Foundations of Play Therapy, Second Edition*; *The Therapeutic Powers of Play, Second Edition*; *Essential Play Therapy Techniques: Time-Tested Approaches*; *Short-Term Play Therapy, Third Edition*; and *Play Therapy for Preschoolers*.